Silvergirl

Jennifer Holly Stephens died on February 25th 1971 at five o'clock in the afternoon. I put her personal things into my student trunk. I finally reopened it in 2003 – over 30 years later. In the trunk I found her diaries ...

Jenny Stephens tragically died aged 24 in 1971 and these are the diaries of her late teenage years, whilst at University, and from being diagnosed with leukemia until her death. She had rejected a career in acting, and obtained her degree in Botany and Zoology, before going into teaching.

Bill Unsworth met Jenny at college and they married after he finished his chemistry degree and before starting on a Ph. D. Bill now lives in Warrington and is retired after a successful career first in scientific instruments, and then in computing and Internet.

Jennifer Holly Unsworth (1946–1971)

Sail On, Silvergirl, Sail On By

Diary of Jennifer Holly Unsworth (née Stephens), 1946–1971

Transcribed and edited, and with additional material by,
William David Unsworth.

Silvergirl published by Ultimate Publishers, UK.

www.ultimate-publishers.co.uk

© 2008 The estate of Jennifer Holly Unsworth
© 2008 William David Unsworth

All rights reserved. No part of this publication may be reproduced, stored in a retrieval system, or transmitted in any form or by any means, electronic, mechanical, photocopying, recording, or otherwise, without the prior permission of William David Unsworth.

The moral rights of Jennifer Holly Unsworth and William David Unsworth to be identified as the authors of this work has been asserted, in accordance with the Copyright, Designs, and Patent Act of 1998.

ISBN 978-0-9558562-0-4

Bridge Over Trouble Water
Simon and Garfunkel – January 1970

When you're weary, feeling small,
When tears are in your eyes, I will dry them all;
I'm on your side. When times get rough
And friends just can't be found,
Like a bridge over troubled water
I will lay me down.
Like a bridge over troubled water
I will lay me down.

When you're down and out,
When you're on the street,
When evening falls so hard
I will comfort you.
I'll take your part.
When darkness comes
And pain is all around,
Like a bridge over troubled water
I will lay me down.
Like a bridge over troubled water
I will lay me down.

Sail on silvergirl,
Sail on by.
Your time has come to shine.
All your dreams are on their way.
See how they shine
If you need a friend
I'm sailing right behind.
Like a bridge over troubled water
I will ease your mind.
Like a bridge over troubled water
I will ease your mind.

© 1969 Paul Simon

Contents

Introduction ix
Diary 1964 1
Diary 1965 65
Diary 1966 119
Diary 1969 165
Diary 1970 177
Autobiography of Jennifer Holly Stephens (fragment) 227
List of Characters and Family Backgrounds 241

Introduction

Jennifer Holly Stephens died on February 25th 1971 at five o'clock in the afternoon.

I put her personal things into my student trunk. The trunk accompanied me through many house moves and I finally reopened it in 2003 – over 30 years later. I could not have done so before. In the trunk I found her diaries (which I cannot recall her compiling or even that they were amongst her papers) and started to read them. The original grief came back but in a way that I could finally cope with and I found out many things that I had not realised at the time. A lot of things remain unknown particularly about her early life. I decided that the story they tell would be of interest to others. In fact there is slightly more to this story – my mother had died early the year before and I had had a heart attack in that autumn and it was after that that I found the diaries and I probably felt that finally I had to come to terms with the events of so long before. The following year I left my second wife and was then able to embark on typing up the diaries and editing.

Initially I transcribed the diary from when she became ill – from 1969 – but I felt that as a story it was too incomplete and unsatisfying. I then transcribed the earlier diaries from before I knew her and with them it became a much more complete narrative. I have only been able to add limited commentary relating to the period before I met her but I hope that altogether it makes sense to the reader.

Abbreviations abound because in a private diary one does not need to explain who people are or how things arose. I wanted to make it clear what was her work and what was my commentary. Accordingly I have done this by the use of two different typefaces.

This is my work.

This is Jenny's.

Sail On, Silvergirl, Sail On By

Paragraphs also usually make this clear as I have avoided inserting my text into her sentences. Also I have added references to films and plays mentioned (e.g. as follows *(Romeo and Juliet)*.

Diaries can be fascinating and compelling reading. The diaries of the politician and historian Alan Clark well illustrate this. They include a mixture of the banal and of historic insights. He seems to worry about money and health out of all proportion to his circumstances. He involves us in his love life and his political career. Similarly in Jenny's diary we have day-to-day trivia punctuated with strong emotions as events unfold. So in the earlier diaries her main preoccupations are with exams and college (and boys) and her parents' expectations and with her amateur dramatics appearances. The pressure does not decrease when she goes to university but increases with the need to cope with independent living for the first time.

In the later diaries the previous worries start to seem trivial as she copes with illness and what will happen when she is gone. To the very end, I was unable to accept that she had a terminal illness. The diaries suggest that she herself thought she had a milder form for most of the time she was ill and that when she realised this was not the case she chose to keep it to herself.

She wanted things to go on as normal for as long as possible. She had yearned to get away from her unhappy home and gain her independence. This came with college and marriage but it was to last all too short a time. She had to give up her job in teaching and no longer had the energy for some of the other things that had interested her. She was a remarkable person with talents in science and the arts and her potential was cruelly curtailed.

I strongly associate the song "Bridge over Troubled Waters" by Simon and Garfunkel with this time in our lives. It was a favourite of hers and hence I start the book with the words of the song and of course it suggested the title.

Honestly written autobiographical works force you to open up your feelings and experiences to the world and this can be difficult. We all worry about what people think about us. Things written and revealed can have unpredictable consequences for the people involved and I apologise for this in advance.

Diary 1964

In which Jenny studies for her exams and copes with family and boyfriends.

The family lived in a Victorian semi-detached near to Raynes Park tube station and to Wimbledon Common. This was 12 Amity Grove. The other house mentioned – Dunmore Road – was the residence of her maternal grandparents. College was Ewell Technical College at Epsom. See "List of Characters and Family Backgrounds" later.

Wednesday 1st January 1964

Am still recovering from last night's party. At 4 am John and I were still in the car. The sherry had been drunk and so were we. John proposed and I believe that I accepted but must tell him tomorrow that if I did I did not mean to get married yet. Infatuation is a strange and wonderfully tragic thing.

Thursday 2nd January 1964

Rose at 10am with great solemnity for today is the anniversary of dear Grandpa's death. The family (excluding Daddy) walked to the crematorium. It is so cold and bleak. They left the 's' off Stephens. Yes he is lovingly remembered, by a few.

Granny looked tired and old. Introspection is inevitable on such a day.

Friday 3rd January 1964

Today I must see John again. Somehow I don't want to. "It will be an anti-climax" I thought and so it was. John looked beautiful but was depressed because he was jealous about last night's party. The common was dark and still; we spoke in low voices. It is infatuation.

Sail On, Silvergirl, Sail On By

The play was over, and I was sad. John said he still loves Linda which begins to make me love him.

Saturday 4th January 1964

So today we must part. I feel tired and depressed and sick at the prospect. The gods of love are cruel. The party consisted of squealing, wriggling females and long haired males. Fascinating. We sat on the bed and watched and watched. In my silver and blue the impression I gave must have startling for people stared. No John I won't marry you, but I like you a lot. Polynesian marriages are grotesquely horrible. Good bye, no, not good bye, Au revoir John.

Sunday 5th January 1964

Sleep did not come at all. So I rose and made a sketch of the boy I loved last night but now by day's gaudy light see him in his true form. He looks more beautiful "for the fancy doth outwork nature" (*Anthony and Cleopatra*). I fear I mustn't see or hear John before he returns. The letter I have written is sadly lacking in something, perhaps it is feeling.

Monday 6th January 1964

7.15 am seems like the middle of the night. I think I will go mad. Same old ugly faces at college. Same feelings of fear and frustration. Oh god why can't I understand chemistry. My cold was worse tonight. There won't be a room. Inconsistent creature. Life is strange without a scarf.

Tuesday 7th January 1964

Zoology doesn't appear to me to be a very enlightening subject after all. Filthy creature, the earthworm. Dilly and I sat and talked among the coats. Cold and bare the cloakroom seems somehow. Pam is a strange person, cold and yet full of life. I don't understand her at all. Perhaps it is my fault. Jerry was so sweet to offer to pay for my "retreat". The gay policeman made me feel happy.

Wednesday 8th January 1964

7 am " Get up!" Our dear and revered father must be preserved as such. Granny looked well. A wonderful sense of achievement of fruition is here with her return. Victoria, Francis arrived yesterday. Too conceited for me. Glass blowing was an anti climax. The legs of the "thing" were actually straight. Mary talked about Dave and I suddenly felt lonely;

January 1964

very lonely. Perhaps I still have got emotions and am not the fool I believed I had made myself.

Thursday 10th January 1964

Physics! Self explanatory I think. After the mid sessional break I rose (practically) to the library to study organic chemistry. Proves to be as frustrating as everything else after all. Brendan and I ate lunch with great solemnity and then harassed the poor harassed lecturers even more by getting them to fill in forms. French as usual was a riot. Being the only girl has definite disadvantages.

Friday 11th January 1964

Surrounded by foaming fizzing test tubes and evil smelling gasses I found myself in the chemistry lab. Eureka. Antimony has an orange colour after all. Brendan was intrigued by the instruments. Mr Mac was as boring and unintelligible as ever. Still a few facts emerge from that ghastly cyclic polymer (to boil a test tube) of words. Crystallisation normally takes place after this in my mind. We sat in the dark and sang happy birthday to the devil with red hair.

Saturday 12th January 1964

Church. Matins to be exact. A few bored members of the affluent society of Wimbledon congregate as "duty", I am told (to whom I wonder) in order to chant with their mouths and not their hearts ridiculous prayers for obscure and obsolete causes. I blush for the whole absurd crowd of them, including myself. If at first you don't work, work and work again. (Otherwise you fail and that is bad for the dignity, so work).

Monday 13th January 1964

"The Longest Day" I don't know what the film was about; but this is mine. Chemistry, chemistry, chemistry, physics. 9 am to 9 pm. They shouldn't do it to a dog! How can you call in chemistry when there is so much maths? Deranged nomenclature. Again Paddy writes to me. Poor boy, perhaps I should really have sent him a Christmas present. Out wood Bound. Where to find God or Life I suppose. This makes me think of John.

Tuesday 14th January 1964

And now it's "today"; for a long time it has been "The Future". Strange it's the same as any other day really. Filthy show, great is my relief that the eternal curse is upon you i.e.

you are condemned to drift in the air without hope and or reprieve. My mind is hugely worrying about something: perhaps it is the exams; or perhaps I am writing too much and anybody reading this will think it is the diary of a maniac. If so read on my friend read on …

It was 7 pm I raced madly for the train and just managed to fling myself in as it jolted out of the station. My hair was lying loose on my shoulders after being tossed about and being hot I smashed down the window and leant out into the cool night air. Did you ever know what it feels like to have the wind sobbing through you hair as you career madly through the night, to feel the light rain stinging your face and to laugh and laugh with the sheer exhilaration of being alive?

The train grew faster and faster, ghost like objects flick past and the tunnels rumble; with a clash and clang their teeth at you. But you're off on your magic steed flying towards the horizon. I drew up the window and sank into the soft seat in a blissful heap; the train swayed and sighed to a stop, for that great monster could rend the soil, conceal its fury with a gentle hiss.

[From the autobiography of Jenny Stephens who spent her younger days doing penal servitude in the solitary confinement of a railway carriage!!]

Saturday 18th January 1964

College, chemistry. The two miserable Cs. Stayed with Granny till 12 pm. The wig suits her but is somehow not "Granny".

On thinking carefully, love is like trickling sand thro' one's fingers. At first it is soothing, soporific, after a while the sweet sensation wears off it begins to hurt, one wants to stop it.

Sunday 19th January 1964

I slept and slept. Enchantment! How I hate, hate, loath, deplore and abhor the "Pioneers". Stupid obsequious girls, pompous supercilious boys. I hate being ignored and made to feel unwanted. Lesley is so awful to me that I want to scream and scream all my fear and loathing of her into the ears of the world. Nobody listens to me.

Monday 20th January 1964

With great solemnity the papers are handed out, and with sweaty palms and shaking hands we set to work. What is this formula – $CH_3C=CH$. I don't know it! With the room beginning to spin as with a cold feeling of dread there is only an hour to go and I haven't even started. And in the end it's alright – 60%. You fool. Rejoice.

Tuesday 21st January 1964

Dissection of the earth worm. Poor things. What a thing to live for. One's destiny pointing towards the slab. To be slashed by eager ham fisted students. The blood seeps between your fingers. The worm writhing in agony. Your heart stops. It isn't dead. God help our ignorance.

Wednesday 22nd January 1964

Glass blowing. Speaks for itself I suppose. My hands don't obey today. Strange when one looks forward to something that is always an anticlimax. So now I control myself. I am a being with no feelings therefore I have no disappointments. Therefore also I have no joy.

Thursday 23rd January 1964

What happened today. Oh yes. Bloody dissection again. At this time there was no blood only mud. Pouring out. I haven't been invited to the party and feel unwanted again. Still I don't care anymore if I work while they play, I will pass and they won't. Boosts my morale if nothing else.

A photo of Jenny appeared in the *Advertiser and Reporter*, Thursday 23rd January 1964 with the caption "Seen at a prize giving at Ewell Technical College last week are Derek Marles, Jennifer Shepherd, Tony Fifield, Rosalind Fortune and Elizabeth Blacklaws". She was very annoyed that they got her name wrong!

Friday 24th January 1964

Don't ever dream again. The worms hung on the wall with guts hanging out, and Eyes. And then one swayed towards me touched my hand, and laughed; it was John's laughter, hollow and mocking and I ran and still it followed, growing louder, I was the wrong way up in bed, my feet touched the cold wood of the headboard. And still it came. Even now that I am awake I can remember those cold morning hours. The cold sweat I was in and the evil laughter, the eyes in the worms. Don't sleep if you have killed something you'll kill yourself.

No letter from John I feel as if I have lost him. Must convince myself I am superior to him or I will die of grief. Why did God make me!

Sunday 26th January 1964

Enchantment. Everything is grand. The sun is shining and of course I get up too late and miss it all. Down comes the rain; and after all I don't go to Church. Hypocrite? Yes but one who has a sense of the truth and its proportion I hope.

Monday 27th January 1964

So indeed he will stay for yet one more week; My little physics man. A new girl joined the class. It was a relief to have another of my own sex in the class. Bit of an idiot but never mind.

Christine talked and talked and talked until I thought that I should change into a raving savage and do a war dance around the refectory.

Tuesday 28th January 1964

Worms again. I led the procession of merry men down to the graveyard where the dead were as yet still living and caught the agonised souls as they wriggled out of their holes. Then we slaughtered them in boiling H_2O. Slit and with disgusted faces chucked them away.

Wednesday 29th January 1964

We had lunch just as we used to in the old days. With Granny at the head of the table and mummy and I either side. Only Grandpa was missing. Poor, poor granny looking so pathetic.

Thursday 30th January 1964

Brendan and I have become very good friends. Platonic absolutely sometimes wish it wasn't. So does he I think. It is good to have a friend. He is going to lend me his scarf for Saturday. Strange as I only want it to impress John.

Friday 31st January 1964

Enderscee was a wretch to make me read in the French class. Brendan and I went for a long walk in the lunch hour. He says he likes me because I am unpretentious. Great stuff. The only thing is I am not. Only one more day until I see John. My God; I feel so nervous. I have hated him very greatly in my dreams. I hope it won't be the same in real life.

February 1964

Saturday 1st February 1964

But in real life it was the same. John is much too conceited for me to ever get on well with him again. Richard came for me at 3.45 and we drove down in the little blue mini, with Liz. John was so pleased to see me it was pathetic. He flung out his arms to me, but he didn't catch my heart for I didn't give it. During the performance I could have cried with pride. He has a wonderful voice. We laughed a lot afterwards but somehow we were strangers. He said he rubs Valerie's hands, just as he rubs mine.

Sunday 2nd February 1964

I couldn't sleep all night. The breakfast was huge and I met a Brian whilst eating cornflakes in the little room overlooking the tree in the sun with the birds nesting on it. John came down early and I went down late as I didn't think he would turn up. He looked very tired. We roamed the streets of Cambridge and then sat on a bench in the sun. Lunch with the Sommers and his parents was a nightmare. Never again. The church service was beautifully cold. Something was between John and I, perhaps we were both too tired. But it makes my heart ache when I think of what a success we were only a few weeks ago. Why, why must it be like all the other hopeless, spiteful affairs I always have? We parted with a lot of feeling on my side and very little on his although he tried to pretend he still loves me and I secretly think it was am image he loved. Not me.

Tuesday 4th February 1964

I wrote John a mad letter after this I'll probably never hear from him again. Perhaps I am mad. But he is too dark and has green, green eyes. So if there is foreign blood in him and we ever by accident had any children, poor little things, they would probably look absolutely Indian or Italian or one of the other despised races. No I will never ever let any of my children go through what I have been through.

A strange reference that I puzzled over. It turns out that the family had a long association with India and that in the family history (more than three or four generations back) there were probably Indian ancestors. This was never mentioned to me whilst I knew her.

Wednesday 5th February 1964

All day today I did revision and a lot I've learnt I must say. Hydra and atomic theory. Granny has gone back into hospital and I think I'll die if anything happens to her. God, why do you let her suffer in this way? She never harmed anything in her life. The wicked prosper, and that's all the consolation we get.

Thursday 6th February 1964

Today we revised from 9 am till 4.45 and overall nearly dead because of it. I still haven't had a letter from John. How dare he whistle at other girls when I am by his side. He is no longer that gently submissive fool I knew before. No a blustering great hulk of fat and fat headedness.

Friday 7th February 1964

Brendan is so sweet and I'm always hurting his feelings. We arranged to go out together on the 22nd. May John have a nice time then because I certainly intend to. He'll probably get off with some foolish girl and then fall madly in love with his image again. Brendan's lucky number is 5 and so is mine. John's is 8.

Saturday 8th February 1964

I can hardly believe it's a week ago I went through all the heartache of knowing that John no longer loved me. How strangely sad.

Mr Mac arrived early. Granny poor Granny is still in hospital. How I wish she was home again. Perhaps she'll come and sleep in our house. Wouldn't that be grand. I do hope so.

Sunday 9th February 1964

Work, work; I've left it too late. Got up at 7 am to go to communion. Must get God's blessing. Went up to the hall in the afternoon. No rehearsal. Please God bless my work in these exams and keep me above everything else calm. What a silly prayer. God has better things to do than dashed exams. What about Granny for instance.

Monday 10th February 1964

Physical and inorganic chemistry exam.

Tuesday 11th February 1964

At 6 am we were woken for today at twenty to five. Granny passed away peacefully and my life is lacking something for ever more. It is void of the urge and drive to work for something. I only worked well to please Granny. Oh God, a calm, if any calm, a calm of despair creeps and soaks through my soul. I can't bear it. My poor Granny dead.

February 1964

Wednesday 12th February 1964

I stayed at home and tried to revise. Work doesn't come easily at such a time.

In glass-blowing the little man gave each of us a glass of orange squash, so sweet.

I walked down the little country lane to the station. It was dusk and wild geese flew in a great V shape overhead, yes Granny is at peace with Grandpa.

Thursday 13th February 1964

We had organic chemistry in the morning and revise like mad and then in the afternoon zoology. We got Fasciola Hepatica.

Poor Mummy, so sad, so lost without Granny, What can I say or do to cheer her up. Oh God, may the twins and I never dispute our parents will as these are.

Friday 14th February 1964

Got a valentine from John. Was by myself all day at college. Still I bought a book and wrote up physics notes. Went to rehearsal in the evening; lost the part of Lottie. It hurt my pride. Russell called for meet at 10 pm. Gave me a little fluffy brooch. Party in a cellar, great fun. Met boy, law student called Tony Compass. Went right up to the top of the old building and got locked in. I think he was a bit mad.

Saturday 15th February 1964

Got up at 11.5 am. Went to Oliver's with the twins. (appoint for the 26th 9.30) Saw Mr Mac's collection of china. Hate Aunty Jean. Played piano. Sat and wrote my diary. I am feeling so depressed about Granny read T. S. Eliot "The Hollow Men", so we are!

Sunday 16th February 1964

Just sat and thought and ate and slept and cried and hated and feared and loathed and wanted to die and wanted to live and felt frustrated and thought of nobody but myself. In other words wallowed in self pity and a lot of blinking good it did anybody.

Monday 17th February 1964

The most terribly tragic thing. Granny is dead and I can't believe it. Oh how does one give way to sorrow, agony, miserable wringing agony, of loss. Her house is so quiet and empty yet so full of memories and all the sad ghosts. The funeral. It was drizzling, the sky was grey, almost as if the whole world was mourning the loss of my poor, poor granny. The cars slipped along, the coffin laden with flowers always, always in front, rocking to and fro. They bore it in on their shoulders. Great Grandpa and I shivered, tears streaming down our faces in the porchway ... but it's all so terrible, horrible. And then all the parasitic relations like a multitude of crows in pinched black coats and dowdy hats, sniffling and making a great show of their sorrow. But she was so very brave. And then we went back to the house and they laughed and drank tea out of Granny's china and ate food paid for with Granny's money and never once mentioned Granny whom <u>presumably</u> they had come to pay last respects to. <u>Cruel</u>, ugly people.

On the Tuesday we laid her ashes next to Grandpa's. Her ashes were white and there were such a very little of them.

So, but for a few photos. Dresses she has sown, children she has born; and memories lingering on our poor Granny is to all intents and purposes dead. But to me Granny is never, never dead because I loved her and always will love her.

Friday 21st February 1964

Brendan and I went for a walk up onto the Downs. The air was cool and refreshing; at a little wayside stall we drank steaming cups of tea. Filthy cups but the liquid in them was stimulating. Went back to French. I was so tired I could hardly move but it took me out of myself. Went to rehearsals.

Saturday 22nd February 1964

Chemistry. Then Mr Mac. Then John; an exciting trio. This boy is becoming a bore. So I did pinch his gloves, well where's his sense of humour?

Sprawling resplendent upon the grassy slopes of St James Park; snugly ensconced upon its benches, dabbling in philosophy and love and I loathed his pompous and supercilious manner every minute of it. Then why do I behave in this obsequious manner?

Sunday 23rd February 1964

Slept in till 1 pm and felt all the worse for it. In thoroughly bad humour.

Went over to Granny's. Oh no I forgot the physical condition has taken over. We mustn't call it "Granny's" any longer but ½ Mummy's ¼ Jean's and ¼ John's. How sweet and world like.

February – March 1964

Monday 24th February 1964

Life. Played with the models of methane etc. in organic chem. amused my mind although I thought I had a higher mentality.

Wednesday 26th February 1964

Went to Oliver's. Murder.

This diary is, I think, becoming an increasing excuse for calculated introspection; for one sits down and recalls a day and tries to write about that day, false reactions creep into the epistle – desirable reactions but untrue. Therefore might be asked, how does one overcome the pathological complaint of inaccuracy. The obvious reply is, of course, have at the time, the desired reactions. This is impossible, so, the diary goes on, a massive little volume of lies, no not lies, that makes it appear mean and petty, a volume rather of dreams pining for what is not, or nearly is and just doesn't stretch to the utmost limits of truth. In other words a typical autobiography.

Friday 28th February 1964

Did a physics paper at home. Gas man called. Went to rehearsals.

Saturday 29th February 1964

Ah, ha, today we pushed a piano from Grannie's to our own house. Brendan is so stupid. Always saying "No Jenny, it's impossible". Nothing is impossible, nothing at all; if only you want it badly enough you can have anything. Anyway we shove it onto the pram wheels and just pushed it over. Easy! Who said it was impossible. Stupid fool.

Sunday 1st March 1964

Yippee I have passed, passed every one. God I thank you.

Inorganic Chem – 79%. Org – 58%. Phys – 50%. Physics – 67%. Zoology – 58%. Botany – 65%

Five stinking exams over. And now I must work till stars spin before my eyes and the Gods of thunder roar in my ears.

Monday 2nd March 1964

Went to physics in the evening. Oh yes I met a most interesting person, interesting because he was so terribly dull and stupid. I travelled back on the train with him and he talked and talked all about nothing at all. Very odd. He's in the building department and heats pipes to cherry red and them bashes them screaming.

Tuesday 3rd March 1964

In zoo. We had to delve inside our mouths and scrape out squamous epithelium. Made me slightly nauseated. Made slides of muscle. Hard and sadistic master of the zoological talents, Luke told everybody that mine was a prize example of idiocy. My-face couldn't have been very easily distinguished from a beetroot!

Wednesday 4th March 1964

Another visit to the Oliver's. She explained all about root fillings apesectomies and how to fill a tooth. I sometimes think about old Dave nowadays. Strange he has the only photo of Granny that I really like. He's the only boy that I'll ever love I think.

Thursday 5th March 1964

The days drag. On and On, into months and years and what have I ever done in my life? Nothing. That's the answer, nothing at all. My trouble is I think about myself too much. Let yourself go, don't care what they think the voice whispers. And then I don't at the time: but afterwards shame and horror at myself. Self respect sighs in the shadows.

Friday 6th March 1964

Today John is going to take out Jacky is he? God speed my dear. Horrible loathsome spidery horror. Fowl pestilence on thee!

Curious how relieved I felt as I fell asleep last night. Tomorrow perhaps I thought I won't be fighting a losing battle, I'll be free to go "where though" tremble the words on my lips.

Saturday 7th March 1964

Alright so John can't treat me like this. Tonight is the "Somebody New" night and so it is. My heart was in my feet, not in the usual place, as I slunk into the Wimbledon Dance hall (8/6 to get in!) a man came up and asked me to dance and I refused and then up floated John (Howe) and off I flew. It was a gay evening; Auntie Jean was there behaving like a drunken idiot. May I grow old with dignity.

March 1964

Sunday 8th March 1964

I slept most of today. You know how (howe) (how funny) it is after an evening on the razzle.

Monday 9th March 1964

My little man on the train hovered in dark corners and didn't even wish me good evening. He's not quite as stupid as perhaps I had thought. Still perhaps he was just afraid of me. Of me, how unreal when I am terrified over all the world if only they did but know it. However you see, they never will.

Tuesday 10th March 1964

Did my first dissection of the crayfish. It has a horrible smell. Putrefying crayfish. Cut out the gut to show nerve centre. Where my child, where? Well it should be there. Typical of all science. It just doesn't apply in real life; just in the funny little minds of men.

Wednesday 11th March 1964

Went out with John Howe. I was half expecting him not to turn up, but he did in the end. So he is going to be engaged to another girl is he? Her name is Jenny, her birthday is on June 18th. Oh it is too ironically. We sat in the car in close proximity for far too long than is good for one. Yes he is all of 23 yrs alright. Oh how I'm muddled up with life.

Thursday 12th March 1964

Slept in and didn't go into tutorial like the wicked child that I am.

Still the dream I had was nice. John H said his usual goodbye with great feeling. How is it that I always manage to infatuate; but never to create a deep understanding love. Granny died a month ago yesterday and I nearly forgot to put that I thought about here <u>all day</u>.

Friday 13th March 1964

God, got a letter from Dave. Wants me to go down there this weekend. Oh god how wonderful!

Went to a dance with John and Alister in the evening. It was all very fine but my mind is obsessed with Dave. Oh how I love him but please god not another anti-climax.

Saturday 14th March 1964

Chemistry. Brendan came over for tea and then we went to see "Gorillas drink Milk". (*A play by John Murphy.*) All about rich American coming back to see poor Irish parents and bringing wife. Very tragic.

Brendan does irritate me. Phoned Robert Burns. Ewell 1413 terribly gusty person.

Sunday 15th March 1964

Got to Sutton station at 1 pm. Robert and Joan picked me up in a little green mini. Roared with laughter all the way there. Dave and I were a bit embarrassed to see each other at first because of our nasty letter writing session. Went into the concert – a bit boring but the music made me want to cry. Then into Horsham for tea. Oh I do love Dave. He's so different from John (B). So very genuine in his feelings. We went back to chapel (I was very irreverent and must apologise). Met Joe then Dave and I went for a walk (in the driving snow) to the pavilion and there we talked and he made love to me; so gently I could have died with my love for him. He told me he'd missed me. I later learnt from Robert that he had been so excited that he ate no lunch. Poor Dave; yet I didn't weep when I left him.

Wednesday 18th March 1964

Slept in. Went to college but did nothing as they were having a 7 a side. Brendan was in it. Went out in the evening with John Howe. Really he is very intelligent, however he is aware of the fact; a pity. We spent a long time in the car talking etc. Saw Betty and Calvin in the pub. I can boss poor old John around like anything. At last I have learnt the way to treat men: – like dirt.

Thursday 19th March 1964

A zoo test was all planned for today. Clive conveniently had an interview at Guys. Only Pam, Steve, Brendan, Richard, Martin and I turned up for the test so it has been postponed till next Tuesday. A thousand curses. Mummy has been awfully understanding. Strange. She met the other Granny on Waterloo, said she looked very thin. Poor thing. Age is such a pathetically ironical thing.

Friday 20th March 1964

I, like the devotee I confess to be, went marching up to the church thinking there was a rehearsal. No such luck. God really called me to him today as perhaps I am to die violently.

March 1964

I nearly got dragged and or really assailed would be a better word into a car with a very nasty little fat greasy Yorkshire man.

A strange incident not referred to again.

Saturday 21st March 1964

I thought I would see John Brice today, no such luck. Dear adorable, hopeless John must return to Cambridge tonight so there will Bacchanalian revels. Anyway I feel too tired too sad, to mad to be nice to anybody; especially a person I profess to hate. So in the end I just sat at home and sulked. Auntie Peggy came around with a box of sweets for each of us. I like her.

Sunday 22nd March 1964

Didn't go to church in the morning. Just stayed in bed. Of course I took one of my secret pills last night, that's why I slept so well!

In the afternoon went up to rehearsals. Farcical. Up again to Church in the evening. A serene and beautiful evening, somebody must be happy in the great somewhere.

Monday 23rd March 1964

All day I have been like a cat on hot bricks. I hate John Brice and yet I'm frightened I love him. When the time came I was foul to him and low and behold he was marvellous, kind and considerate and so sweet. He actually sat down, sang and played his own accompaniment on the piano. As we sat in the car we talked of love and marriage and what our children would be like. Swarthy like us, so they can never be. A man crawled to the window and pressed his face against the glass, my heart felt cold and sick with the sight.

Tuesday 24th March 1964

Nothing memorable happened today. I still feel very, very depressed. Almost a pain in my mind but I don't know what it is. Perhaps I'm insane.

Wednesday 25th March 1964

John Howe is engaged so really how can I go out with him. An insult to me and insult to her, an insult to himself. We sat in the car the whole evening and talked about ourselves and life and love etc and the usual things one does talk of before one says " Goodbye" for good. I was very magnanimous I know, yes I am capable of it when I want to be. Reassuring. We parted as friends but I loved his deep respect for me. Respect is a much more wonderful thing than love, for the latter is superficial i.e. flesh like respect is pride it is a fine thing on its own. I honour John's respect for me.

Friday 27th March 1964 — Good Friday

As I am, so must I see. Today I went to the RC church. God lies resplendent in this great tomb; but perhaps after all, it is only an edifice. Man's edifice, his concept of God. During the service a strange love, almost pain, for this wonderful gift of life God has bestowed on me was overwhelming. I was swept by this love to the foot of the cross and found myself as were others kneeling before it and kissing those poor bleeding feet. For years and years, perhaps since I left the convent I have been searching for the peace I found as I walked back down the aisle. People may laugh, but I believe in God, but I still hate those people he made. So I must hate myself and yes I suppose I do, more, in fact that I hate them. But then as I am so must I see.

Sunday 29th March 1964

Easter Sunday. Last night went to see "Jason and the Golden Fleece" with John Brice. Awful. Then went to a party. How I hate him! Bawling, pugnacious moron. How dare he say such obscene things in such a loud voice, now it reflects on me. Pauline chasing him like mad. Drank 9 sherries and felt positively foul this morning. Vomited heartily. The other Granny came to tea and lunch. Don't like her terribly. Rather hard and sarcastic, but beautiful manners.

Monday 30th March 1964

Slept in till 10 am. Did 3 hrs work. Chem and chem. I hate a certain somebody. Pater I think we address it. Just because Mummy had her hands in a certain position he snapped at her and then rubbed coal dust on them and roared with nasty laughter declaring "now there's something wrong". I loathe him. Perhaps it is not capable to have the capacity to have so much hate and that's why it all comes bubbling out. One day when he is old and dependent God help him. I have decided to marry an old man.

Tuesday 31st March 1964

That veiled and terrible guest, trouble, is on the door step again and soon he will be knocking. I feel it in my very bones. However he brings for us, if we accept it the strength of self control. If we must bear it let us bear it well, with high heads, let none of the weight fall on other shoulders. Though my heart is sad within me I must treat others with a kindly presence, considerate words and helpful acts. For that after all is the very trial we are put upon the earth to bear.

Wednesday 1st April 1964

The hot tears I shed are my tears; my own tears and may no eyes but my eyes see them. So John B cannot come today after all. I'm glad, glad is it that makes me hate him when I am away from him and yet desire him so very much when he whispers those sweet words of love. Please send love, for it is only himself that he really is in love with. Perhaps its because he is like Grandpa. Stupid fool that I am! Narcissist would be more appropriate.

Thursday 2nd April 1964

Today I have been very "Hysterical" as Mummy would say. Rose at 11 am very bad. Really I must work harder. The shame of failing the exams would be so awful. I walked down to see John with a rose stuck in my boot. He actually noticed. Marvellous. We just drove around as usual for about an hour and then sat on our favourite haunt on the bye pass (Kingston) and talked and talked. I was positively beastly and so was he in a charming sort of way. I am sure he is not really going to a party in Brighton.

Went to rehearsals in the evening. Oh it is wonderful to be able to mould a part into a living vital personality. So now I must keep the au-pair accent after all. Went to see Tony on the way back, as usual only just got out of his bedroom a virgin. I suppose I should be flattered.

Saturday 4th April 1964

I slept in till 2 pm and then pretended when they came back that I'd been up for hours. Mummy taught us how to play whist. Rather ingenious. But oh, how she goes on and on about my future career, just because they are supplying the money for any training I might have does it mean they can treat me as a mere investment? I wonder. But I suppose I am being unfair; as usual.

Sunday 5th April 1964

I hate the Pioneers esp Robert Sommers. John turned up in the hall to say he couldn't take me out as he is going on some boat trip. I honesty couldn't care less. Moron that he is. We walked around the church in utter despondency and hated each other; repelled each other would be a better word.

Sail On, Silvergirl, Sail On By

Monday 6th April 1964

A state of apathy is fast closing in on my mind. For days I haven't done and work. "Tomorrow and tomorrow and tomorrow creeps on this petty pace from day to day" (*Macbeth*). It is a petty pace too. Oh well you're only young once. It's the first time, the first time that counts as one has no 2nd chances in this life. I'm going to die young anyway.

Tuesday 7th April 1964

Went to Oliver's. Hell, as usual, didn't help matters with my present state. I think I'll write to John and tell him I never want to see him again. How easy it would be yet how I fear doing it in case he really loves me after all. I suppose I really love him in spite of myself. Crazy.

Wednesday 8th April 1964

Again walked across the common to Oliver's. Met strange boy called John. I appear it would seem to be haunted by them. How strange.

It is a beautiful day and at last I feel happy. The thought of John Brice make me sad even in this sunshine though. I hope he won't be too hurt and go and fail his Tripos or something awful, I'd feel so guilty.

Thursday 9th April 1964

Tripos, "my dear", Tripos. I didn't even get ready to go out with John in the evening after returning from my 1st day back at college. I was so sure it was the end. However we went for a walk on the common, found a gorse bush and sat and talked under it. He showed me all the positions for copulation which I found terribly amusing and rather thrilling.

Friday 10th April 1964

Today I was very wicked and didn't go into college until the afternoon. Well I managed to do some work. In the evening had French class then rehearsals, then no 21. I just hate people. Old Phillip actually offered me a lift but in the end I came down with John Doswell. John Brice returned to Cambridge today.

Saturday 11th April 1964

Went to college, for chem. Pretty boring proved for zinc, white precipitate. In the afternoon went running on the common with the twins. Boy! Do I feel stiff. I can hardly move! Wrote to John B.

Remember poor old Granny today. How I miss her.

Sunday 12th April 1964

Went to see other Granny. Proved as always a pretty boring ordeal, with Daddy being sickly sweet and Mummy vainly trying to make conversation. Everybody was relieved I think by 6 pm. Daphy as always shows off to the full, however, I for one treat it with the contempt it deserves. Poured with rain on the way back.

Monday 13th April 1964

Went into college late due to a visit to the doctor about a rash on my back and hands. Brendan accused me in no uncertain terms of doing it on purpose. (Well who can speak for the subconscious.) Went to evening class, old Wilkins (Walton) was there. I think he is terribly nice, primarily because he amuses me with his Grandfatherly air and boyish looks.

Tuesday 14th April 1964

Did a zoo, prep of a striated muscle. Had a lesson with Mr Pike (physics), awful. He gave us a vast sheet of exercises to do by next month.

Well must do some work, I really have to get through these exams.

Got a letter from Paddy and one from Valerie.

Wednesday 15th April 1964

Slept in. No Oliver, no college. Went in for lunch and then in the afternoon for a drive in Steve's car, then glass blowing. Went for a run on the common in the evening, don't feel quite so stiff this time.

New boy in our class called Ling. David Ling. Minute but highly intelligent.

Thursday 16th April 1964

The rain is falling in thick heavy sheets, the time is 7.15 am and I'm supposed to be doing some work. It's the hosts heavenly sound as it drums on the roof and patters down the drain pipes. This morning I slept in as Mummy forgot to wake me, which explains I suppose why I feel so exhilarated now. How the thunder crashes!

Friday 17th April 1964

Stayed at college all day today. Brendan was his usual inspiring self. We had a frightful row over the way he says his grace making a very obvious sign of the cross and muttering loudly, it seems comically false to me however he declares hotly that he means it. Poor old O'farrell. Idiot!

Went to rehearsals in the evening, only a few more days. Glory!

Saturday 18th April 1964

Went into chemistry in morning. Played cards all afternoon. Very wicked but great fun. Watched Juke Box Jury and Taxi and thoroughly enjoyed both. I really am getting terribly lazy. In the evening what was left of it ate a huge supper; a blissful day of nothingness.

Sunday 19th April 1964

Slept in, rose at 12 am. Hurriedly learnt my lines and bombed up to the hall after ceremonials. Sunday lunch. Rehearsal went well, stayed in the hall for tea. Church missionary do after. Interesting. Careered back to watch Hamlet. Stupendous! Only the TV blacked out ½ way thro' it, maddening.

Monday 20th April 1964

Rolled in at 11.30 pm for organic chemistry. It was practical and we distilled alcohol (ethyl). Old Ling splashed acid in Dilly's eye and roared with laughter as she almost cried with agony. These Japs.

Went to physics class in the evening. Got a letter from John Brice. A really foul epistle, ragging me like mad with great exclamation marks and references to very private relationships we've had. I really is too bad of him.

Went down to 39 Pine Walk for supper with the Chamberlains. Felt totally inferior as usual, Jill and Annette talked about their boy friends. I smiled secretly. Why does one have to talk so much about a boy you go out with to others. It's far better to have it as a secret between you and him.

April 1964

Wednesday 22nd April 1964

Felt terrible tired God knows why. I slept in till 10.30 am. In the afternoon went out on the field with Steve, Clive, Martin, Brendan ran 100 yds and came last. Disgraceful. Did glassblowing, the man, Mr Davidson, showed me how to make a beautiful curly glass snake. Mine turned out a bit crazy and dilapidated. Never mind. Slow woman! Not very funny.

Thursday 23rd April 1964

What a really pathetic day it has been. Pam and I went out for walk, miles and miles over fields and hedges and got lost. We were 30 minutes late for Botany. Oh well we found 2 black hats which we kept. The world seems determined to be dismal. It started to pour with rain and the thunder crashed until it seemed the earth would crack with the noise. Very terrifying.

Friday 24th April 1964

We did the plotting of a cooling curve for teraphalene this morning which was on the whole a very pretty experiment as the t. crystallises but into long slender crystals which glisten with an almost uncanny brightness in the sunlight. Yes we actually saw the sun today. Heaven. In the evening dashed home, swallowed a hurried supper then to rehearsals.

Saturday 25th April 1964

I feel terribly happy today perhaps it is because I have for a change been pleasant to humanity in general. Old Ling " walked me" to Ewell West Station as he put it. An odd little chap. I suppose really I should be learning my chem. But I can't be bothered. I am getting terribly lazy and lethargic. Wrote a beastly letter, but rather subtle, to John Brice.

Sunday 26th April 1964

"Sleep that Knits up the ravelled sleeve of care, sore labours of bath". (*Macbeth*)

Glory, I should I was tied in knots and drowned this morning. I slept till 12 am. Shocking but bliss. Went and sold tickets to Brices. Mr B. very cynical but a sense of humour. Mrs B. smiled at me, rather too sweetly for my liking, I am afraid that whatever her hopes I am not going to be no daughter-in-law of hers.

Monday 27th April 1964

Do I live to live or live to die? The latter part is of little concern to me for I am but a living thing.

I went to evening physics class and as usual felt totally inferior. How I hate people and their fake pride.

Tuesday 28th April 1964

Today rehearsals have started with a vengeance, of course, I arrive 1/4 of an hour late and Maurice has a secret fit in the corner. Well I can't help it but must remember those words I read "Do not dare to live without some clear intention toward which your living shall be bent" (*Phillips Brooks*). Oh so true, I say.

Wednesday 29th April 1964

Again I find myself tripping up to the hall. These are fine clear evenings, the smell of spring is in the air and I somehow feel happy as I strolling to the hall swinging my bag with the books poking out of the top. Only the string does cut into my fingers. So sad I remember how carefully poor Dave threaded them into the bag.

Thursday 30th April 1964

First night nerves. My tummy felt highly peculiar as I walked onto the stage shouting "You will have to wait ..." But after a while I loved it and felt completely in my element and at ease. The feeling of power as one recites one's lines with feeling and depth, the subtle pauses and the roar of laughter as they understand the joke.

The Pioneers was a club for all young people in the West Wimbledon area. It met at Christ Church Hall. In the Pioneers' dramatic society's May 1964 production of "When we are married" by J. B. Priestley Jenny got top billing as Rosa. John Doswell also appeared as did another friend she kept in touch with, Anne Marie Bundell. The final play for that year was Jean Anouilh's "Ring around the Moon" in which Jenny played Isabelle, a ballet dancer.

Friday 1st May 1964

Tonight, Mummy, the twins, A. Dorothy, Jill and Annette and U. will come and see the play. I felt so excited when they rushed up to me saying how good I was and how did I manage to keep up the accent etc etc. I will never forget the look of sheer, hero worship in the Daphy's eyes as she congratulated me. Somehow life is worth the living again.

May 1964

Saturday 2nd May 1964

The performance went like a bomb. We had a full house with people standing at the back. Brendan comes as did Victoria and her friends. Afterwards we had a wild time on the stage and lots of people said that they thought I was foreign really. (Rather a back handed compliment I thought). Afterwards we strolled down to Margaret's house and had another booze up with dancing etc. Walked home with Alistair (+ motor bike).

Sunday 3rd May 1964

Oh how wonderful to sleep and sleep and sleep. We did another performance and John and Helen gave me a lift down. (At every performance, I forgot to put it down, I read Pilgrims Progress. Really very enlightening.) Phillipa and I made ourselves up as witches. I do hope this tooth doesn't come out. I'll look hideous.

Monday 4th May 1964

Mummy looks very tired, I think she has got flu. I often secretly wonder how much she really does miss Granny. More than any one realises shouldn't wonder. How terrible to loose ones mother. I never really thought about it like that before. Poor Mummy is an orphan now. Oh gosh I am so horrible to her sometimes.

Tuesday 5th May 1964

Had a sore throat all day, feel awful. Went to bed early and washed my hair and then brushed it with brilliantine which I am told is supposed to make it look shiny. Had a frightful row with Brendan about the Immaculate Conception. I myself think that one cannot have a child if coitus hasn't been performed. (Genteel way of putting it).

Wednesday 6th May 1964

Got up at 10 to 8 and sat listening to dismal music in the kitchen then marched across the common to Mrs Oliver's; next appointment July 7th 10.30. She inserted needles into my tooth again to drain it again. Ouch! Didn't go into college, felt too ill.

Thursday 7th May 1964

A flirtatious and quarrelsome day. I don't know why at all, but I had lunch with Brendan, Steve, Bince, Christopher Cutler and Brian and was made a terrible fuss of and thoroughly mocked. It was rather nice to be the centre of attraction again. I wore the blue and white striped shirt, perhaps that did it.

Oh it's a poor stupid melancholy little world at the moment. I feel so depressed. Rosy is in a bad mood again.

Friday 8th May 1964

I think something spectacular is going to happen on this day, perhaps I am to go to heaven. But actually nothing spectacular did happen at all. It was a rather boring and uninteresting day, with Enderslee at the end of it. I posted off a letter to Dave and was given 3 beautiful rabbit skins by the B2 students, positively exquisite.

Saturday 9th May 1964

Went to chemistry in the morning, did no work at all in the afternoon and then went out in search of a fair in Putney with Brendan in the evening. We went past a churchyard with all the graves white and awful in the moonlight. How I would hate to be dead, a mere nothingness, our life is so short, so very short. (Russell came round – his father is dead)

Sunday May 10th 1964

Got up late as usual. We all sat and watched the new T.V. in the afternoon (it came yesterday). I think myself that the Beatles are positively foul. But everyone to their own taste I suppose. Went up to the club in the evening. I should have gone into the church but stayed in the hall and did the washing up instead. I suppose that God appreciates that much more than going into church and thinking blasphemous thoughts really!

Monday 11th May 1964

Received a very strange letter from Dave. I appears he has met a new "friend"; I hope it isn't a male one again. If it's a woman then I've had my day and it is all over, but couldn't bear him to go through that awful phase again. Got a letter from Alison.

Tuesday 12th May 1964

Oh it's been so heavenly, so hot, we all ran onto the field and flung ourselves down on that gorgeously soft clover. It must be the earth in ones flesh that makes nature smell so sweet. I'm beginning to think I'm infatuated by Christopher Cutler, so silly because he is so terrible ugly. Wrote to Paddy. Got a letter from Valerie.

May 1964

Wednesday 13th May 1964

Received letter from Paddy asking me again to meet him this Saturday. We must see what happens. Stayed at home all day and revised (like Hell!). How I wish I could find a friend who takes me as he finds me and sees my true self through all the confusions and imperfections. It would be so lovely, how I wish it.

Thursday 14th May 1964

Did spermatogenesis in zoo. Very interesting. Didn't do any prep. Just feel too tired. It is a shame I'll just be starting exams as J.B finishes them. Merciful really I suppose. Oh I don't know he can be great fun but rather boisterous. I do miss him really in my inner heart only I won't admit it. Silly Girl!

Friday 15th May 1964

Brendan and I found a little secluded spot beside the railway bank and learnt our notes all afternoon, it was really very cosy. I ate the most huge apple. B told me a filthy joke about dripping tampax. I always thought he was good and innocent. We live and learn. Didn't go to French, went to rehearsals to discuss new play. Romeo and Juliet. Ha ha.

Saturday 16th May 1964

Went to college. Pam wasn't there and it seemed strange without her somehow. In the evening went to Waterloo to meet Paddy, at first we didn't know what to do and just wandered by the river. Talked a lot about the shooting lodge and Pat, and Brian and Nathan. Paddy's really terrible shy, then went to see "Oliver" in the evening. It was fantastic and I of course had to go and faint in the middle of it. Sickening!

Sunday 17th May 1964

Got up at 11 am. Dissected a poor earthworm and then went over to see Victoria and Aunty Jean who are moving out today of No 7 Dunmore Road. Went up to see old Mavis in the afternoon, she's really rather pathetic. How I hate the way Rosy bosses Daphy around it's so pointlessly pugnacious.

Monday 18th May 1964

Meant to get up and attempt revision but somehow it was nearly 11 am before I actually did. Did some work on the halogens in the morning and then in the afternoon cycled over to Granny's, met Tony on the way and had a long chat. Daddy has been foul shouting and yelling and calling Mummy "Mohammedan cow". Such a spiteful, petty man, and the sun shone brightly too.

Tuesday 19th May 1964

Nothing of importance happened today. I tried my hand at cooking again and managed a rather delicious Bakewell tart. Did some revision. Then went over to Granny's. The tortoises really look very healthy. Wrote letters to Valerie, Paddy, John, Dave, Alison, Eugen. Mammoth mounds of correspondence! It was a heavenly day.

Wednesday 20th May 1964

Only one more week and Dunmore Road will be auctioned. Oh I can't bear it. Everybody is so terribly depressed at the thought but it has to go. We, Victoria, the twins and I ran and ran around the house just to remember it. I must have one last bath there before it is sold. It seemed strange somehow being able to run around the house screaming without being told off by Granny or Grandpa. I do wish with all my heart they could still be here to tell us off as much as they like though.

Ate a forlorn lunch at Dunmore road by myself. It reminds me so much of last summer when just Granny and I used to study in the afternoon, she was such a wonderful, wonderful help to me.

Friday 22nd May 1964

A diary, I presume should concern, solely oneself and ones day to day activities rather selfishly but then one is an individual, when I am dead there will never be another me so must write and write truly about myself so that other people remember me. At first their memories will fade whilst what I have written will remain long after even they are dead, "Time laughed at everything, but my diary laughed at time" (*Ann Franks Diary*)

At 1 o'clock this morning I was flushed and excited and dancing with Rodney Rye the millionaire's son. An enchanting feeling. I do so thank God for giving me the power to be able to dance, to dance, fast fiery dances besides!

Sunday 24th May 1964

We went over to Dunmore Rd for perhaps the last time, poor, poor Granny and Grandpa. But the house is beginning to seem less strange now without them. It just shows even those whom we love most dearly we soon, oh so soon learn to live without. Time will cure everything, yes it most certainly will. I suppose it's a blessing.

May 1964

Monday 25th May 1964

Went to college for organic chemistry, at long last the light is breaking through on that dismal and miasmic gloom surrounding the subject.

In the evening I went up to the library for an hour, came down, ate beans on toast and then plunged into 3 solid hours of physics. Chronic! But worth it I hope.

Tuesday 26th May 1964

I felt frightfully embarrassed all during the zoo class because I was convinced the button at the back of my shirt was undone and everybody could see my patched up underwear. However on dashing to the cloakroom in the break I found it wasn't. Relief! We went over to Dunmore Road again, oh so sad. I just cried and cried.

Wednesday 27th May 1964

We all thought it would be the last time we set foot in no. 7 but it wasn't. Glory, glory to what ever God is giving us. Mummy, A. Jean, Derek, Daddy, M. Fisher, M Baker and I sat in awful suspense "£3000" said a man "£3100" squeaked Daddy and so it went on. And we got it for £4900! Marvellous!

The grandmother's will had left an eighth to John, an eighth in trust for Victoria and three quarters to Cynthia, Jennie's mother. Auntie Jean Amy's other child was considered too untrustworthy to be left a legacy. However Cynthia had been asked to make sure that Victoria was cared for.

All afternoon I watched Brendan pole vaulting, he just lost his championship.

Thursday 28th May 1964

I just felt it was going to be an unlucky day and it has been. In the morning I especially went into college on the presentiment that I would miss something if I didn't and wasted a whole morning as we couldn't find a classroom. Afternoon – genetics, dashed interesting. Evening I went to see Robert and he showed me around Ewell Castle grounds. I felt frightfully uneasy with him, goodness knows why.

Friday 29th May 1964

Brendan and I again found our "little place" near the railway and revised and argued etc. In the evening I went up to rehearsals by special request (I was very flattered) and performed a very melodramatic part which I fear Maurice will give me. We then went along to the pub, it's interesting psychologically how much attention one can get if only one is unusual for I found myself the centre of attraction merely because I wore a sprig of eucalyptus in my duffel coat. Strange. Rodney brought me home. Over sexed wretch! Felt rather unwell, took rabbit run over to Granny's, read D. H. Lawrence "Sons and Lovers". Superb.

Sunday 31st May 1964

I still feel far from well and haven't done any work. However tonight I will swear to God on my bible to pass these exams so it's his will I do or not.

It is strange how all the boys hate John Br. So much, I wonder if it's jealousy, wouldn't be surprised.

Monday 1st June 1964

I wandered in for organic chemistry had lunch and then went home again. On the whole felt positively wretched but crawled off at 6.30 to physics. Perhaps the complaint is psychological because as soon as I started working at the physics problems I felt fine again. Very odd. I really don't think I am going to pass these exams.

Tuesday 2nd June 1964

Today I've had the most terrible row with Brendan. How dare he say that I act in a supercilious fashion. Stupid boy. In the afternoon Dilly and I had physics and old Pike went round the class asking us definitions. Pathetic. I was filled with chagrin when my own came as I just couldn't remember what a watt was (!).

Wednesday 3rd June 1964

The trains were packed as it's Derby day. After lunch Pam and I hitched up to the downs. First of all we got a lift in a van with a little old man and jolted noisily along. Then we got a lift from two awful convict types in a black saloon. Everywhere was packed with swarthy gypsy men in bowler hats, screaming women, and air was tinged with the fragrance of damp earth, onions and horses. A shudder of excitement went through the crowd as we jostled our way through the crowds frantically sucking lollies. On the way back the car was a handsome "Dodge", a huge American car.

June 1964

Thursday 4th June 1964

Today is Granny's birthday. I whispered a rather foolish "Happy Birthday" as I got up.

Friday 5th June 1964

After staying up at the cemetery with Victoria for about 3 hours last night I felt as if I was in for a nervous relapse this morning. It was so peaceful up there though with the rooks chattering in the poplars and the rows of gravestones very white in the twilight. We put 3 roses on Granny's and 3 on Grandpa's. It's so awful to have a bare patch of ground the size of a tennis ball the only visible sign that one ever existed, but that's what they wanted.

Saturday 6th June 1964

Today we had chem. prac. A most terrible feeling of nausea swept over me as I walked in and started feverishly setting up apparatus. Afterwards I was told I had every titration wrong. I could weep. Brendan came and cut the lawn. "Some ladies do."

Sunday 7th June 1964

I got up very late and tried to wash the mud out of the cuts in my hands. I must be mad to go to bed with tetanus bacilli crawling all over me. Hope I don't get it. Went over to Granny's in the afternoon to do some gardening. Only few more days till the exams. I must really start working!

Monday 8th June 1964

Diana, Brendan and I went in for organic and found to our dismay that we were the only ones present. Still we picked up a few hints for the exams.

I wore my "unlucky" brown dress today, but somehow everybody admired it and it brought me luck. Old Welton said it took his breath away. Silly fool!

Tuesday 9th June 1964

We all went traipsing in because we thought we would have zoo. prac. We didn't. Typical, so that's another morning wasted. I got good luck card from J. B. He can keep it. Got a strange letter from Dave saying, for some apparent reason, that he never wishes to see me again. Actually the feeling is quite mutual although I do try and pretend that I feel something.

Wednesday 10th June 1964

We went rock-climbing in the afternoon and got lost in Steve's car (in the country!). Richard, Brendan, Pam, Steve and I we had a simply glorious time scrambling up and over rocks and running through the rippling grass. Richard found a birds nest with 3 baby birds. I laughed until my sides ached to watch him crawling thro' the bracken looking for them.

Granny died 5 months ago today. Poor Granny. I do wish she'd lived to see this lovely weather.

Thursday 11th June 1964

1st Exam. In the exam room one either becomes a professor or an idiot. In the former case the anxiety disappears, your heart swells inside and with great deliberation hardly able to wipe the smile from your face you flourish the pen as it flows over the paper. But to feel an idiot, your palms sweat, the pen keeps writing the wrong things everybody is smiling secretly to themselves you want to scream and beat the ground with your fear and hate. The pen splutters and blots, the minutes fly past as despair comes sobbing into your brain. It is the end.

Brendan kissed me for the first time today. Our friendship has lost yet gained an essential something. It was a very rough kiss and yet something hard ached inside me as his hand crept down over my blouse and I sprang away hastily and reproached him strongly. What a crazy idiot I am!

Saturday 13th June 1964

Paddy and I wandered around the bookshops of Charing Cross Road, which I might add are really rather exciting. We charged into the Dominion Theatre and watched "Cleopatra" with great earnestness and then we went home. Not madly gay I suppose but relaxing.

Mummy will probably come back on Tuesday. However lets hope the rest will do her good. I feel frightfully guilty at letting Rosy do so much but really how can I when I these b. exams almost on me.

Monday 15th June 1964

Brendan met me for lunch and we wandered to the railway bank afterwards. He declared in hot terms that he loved me dearly, which, although it may appear conceited I really believe, poor old Brendan. At first, according to him, he found merely the woman in me attractive now it seems it is myself that he loves. My feelings towards him are rather mixed, sometimes I feel strongly attracted to him and yet at others he annoys me intensely; I suppose that's one calls "Love." Rather frustrating as I sit close to him for every lecture every hour of every day practically.

Tuesday 16th June 1964

I received a letter from Paddy complete with photos. Mummy came back very late on Sunday night. I have actually managed to start revising my chemistry. Oh if only I knew what topics we are going to get!

Wednesday 17th June 1964

Just sat around thinking that this is the very last day I'm ever 17 again.

Thursday 18th June 1964

Great shrieks and yells of "Happy Birthday Jenny". I suppose it all compensates for growing 1 year older! Mummy gave me two most heavenly rings. One the shape of fish coiled together to for a setting. And another of silvery material, and laid with sparkling jewels (glass actually I think but oh so exquisite).

I received a card labelled "Happy Birthday Sweetheart" from Paddy and a screaming one from Brendan telling me not to go out and have a good time without him. I won't. We had a glorious tea (spoilt a bit by Daphne getting 'moody') but still jolly sweet of Mummy as she wasn't feeling very well.

Friday 19th June 1964

Brendan and I came in for lunch. Joe brought me 4 adorable baby guinea pigs and every girl in the cloakroom has a secrets swooning fit over them. We (B and I) went to our bower afterwards and he started kissing me so passionately I was a bit afraid. However he suddenly declares "I can never marry because of our religions"; Typical of the man. I got the part in the play, Rodney drove me home and made violent love once more. I almost lost my virginity (in a car of all places really).

Saturday 20th June 1964

Brendan's going to a party tonight and I'm so frightfully jealous and afraid he'll meet somebody new. Strange how much I care about him. I just hate life at the moment and spent all today revising.

Sail On, Silvergirl, Sail On By

Sunday 21st June 1964

Got up at 11 am. Washed my hair. Sat around in my bedroom thinking of Brendan. I really must do some work.

Monday 22nd June 1964

It's a horrible thought but I'm convinced I am really psychic. I knew in my bones that B. would meet some girl at that damn party and he did. Penny (name and nature I shouldn't wonder). His mouth was quivering with secret emotion as he told me. My God how it hurt although I didn't, I hope, show it merely saying " if I am supposed to be jealous, forgive me, but I am not" (inside my heart was bleeding to bits though). But as always I shall woo him as though I love him, poor Brendan he shall pay for his calculated little piece of malice, by God, I swear it.

Tuesday 23rd June 1964

Tonight it was a beautiful evening, clear as a bell and with that warm earthy smell of recent rain still lingering mysteriously over the damp earth. As I strode through the grass it " shushed" pleasantly. The sunset was superb like the slow and agonised demise of some huge golden bird sending hot ears of blood into the very air itself. A struggle and then the last glistening feather sank softly into the darkness.

Wednesday 24th June 1964

Brendan is paying with every ounce of his heart now. He is afraid, anxious to please, perplexed and angry that his conversation is ignored by everyone, that I don't wait for him for lunch anymore and that when spoken to I answer in cold, satirical biting tones. Ha, my little darling just see what comes next to you!

Thursday 25th June 1964

Today we had our organic exam, I have been reading a book and really repent of being so cruel to Brendan, I did my best to make up and he responded admirably. I suppose everything is alright except for that beastly little something. However I am beginning to feel I have fallen in love for the very first time, strange how it gnaws at my soul.

Friday 26th June 1964

We met for lunch and exchanged shy secret smiles. Afterwards we went to our bower and talked and talked all afternoon. I feel sick with love to be even near him and at last I think he knows it fool that I am for this is the way to lose him

Saturday 27th June 1964

B. came over at 3pm. We went over to No. 7, mowed the lawn and then went up to the common and danced round and round the golf course. Hot and tired we went for a drink at 10 pm and then purchased a bottle of rum (4/6d) and drank it secretly in a gorse bush. To test B. religion I told him that couldn't touch me unless he made a sign of the cross first. Oh how I regret having said that, for almost in tears he was so distressed he told me that his religion meant more to him than I did, so he had better leave me. In the quiet of Dunmore Rd I just lay feeling wretched.

Sunday 28th June 1964

John Brice arrived looking positively beautiful and of course I said "yes" when he asked me out. We went onto the common and he started putting his hands in all the wrong places. It made me angry for after B's great respect for my body I felt degraded and cheap, so I became cold to J.B. He really is a silly fool and so I suppose am I. "The octopus had 8 testicles wrote the student. What a lot of balls retaliated the examiner." Not very amusing.

Monday 29th June 1964

Went onto the downs with B. great fun!

Tuesday 30th June 1964

Glory! I never really thought in my wildest dreams I'd make it into B2 with honours! (to be truthful I really wondered if I would make it at all). I told Lawrence I wanted to be a speech therapist, god knows why. Rosy and Mummy are supposed to be ill today. Before, I was terribly worried about M. She really was ill. However I'm inclined to wonder if it is "workitis"!

Wednesday 1st July 1964

I received a letter from Valerie asking me down to stay, however how can I if I am going youth hostelling. Gosh it should be fun, we've decided to go down to Cornwall instead of Scotland, which really I'm glad about. Went to our bower in the afternoon. Evening work, work. Botany is so boring though.

Thursday 2nd July 1964

Botany exam today, cripes. I don't know a thing. We have got the snapdragon and by a lucky chance I guessed it was scrophulacea. Went for a long walk with B. on the downs afterwards. Then back for J.B. He was positively foul this evening, don't know why I bother with him really.

Friday 3rd July 1964

Brendan and I came in for lunch and then went shopping in Epsom, I bought new sandals, stockings, notepaper etc. Old Brendan had the cash (£6) so it was alright. In the evening went up to rehearsals. Ended up on the floor of Rodney (millionaire's) house. Awfully low I suppose (joke) but felt in a primitive sort of mood. Got back at 1 am!

Saturday 4th July 1964

Went to dance at Ewell Tech. with B. (should have been going out with John Brice and really it would have been better if I had). People were shrieking and swaying on each others shoulders, hanging out of windows, crying, and the noise, the drums throbbed through ones soul. I thought the roof was going to fall down. Met B's parents. They disliked me.

Sunday 5th July 1964

The twins birthday. Gave them stockings. We went up to a service at the crematorium. Oh, it was so sad. We were all very hysterical and didn't feel much like having a birthday. There were a lot of tears and Mummy lost her temper. In fact is a horrible memory altogether and I don't want to write about it. Went to No 7 with J.B. He cheered me up greatly. Showed me various positions again. Awfully dull.

Monday 6th July 1964

Brendan came over with the news that we can't go youth hostelling. I was so angry and upset that I made an absolute fool of myself. We had a frightful row, but he stayed all afternoon and evening. We went to see "Gigi" and when he'd gone I wrote him "the" letter, like a fool.

Tuesday 7th July 1964

Arrived at B's house looking like nothing on earth (on purpose). His mother wasn't impressed with me. So by God she won't be. Cycled over. Sat around with B. then cycled home. Of course he shows me a "short cut", which takes about 10 minutes longer. Anne Marie came round and tried to convert me. She actually succeeded.

Wednesday 8th July 1964

John Brice again. We went over to Dunmore Rd and "mucked around" in the dining room. He read to me out of a Chinese book from right to left. I laughed in a hollow sort of manner at first, but honestly, ½ hour of it is a bit much. Then he became awfully loving and, of course, like a fool I responded. Finished off the bottle of sherry, or rather J.B. did.

Thursday 9th July 1964

Met Brendan at college and paid my fees. We went for a walk n the downs which was quite pleasant. Probably we'll go abroad for a year when we're married. Then met Robert, + umbrella. We ate raw beef in the Green Man and he told me how Dave was really a few screws loose. However I still like Dave even after the way he's treated me. Robert says he's (R.) entirely on my side. Joy!

Friday 10th July 1964

Went cycling to Reigate with B. Had a frightful row in the woods. I pinched his side between my nails a little too hard but he still didn't hit me. Then we made it up in a loving fashion and I gave him dancing lessons after lunch. We stopped at pub on the way down. Went to see Tony in the evening. The likeness between him and B. is uncanny. Ended up only just escaping a virgin again but I don't mind T. He's a great friend of mine. It's so marvellous to be able to talk and flirt with him and know that neither of our hearts is broken.

Saturday 11th July 1964

Went out with J.B. to "Green Man" and then to Epsom downs. He was in a bit of a mood and kept poking me, which, frayed my temper so I bit him (he nearly broke my arm for the trouble) and then he sulked and nothing I did brought him out of it. So we went home and at last he thawed out and we laughed about it. By unanimous vote the affair with J.B., is over but it ended on a happy note which I'm pleased about, it's always better to part friends.

Monday 13th July 1964

Phoned up B. at 12 o'clock. Did some shopping in Wimbledon. B's father in hospital.

Brendan came over at 3 o'clock and drove us up to the common, where we went for a walk. Met Susan Miller but pretended not to see her. B. had to be home by 8 as his <u>dear</u> mother worries otherwise. Oedipus complex there alright.

Tuesday 14th July 1964

Went to Oliver's. B. picked me up at the fountain on W. Hill. Met his brother for lunch and pinched gorgeous glass. Finbar is a strange character, I'd say there was VD in the family though as his head is too big for his body. Went to Lloyds and Stock Exchange. Had supper in a glorious restaurant with shells all over the walls. Saw "Mad, Mad, World". Very funny. (*Film with Terry Thomas et al*)

Wednesday 15th July 1964

B. came over at 4. We went up to Canizzaro and on arriving back were greeted by shrieking Rosy and Mummy in a bad mood. I could have wept as I do so want B. to think that we're a happy family. Then I lost my temper and made a fool of myself. At last we (B and I) set off for the dress show. It was interesting to see the old school again.

Thursday 16th July 1964

Did a launderette. B. came over at 4pm. I'm frightfully apprehensive about Sunday. Mummy has declared that she is going down to see the people. B. and I went up to Canizzaro again and again it was really pleasant, he cycled over today and took my photo. Dear old B., went home at 11pm.

Friday July 17th 1964

Went down to B's school. I wished in a way he didn't want me there. We sat beside the river Wey. I suppose really I get on better with him than any other boy, merely probably because I feel superior to him. He drives fairly well now and has certainly developed the driver's "cantankerisity"

Saturday 18th July 1964

Oh dear, one more day at home. M. we took to see them today. I went to Mrs Oliver's. Then B. and I went out for our last walk this hols, very sad. Old B. depressed and trying to be so melodramatic, after all it's only two months. I was at home by 10 o'clock.

July 1964

Sunday 19th July 1964

Mummy accompanied me to Liverpool St. and I just caught the 10.36 am to Cambridge. To be truthful I felt like a jelly until I saw the daughter and she was just such a meek little woman I was too fascinated to start thinking about myself. Dr Keiling, well at first I was petrified, a stern look very erect, diminutive woman eyebrows pencilled in heavily. We saw the daughter off on the 6 something train and the doctor drove us home in her crazy old car. Mummy phoned up at 10.

Monday 20th July 1964

Rose at 9 and ate a very strained breakfast in the "upper kitchen". Old K. isn't bad really, but frightfully talkative! We started French lessons. I went into C. centre after lunch.

Tuesday 21st July 1964

We had a French lesson in the "study" this morning and she showed me her paintings some are really rather good. After lunch I walked into Cambridge along the river. First I went to the Fitzwilliam museum, beautiful paintings, and sculpture; later as I walked down St Andrews St., I met Hobbes of Keys College. He showed me round one of the colleges. Odd boy.

Tuesday 22nd July 1964

Today it was flap, flap, as I was to go to the Art's theatre to see "Midsummer's Nights Dream", when I eventually arrived it was sold out. Joy! So, like a mad idiot I went and haunted the place that I stayed in last time I was in Cambridge. I got so depressed.

Thursday 23rd July 1964

We had a lesson during breakfast. Really it's a bit much but I suppose it's sweet of her to try so hard. I got a letter from Brendan, very touching. In the afternoon I walked out into the country, nearly got scooped by a car. On returning picked goosgogs. Heavenly! It was a hot clammy sort of day.

Friday 24th July 1964

We were supposed to be going into town today, but the creosote man called, so no town. In the afternoon I sunbathed on a bench in the grounds of St Johns and then met

John's (H) friend in the court of Keys college, he's rather lovely, but frightfully stuck up. The place is crawling with the French. Ghastly.

Saturday 25th July 1964

Into town this morning. Wow, was it hot. The sense of frustration was exquisite as I fumbled with the basket (on wheels) shoved past milling bodies and had to keep hunting for the doctor in the horizon of hats. We had a cold lunch, chicken and had a lesson on returning. In the evening went to see "Midsummer's Nights Dream" at the Art's theatre. Funniest production I've seen for years.

Sunday 26th July 1964

Today is the "day of rest" or so we put it in the Keiling household. We arose late and just pottered around after lunch I went for a walk to the chapel, but found I was too late for a service. Heavenly hot day.

Monday 27th July 1964

I roared into town at about 4pm just in time to catch Peter Grimaldi, John's friend. We sat on his scarlet sofa, drank sherry and talked about religion. Highly intelligent boy, however, he has the usual masculine character, conceit. My shoe broke and I had to walk home in bare feet!

Tuesday 28th July 1964

Had a bash on the typewriter in the evening after sitting on a bench on St John's college talking to Lawrence Paine (in every way) who is a friend of John Brice. Small world. I don't think Old Keiling is too well. Received and answered all the letters.

Wednesday 29th July 1964

Got a letter from Mummy saying J.B is looking very unhappy. I feel very guilty. In the afternoon after a French lesson went into town and sat on a bench in St Johns. "May I sit here please". Lawrence Paine again, oh dear. Went up to his set for tea, then he ran to see his beloved choir boys. I think like Oscar Wilde he's a sodomite.

Thursday 30th July 1964

Today I was supposed to be meeting old L.P. for tea. I found him sitting on the banks of

July – August 1964

St. Johns part of the river, on the eternal grey blanket spread out carefully so that there was just room for me!

Really I was very flattered as a sumptuous tea, with cake was carefully laid out in the set. He's a crashing bore tho! Afterwards we went to chapel.

Friday 31st July 1964

Perhaps it's dangerous to write about people in one's diary. Frankly, I'm of the feeling that a diary is a private epistle and shouldn't be read by other eyes. Essentially 'human' approach to an embarrassing situation! We went round to an exhibition of contemporary art. Hideous. Saw L. for a brief half hour and offended him by telling him he is a fool. Well so he is over some things.

Saturday 1st August 1964

Egoism should be one of the cardinal sins if it isn't already; I cannot bear the way old K goes on and on talking when she knows I have better things to do. Why is it that she can go out all day (as today) and leave me at home, yet if I want to go in the evening "It's a bit risky".

Sunday 2nd August 1964

Went to 8 am communion. French family came for afternoon tea and old K got in a most tremendous flap. So I went to play Brahms's German Requiem as loudly as I could, it's a pretty booming piece anyway. The tea wasn't much of a success as, as usual, K. bored everyone to tears by extremely lengthy stories of her life. The poor little girl was a mongol but highly intelligent. Mrs Whatever her name was had really the most beautiful eyes I have seen for a long time, and she had gold fillings in her teeth!

Monday 3rd August 1964

Wrote to J.B. Wow was it hot today! Millions of people out on the backs.

Tuesday 4th August 1964

Law. Paine is such a bore I've decided that I won't go and sit on the backs anymore! Old K. and I went on another shopping spree and I bought a marrow and attempted marrow bake. Hope it works. Elizabeth arrived at 8.30 pm. Such a sweet person and so marvellously unselfish. K and she sat up till midnight talking. I wonder who did the talking though.

Wednesday 5th August 1964

How I hate K. Will you never stop bossing me around? Alright so I move a little faster than you, it doesn't mean I'm going to break everything. E and I went for a walk in the country side. She told me that if I didn't get away soon I'd go mad!

Thursday 6th August 1964

E. and I crept out at 9 a.m. after K had disappeared to her lectures. Silly fool. I'm sure she doesn't take in half of it. E and I went for drive after lunch and in the evening dashed off to the theatre and left K talking to herself. After the play we sat in the roof garden and ate bacon and eggs. Heaven after K's diet. Had a row with E. over washing grapes!

Friday 7th August 1964

Went off at 7 am to new hospital and pushed trolleys and patients around for 5 hours. I thought I was going to faint afterwards. K. had lunch ready for me afterwards which I thought was very kind. However, she was awfully cold. Elizabeth had her operation and then went home. I went to bed very early.

Saturday 8th August 1964

I went out with Lawrence in the evening after a frightful row with old K. We went to the "Monks Head" and drank wine there and in his set. I really think he wanted to kiss me but is too much of a prig to try, progressing only as far as putting his arm around me on the sofa, upon which I leapt up and sat on the opposite chair. Poor L.

Sunday 9th August 1964

Absconded today after row with K. Went to say good bye to L. then caught 5.35 to Liverpool St. Travelled with fat American. Everybody was pleased to see me, however it's not a nice feeling to run away.

Monday 10th August 1964

It seems awfully strange to be at home again. I rose at 9 am and didn't really do much till the afternoon when the twins and I cycled up to the common and picked blackberries. We made a heavenly tart with them. Mummy has put on weight and looks awfully tired.

August 1964

Tuesday 11th August 1964

Last night I phoned J.B. in an Irish accent and was invited round. The German Frau turned out to be Danish, he was polite but cold and merely pecked me on the cheek when we parted. I told him about B. which was a mistake as he looked frightfully hurt.

Wednesday 12th August 1964

Daddy's started his Damned nonsense saying I'm a "slut" and various other detrimental things. I loathe the way he always takes it out on Mummy. Really I'm so ashamed for having such a loathsome thing for a father. Humanity? Lump of selfishness and sin if you ask me. How I hate him. By God he's not kicking me out for he brings me into the world, and ruins every chance I ever have surely if he is to earn the title "father" he can provide me with training or a profession at least.

We cycled to Chessington to pick blackberries.

Friday 13th August 1964

We went shopping. Got a p.c. from B. Up in the evening to the club. Ended up with Maurice not turning up and Lesley F. making a fool of herself by trying to be funny. Went pub crawling. Old Rodney took me home again. At one point I thought I was dealing with a maniac as he suddenly cried "put your arms around me". I got out as quickly as I could.

Saturday 15th August 1964

Slept in and went over to No. 7 in the afternoon. Oh dear the lawn does need cutting. D and M went to see A. Peggy while R and I stayed at home and watched a really exciting Dr Who! I did a bit more electrolysis and retired for the evening at the early hour of half twelve. Oh yes I had a bath!

Sunday 16th August 1964

I didn't go to church today but instead sat in No. 7 garden and tried to get a sunburn. In the afternoon tripped over to see Maurice, he doesn't look too well really. Gorgeously hot and sultry day. I think perhaps there will be a storm. The sky isn't as blue as it was in Cambridge.

Monday 17th August 1964

Sometimes I like writing this diary but by Jove sometimes I have awful qualms that perhaps alien eyes will read it. If they do I think if a conscience possessed them it should be a guilty one. I'm sick of the twins. D.s egoistic attitude to the rest of the family. Really it's just too bad if we all have to live together and two of us persist in having tantrums and being persistently spiteful. I really am beginning to hope that there's such a place as hell for if I'm going there others are as well. Praise be.

Wednesday 19th August 1964

Linda Randell came over. At first she was very sweet. However after an hour or so I didn't have a very high opinion at all. She brought over her drum and made such a noise. D. was showing off as usual and making an utter moron of herself.

Thursday 20th August 1964

The poor guinea pigs were very ill today so we scrubbed out the whole caboodle. In the morning cycled over to see Gt. Grandpa and sat for an hour or so listening to the dismal voice of the past. The poor guinea pig is really in great pain. I wish I could put it out of it somehow.

Friday 21st August 1964

Brendan came back today. I received a dismal letter declaring that he hadn't heard from me for weeks. Really he sounded awfully depressed and unfriendly on the phone. Perhaps he's just tired. Last night at home before we depart (in peace).

Saturday 22nd August 1964

Glory, bustle, bustle, off to Devon. Do hope the holiday is a success. We arrived very tired and irritable at Torquay station 1 ½ hrs later than expected. Mrs Goodwin is really very pleasant and we sat down to a huge supper of onions, beef etc. Later we went for a walk.

Sunday 23rd August 1964

Today I had my first bathe and of course went roaring in with my watch on. The Wetons arrived in the evening. Great fat jolly people, but rather coarse. Oh it's so lovely to be in Devon again.

Monday 24th August 1964

The weather was very dreary and so we decided to go shopping. I now have the most glorious suit of royal blue with a pale pink blouse to match. Very smart. Trying on clothes is such a tiresome business as one feels such a cad when really one doesn't want to buy. I feel so sorry for the poor assistant.

Tuesday 25th August 1964

I was violently sick and slept all day.

Wednesday 26th August 1964

Oh dear, tea with Lily and co. Not really tremendous fun. We all solemnly ate crumbly cakes and swallowed luke-warm tea. A typical tea-time atmosphere reigned which always makes me want to giggle. Oh the relief when it was all over!

Thursday 27th August 1964

After the most glorious day on the beach, during which I was in and out of the sea all day we were solemnly taken for a drive by Barbara to "see the lights". Really rather awful however we "ooed" and "aahed" in the right places, I hope.

Friday 28th August 1964

Barbara again took us for a drive this time to Teignmouth. The air good and feeling of perfect contentment makes one so ravenously hungry. Received a letter from Brendan. Dear old B. I went swimming all day.

Saturday 29th August 1964

We travelled for hours as really I couldn't leave without visiting Buckfast. It was an anti climax but I bought a crucifix and some holy pictures, not bad. Everybody was very tired. We saw entrance to Ingsdon from bus.

See Autobiography section for information on the convent school Jenny had gone to at an early age.

Sunday 30th August 1964

Only two more days in this lovely place, it's a crime. Mummy has really become rather friendly with old Goodwin. They both declare that their active interest in other peoples affairs is "for the good of mankind". I myself think (secretly) that it is a euphemistic was of saying "I'm a gossip!"

Monday 31st August 1964

The sea was so high today. Hissing and roaring on the Abbey sands wall. I felt very small and insignificant besides it. It is such a wonderful liquid glassy blue colour.

Tuesday 1st September 1964

I had a last look at the sea before catching the 11.55 from Torquay. Pleasant journey. Brendan took me out in the evening and we went to the Rawlpindi on Wimbledon Hill. Marvellous. It was marvellous to be together again but somehow I kept wanting to burst into tears. Idiotic.

Wednesday 2nd September 1964

I travelled up to Leicester for an interview and got lost. Had IQ test and 3 interviews very nerve racking. On returning here rather cold talk with B. on the phone. Victoria came over asking for money as usual, she's become very pretty but very common.

Thursday 3rd September 1964

Didn't get the job today so read poetry and applied as a " cha" unsuccessful. In the evening went over to B's, we ate baked beans ugh! Then hared over to Fox and Grapes for a quick drink. They were filming a commercial on the common and had great hoses to try and simulate rain, great fun as everyone was waddling around in galoshes and with umbrellas.

Friday 4th September 1964

I just hated today. I phoned Brendan in the evening and he was foul, then I stalked to drama and made a thorough mess of my part. Old R's got a new girl friend and I'm frightfully glad.

Saturday 5th September 1964

The others return. I spent the whole morning cleaning and cooking. Brendan called at 3 and we had the most heavenly afternoon on the common. Really I did enjoy it. In the evening we drove to Ewell, sat in the Green Man, then drove back to the common and talked in the car till 11 pm. B. gave me a huge box of Turkish delight and a lovely brooch. He tried a ring on my engagement finger!

September 1964

Sunday 6th September 1964

"If you can fill the unforgiving minutes with 60 seconds worth of distance run." (*"If" by Rudyard Kipling*). I wonder if I do. Somehow it's strange to be going back to college. I feel like a sea creature; flung out at high tides but gradually flowing back into the great sea again.

Monday 7th September 1964

My own inward soul; wasn't it Jesus who said "God is within the man himself". God is surely our own unconscious faith over which our will has no exercise. Why are people always rushing out of themselves? Why do they want excitement today. I started working at Kingston hospital, these poor women.

Tuesday 8th September 1964

I seem to spend all my time here scrubbing window sills and washing up. Miss Marshall is really very sweet; I do like her. Brendan seems very cold towards me now. It terrifies me to think that even he can learn to hate me like most other people. Still one can't buy affection.

Wednesday 9th September 1964

It's really very surprising how, if one is kind to a person in trouble, they learn to love you. Just a warm smile to a patient makes them fall over themselves to be nice to you. Strange, I suppose the old saying is true that life is merely toil and trouble, two things stand like stone, kindness in another's troubles, courage in your own. (*Adam L. Gordon, Australian poet, b. 1833*)

Thursday 10th September 1964

My day off. I slept during most of it. In the evening met Brendan. We were very cold. Had a golf course dance. Irritated each other then came home. I'm sorry it's not working. Mummy looks very tired.

Friday 11th September 1964

Back to work. Had the most awful time cleaning windows only 4/- an hour. They shouldn't do it to a dog. Went with B. to a barbecue, not terribly good. He is really a hopeless dancer. Suddenly I got one of those strange moods that I used to have (I can still vividly remember them as a child), I couldn't stand the noise and the bad dancing so I ran, just ran away from B. and everyone else. So silly as old B. must have thought I was frightfully ungrateful. He made a great fuss of me and everything was alright again. Strange.

Saturday 12th September 1964

Had a row with Shirley. B. took me for an hour onto the common.

Sunday 13th September 1964

In to work again. Really this is getting tiresome. I'm also absolutely fagged out. The patients are marvellous and so are some of the nurses. At least that's something I suppose. Church, God and religion seem to be going for a burton these days.

Monday 14th September 1964

Goodness knows how the wards manage to get so dirty. I returned in a very bad mood having tried to phone old B. He had a guts ache. How pathetic. Tomorrow he has to collect his parents from the airport. Joy!

Tuesday 15th September 1964

I had to work late and really didn't know what to do for supper for the poor patients. A. Jean is kicking up a fuss about the new room she must have this and must have that and the other. Honestly it's too bad. Glory tomorrow I have my interview how awful.

Wednesday 16th September 1964

I sat in this dingy hall with approx 12 other girls and trembled, 1st a phonetics test. Then other interviews with head etc. Met Val after, we went round the Chinese exhibition, "Railway of Death", It was terrifying.

Thursday 17th September 1964

How can human beings treat others like that. Let's pray for peace. Afterwards we went to the Savoy. Just as we were running guiltily upstairs a great shout of " come down". We came down very ashamed but he let me to ladies. Very sumptuous!

Friday 18th September 1964

Worked late today. Rehearsals. Maurice does get so irate, poor old chap. Afterwards we went to the Chinese restaurant and ate lobster balls. Met bloke called Chris, with most heavenly voice. Rod brought me home, he's quite mad! Oh dear I feel so tired. Work tomorrow.

Saturday 19th September 1964

Off at one and tore home to meet Brendan at 3. I got there at 5 to and he at 15 to. We are both angry because we thought the other was late. Had dismal time on the common just trying to make conversation. Old B. certainly has an eye for the girls. I suppose it's flattering that he looks at other women even more so that they look at him.

Sunday 20th September 1964

Last day at work. I had rather mixed feelings. The patients were sweet and gave me chocs galore. I think the most rewarding things were those beautiful smiles of gratitude though!

Monday 21st September 1964

Back to the jolly old Tech. for another year. Joy! Clive was being his old horrible self teasing me about Brendan. Talking of him (B.) I was given the most filthy look from that quarter on my first greeting him, later he told me that it was because he hated seeing me with others. I suppose I should be flattered.

Tuesday 22nd September 1964

Lord, I feel depressed, perhaps they've let off an H bomb. Autumn is really the most beautiful of the seasons; Spring is cold and fresh and young summer too bright, winter too cold but autumn so peaceful and calm with old gold sunshine and all the berries.

Wednesday 23rd September 1964

B. Was in a hell of a mood; we decided to walk to Epsom during our lunch break. Completely forgetting of course that it was a Wedn. Didn't help much. Did glass blowing in the pm and felt very odd as was the only old hand. In the evening went to boring rehearsal. Told old R I didn't want him to kiss me. He went off with a great rrrrrr.

Thursday 24th September 1964

Zoo is really rather pleasant esp. if you're treated as one of the elite. We had chem. in the pm and sat on the field for an hour. Had lunch in "our bower" as usual, B. is so wonderful.

Friday 25th September 1964

Went up onto the downs in the pm. Glorious, really heavenly. Had lunch in bower. I've never felt so happy! Old B. kept talking about how we "fell in love". It's awfully exciting. Yes I suppose he's right. Love is a possessive thing. Funny how I feel so attracted to B. now.

Saturday 26th September 1964

Did practically nothing except sleep. B. came over at 6 and we went to Gillian's party. I was wearing my mauve sparkly suit but with an oh so revealing blouse underneath. I don't really think B. enjoyed himself tremendously, we danced and played word games and then walked back from Surbiton. Joy!

Sunday 27th September 1964

Slept till 1.30 pm, wicked so very wicked. In pm went over to Dunmore Rd. The garden has a strange serenity. Oh I do adore Dunmore Rd. Daddy's done it up for A. Jean. This autumn weather is just bliss. How awful to think of the cold and winter yet to come. Must do some work. Did a caraway seed cake.

Monday 28th September 1964

Met B. in chemistry lab. Was the first to finish today, it was a great feeling. Had lunch in our bower, it was a bit chilly today. B. talks in such a matter of fact way about how we are going to get married. It really rather takes the thrill out of it. He wasn't well at all today. Allergy again.

Tuesday 30th September 1964

The morning was my own and I felt so damnably depressed. Yes Jane (= period) a week late. At least Mummy's fears of my being pregnant allayed! In the afternoon after a rather morbid lunch with B. owing I suppose to the fact we was late, and I have the most frightful back and tummy pains. I had a physics afternoon and felt like howling with rage all through it. Most strange.

Wednesday 31st September 1964

I'm beginning to rather dread Pike's physics lessons with old David Ling. B. and I had a good old heart to heart during lunch and been reconciliated again. It's really most odd how sometimes I hate B. and at others I love him so much I find it an almost physical pain in my mind.

Thursday 1st October 1964

Lordy how I have been dreading today. Our new chemistry man is really like a wicked goblin. The threatened test was merely oral but still frightfully nerve racking. The rooms are so beautiful at college in the late afternoons with the golden sunshine, almost serene. I went to see a Billy Graham film and had a really terrific hate for B. as he left me in the lurch very badly. I sat in the dark pit of the audience and wept my soul out silently. How could he be so cruel.

Friday 2nd October 1964

B. was all apologies but something seems to have gone wrong with my affections, he doesn't mean an awful lot to me now. Went to bed with severe laryngitis.

Saturday 3rd October 1964

Stayed in bed all am. In pm cut down hawthorn tree at Dunmore Rd and had huge bonfire. Cleaned my room. B. arrived at 7 and was escorted in ceremony upstairs to my room. Was very amorous at first and then I gave him a "be careful look", which set him on the reverse road and he helped me with chemistry problem. Told me in confidential terms about the jock strap! He had his first game at the rugby club and lost. Poor old B.

Sunday 4th October 1964

Just as I was settling down to some work Alistair and John Doswell call. Rehearsals. Maurice was positively elated that I'd got into the Central School of Speech and Drama. So am I really!

Monday 5th October 1964

Goodness knows what the matter with me is. I want him to be nice to me and somehow he seems to be the reverse. I must be absolutely crazy as I almost told him that I don't want to see him again. The look of terror in his eyes made me hesitate tho' as it really would be the end of all my hopes and prayers. I just couldn't bear it. So I pretended I'd had a dream.

Sail On, Silvergirl, Sail On By

Tuesday 6th October 1964

Lunch today was a tense affair as B. wanted to get away from the miserable wretch Jenny. I could feel it in my very bones. I'm quite sure he finds Lindsay damned attractive. Oh well I suppose it's really rather flattering as he does love me more than her although she's beautiful. Joy?!?!

Wednesday 7th October 1964

B. and I had lunch in the Green Man and then went walking on the "LCC land!" Oh dear it's really getting so cold and I do hate winter with all those beastly chilblains and numb fumbling fingers. The leaves are falling fast and furious now. I still remember Lavinia telling me not to watch the devils dance of the leaves whirling round on the pavement.

Thursday 8th October 1964

Today it poured and those gay crisp leaves are lying sodden and sullen in the gutters or plastered onto the ground. Poor things.

Friday 9th October 1964

B. didn't turn up today as he is going on some boat trip to the Isle of Sheppey. I feel positively miserable without him. Stupid creature am I. David Ling giggled besides me all through French and then got this other David to give us a lift home, it was rather exciting whirring along the wet roads.

Saturday 10th October 1964

Gardening. Its very hard work but really I do love it. Rosie and I dispose of the Hawthorn tree. Rather like a film "two hunched figures appeared out of the sleet hauling the 20' tree, hurled it over the "No tipping" sign and scampered off into gloom, pram wheels bouncing behind them!"

Sunday 11th October 1964

In the am we tripped up to the Kirk. Not terribly inspiring. The book of Rev. is really weird "Write the things which thou hast seen, and the things which are and the things which shall be". John 1.19. Might almost be the title to this diary.

Monday 12th October 1964

B. Chemistry. So depressing first thing on a Monday morning. On reading this diary just now every 2nd word seems to be "Brendan". I do think I'd better desist and start writing about something interesting. Perhaps he is my main interest in life though. Lordy, now awfully depressingly melodramatic!

Tuesday 13th October 1964

Went for my 2nd French lesson, she's a funny old thing. So frightfully strict and sarcastic. If you ask me most French folk are. Take old K for e.g. Sitting in our bower you can see the sky now as the trees have almost lost their leaves. I sat in the library and worked all pm. In the evening dyed my blouse green!

Wednesday 14th October 1964

Lordy, the last day I ever do glass blowing. Well it isn't all that inspiring. Mummy says I'm letting B. have his own way too much, Glory perhaps I am. Enough of that hackneyed subject tho! I went to see Tony tonight. He was very amorous and really rather sweet. Funny how we stay "just good friends" tho!

Thursday 15th October 1964

Oh dear, more rows with Clive. I do hope he does take Lindsay out. It would be so lovely to have two couples in the class. C. is always mocking me about religion, politics and B. Sickening! Politics; I stayed up till 1 am just to hear stupid men making facetious remarks and labour got in.

Labour under Harold Wilson got in.

Friday 16th October 1964

Clive and I were furious today. Labour, my goodness. B's going to wear his white shirt and old public school tie. Silly foolish boy, he's only trying to be like Clive and I, who have been staunch supporters of the blue cause for aeons. I suppose it's rather pathetic really. Nearly forgot he was "depressed" today!

Saturday 17th October 1964

Gardened in the morning and trotted around after B. in the late pm. He's frightened we're making it too physical. I'd be interested greatly to see why he says this, as I know damn well (and so does he) that we're not making it too physical. Something's going on in that funny little head of his. I think perhaps I'd better say "no next Saturday" and see what the outcome is.

Sunday 18th October 1964

Rehearsals are moronic. Espec if a certain person we know won't ever bother to learn his lines!

I hate hate hate ^{1000} B. No more to be said. I just hate and despise him.

Monday 19th October 1964

Started dissection of the dog-fish. Great fun flinging gut around. Jolly nice boy in zoo who always helps me with my microscope! The red haired girl on the train is just how I imagined Mummy to be when she was young. Perhaps not so shy though. Ewell West, Stoneleigh, Worcester Pk. Dreary monotonous voice.

Tuesday 20th October 1964

Had French lesson. Just as I was turning the corner near the dentists Tony and Jim came round. They laughed so loudly at my marvellous hair style. Rotters! Wendy made me heavenly dress.

Wednesday 21st October 1964

B. was extremely loving in the pm. But I'm afraid I didn't respond. Moron. We didn't go sailing. I was rather relieved. Really B. is incredibly selfish and not a bit kind hearted as I thought. Still better to find out now ... In pm rehearsals with Maurice. Jane Sherwin appears to have taken a great liking. Wonder why? I suppose I'd better write to Paddy.

Thursday 22nd October 1964

Did dog fish dissect. Stupid old B. will never make a doctor if he treats the poor thing in such a ham fisted manner.

Thursday 23rd October 1964

Tonight I did no revision, and just sat and read about telepathy and fore knowledge, frightfully interesting really. Had chemistry test. Oh so delectably foul!

Friday 23rd October 1964

We went onto the downs this pm. It was glorious. How I love autumn with that faint tang of winter in the air but still serenely beautiful. How sad it will be when all the leaves fall. We collected pocketfuls of chestnuts on the way back. It's heavenly to be alive. Shall I, shan't I become RC??

Saturday 24th 1964

Slogged away in the garden and made 2 flower beds at the end. In pm went onto the common with B. I suddenly began to laugh and laugh and laugh. I knew if I didn't go on I should begin to wail out my secret heart to B. about Granny's death and so I just laughed and laughed until I had no more strength in me to do anything. That way I keep my secret feelings secret.

Sunday 25th October 1964

Tried a new rinse in my hair, unfortunately or perhaps fortunately it didn't work. In pm rehearsals. Maurice is in hospital so Rod took them, he shouted away at Pelham but I don't really think he dared shout at me. I've got a whacking bruise on my b.t. after being thrown around by Phillipa.

Monday 26th October 1964

B. was in a good mood, so was I, we got on like a house on fire I'm glad to say. L wasn't there perhaps that explains it. More dissections of the dogfish. I really think I'm infatuated with Fluke. Oh how awful, but my heart does pound so when he looks at me!

Tuesday 27th October 1964

Went to another gruelling French lesson with Mrs Kemp. The twins had ½ term so, no school. I went haring into college with old B. for lunch. He was in a bad temper. Poo. Who cares. Wow it is cold now, and I feel so damnably depressed too. Woollen gloves and black stockings to the fore I think. Tomorrow we should be going sailing.

Wednesday 28th October 1964

No sailing. Praise the lord. I went with old B. to Carshalton. B. and me up to see Aunt D. B. walked up with me. I sat through their boring slides, a very uncomfortable tea and one Jill's 28 page letters. Lordy was I pleased to flee back to old B., even if he was a bit grumpy. I could have sat down and howled on my way home.

Thursday 29th October 1964

Dissection of df again. My back was breaking but I felt particularly martyrly and kept everyone laughing. My hands rather shaky and the old arteries though twang, twang. Oh the dear Fluke was rather bitter about the whole thing. Well I can't help it if df are rather expensive.

Friday 30th October 1964

Rehearsals. We went up to the downs and it was rather dismal and I really think we'll have to stop going soon. Maurice was foul to me. I could have wept. Instead I became very sarcastic and spiteful. Well damn it all, how on earth are you meant to act out a joyful scene with someone scowling at you?!

Saturday 31st October 1964

Life is so mundane. Mummy's ill so I had to make lunch etc. The mad bulldog on the common gave me the willies. I hate the pubs and the noise and the smell of beer grated as I gulped it. Nobody looks really happy in a pub. Either too selfish, self conscious to bored or too sloshed. Ugh.

Sunday 1st November 1964

I cut my hand yesterday gardening. I walked back from rehearsals holding Mike's hand. Rather nice to hold someone else for a change! The lights in Worple Rd are bilious – horrid orange. I watched a fantastic film – "Kitty". Glory alleluia. Winters almost here at last.

Monday 2nd November 1964

Dog fish dissection again. And chem. in pm. <u>Too</u> much. Old F came round and asked us about careers. I nearly swooned with embarrassment when he perched himself on the bench in front of me and began to have a tete a tete. Cos, he's got marvellous eyes. How vulgar, how positively vulgar. My feelings for B. rather evaporate when Mr F is in the vicinity though.

Tuesday 3rd November 1964

French with Madam. Thoroughly boring day. Some other girl in the college is keen on old B. Flattered I'm sure. Oh and to hell with the whole damned affair, I'm sick of being sweet and kind. I just cannot be the recessive character in a partnership. Sad but true. Whow. No sailing. Went for interview in the morning. It was all very cosy, in front of a fire and in deep chairs, only thing was I kept sinking into the depths of mine. I know I haven't got a place. However does it matter – I think not.

November 6th 1964

Went up onto downs, not particularly inspiring. But then old B. isn't really. Got a letter from John B. whoopeeee! I had to turn him down though as I had promised to go out with old B. tomorrow. Damn. Had rehearsals and really felt quite awed as everybody stopped and listened in silence, absolute, breathtaking silence as I threw my melodramatic fit. Oh I do <u>adore</u> that scene in my part.

Saturday 7th November 1964

Went to old B.s for firework display. Very pretty but pretty cold. So are most pretty things – take B. eg cold old B. ugh " No Jenny we mustn't touch each other in public, someone might see" Oh my dear!

Sunday 8th November 1964

Meant to be going out with J.B. but rehearsals instead. My dress has come. Positively gorgeous. The scenery is going up at last and the play is going to be a success. Oh I do hope I'm right. Poor old Maurice is frantic with worry.

Sunday 9th November 1964

Zoology and cranial nerves, bliss, I adore doing little delicate operations on my dogfish. Thank the lord it's not really alive now. How many arteries did I cut. 3 oh glory. Poor old Desmond Dogfish. Old Flukes was very nice to us again. Lindsey brought me some elastic bands.

Tuesday 10th November 1964

Tonight first dress rehearsal. John and Helen gave me a lift up and as I went in my costume I was ready before all the rest and had to sit around shivering. No make up. At college I did feel depressed. Old B. was very kind but he still seemed pleased to go off with Lindsey. It was a cold blustery day.

Wednesday 11th November 1964

Went in time to see the others before they went up from their break.

Evening. Make up arrived. I practically made myself up. Phillipa was bustling around making catty remarks as usual. Oh that heavenly feeling as everybody congratulates you after a good performance. No sailing today.

Thursday 12th November 1964

First night. Oh the excitement and butterflies. We all gave a marvellous performance and it gave me quite a kick the way Pelham kissed me. Afterwards John gave me lift and I flopped into bed tired but wonderfully elated. Oh joys of acting! Well rather euphemistically put still its great fun!

The play was "Ring around the Moon" by Jean Anouilh.

Friday 13th November 1964

Tonight, Mummy, twins, Chamberlains and Granny came, the latter was in a bad mood. Ugh I tried to put it all in the past but, probably because I was trying so hard it wouldn't come out properly. Pelham acted very well tonight though. My he is good looking.

Saturday 14th November 1964

Last night. It's rather sad and B. came and sat mournfully in the audience. After all the curtain calls and clappings etc the press took photos and off we went to Pete's party. Old B. was a bit of a damper at first as he would talk about people at college and other mundane things. However he was very attentive and told me I was a marvellous actress. We went and came back in Richard's meat wagon. Poor old B. had to walk all the way home. Thank goodness we don't behave in such a sloppy fashion at parties. It does look disgusting to see all those couples necking away.

Sunday 15th November 1964

Felt very depressed. Wrote to J.B.

Monday 16th November 1964

B. went for an interview with Buchy. today. Poor old B. His face had one of those stupid nerve rashes on it when he came up. Clive of course has to be frightfully rude about it.

Talking of Clive he says he wouldn't touch Lindsey with a "barge pole". Strange. There was dead silence in the zoo room, looking ahead of me rows of heads crouching over dogfish and poking around for all they're worth. Nobody understands my sense of humour. Very sad!

Tuesday 17th November 1964

Madame was very sweet. Went in for lunch, had it with B. He told me about his mother's new washing machine. Really, what a lazy woman she must be. Maid, fridge, Hoover and everything. Still old B. assures me I'll have them someday!!

Wednesday 18th November 1964

We didn't go sailing as usual. Old Skinny's really got her teeth into B. Oh she's such a cat. Why does she have to have everybody's hearts. It was gorgeously gusty day, but I felt too depressed to notice. I'm getting fed up with B. again. Hope to God he doesn't find this diary ever.

Thursday 19th November 1964

Heard from J.B. Joy oh joy. He can make it on Saturday. Wrote by return of post too!

There I sat in organic feeling pleased as punch as he read out the marks. 3/10! Oh no bottom. How awful. B. was marvellous and pretended not to notice. He really is a decent chap. Old Raferty had lunch with us, very embarrassing.

Friday 20th November 1964

Borough News "Star performer pretty 18 yr old Jenny Stephens. Architect of play's success." Wow! Felt marvellously elated. B. was all over me and very humbly asked if he could take me out. I felt such a cad as I smiled sweetly "Oh thank you Brendan". Rehearsals, Maurice was very jubilant at my success. Now for the review.

Saturday 21st November 1964

Met J.B. at the Waterloo Station. We were a bit embarrassed to see each other at first after a nightmare ride in his van through the noisy London streets arrived at a quiet dingy suburb. Lordship Park. We ate fried eggs and had a pretty uproarious time harping on all the memories we shared. Then off for a mad pub-crawl. He drank 3 pints at the 1st sitting and after about 5 was getting very amorous. I mixed them, vodka, beer etc. Back to the flat and I sat on top of him in the great armchair. J. kept saying how good it was to see me again, how beautiful I looked etc. Very embarrassing but wonderful after the mundane fashion Brendan treats me. I suppose J.B. was right we did behave as if we were madly in love with each other. Bergit appeared to have been forgotten, oh dear so had I. J.B. drove me back miles and then kissed me passionately. Wow that solar plexus.

Monday 23rd November 1964

B. wrote me a very touching letter saying he hoped I was better after Saturday. I suppose it must have sounded like I was dying on the phone although I didn't mean to make it sound that bad! B. had interview at Barts. Thinks he's got in, silly fool. Phoned him at 8 and had a long tirade. Very boring. Mummy grinned knowingly when I came in after ½ an hour's natter. Little did she know who did the talking! Not me.

Wednesday 25th November 1964

Went to little Aunt D's with B. Oh he's so boring, got clothes. Went to Kingston. B. in a bad mood. I'm fed up with his moods, drank warm tea in a little café.

Thursday 26th November 1964

Had chemistry test got 6/10. Joy! Felt in a good mood. Skinny old Ann Skinner sat and leered in org behind us. I was wearing new grey jumper and she kept putting in the label. Pathetic the way Mike and Steve sit behind her. I hope she falls to bits with all the rattling bones. Ugh! Had pseudo conspiracy with B.

Friday 27th November 1964

Felt depressed and didn't go to rehearsals. By accident with a wicked gleam in our eyed pinched a pink spotted pillowcase and a pair of pants ha ha. (in launderette). It was cold in the night and to hell with this bloody dreary existence. So there!

Saturday 28th November 1964

Went to damn awful play. So boring. Went to Oliver's in morning. Painful to say the least. Hateful Dr O'Farrel wouldn't stop staring at me, and Mrs O'F was hellishly boring. B. is really getting beyond himself, hate, how dare he. My soul was just brimming with fear and hate when I saw him. It's quite true, he is getting too cock-sure!

November — December 1964

Sunday 29th November 1964

Got record player on Friday and played it most of today. Marvellous. It's getting very cold and do I detect snow in the air. "Famine relief wrists" Stupid fools, my poor flat wrists, but if I eat too much I get a double so what do I do! Ahem.

Monday 30th November 1964

Old Fisher came over with a solemn face and gave in her notice. Poor thing is moving next door to Martin's. Russel called. I wonder who will die now. Had row with Rosy, she said some really terrible things to me and ones which I shall never forget. Did tons of French and felt very depressed. Loathe Brendan.

Tuesday 1st December 1964

French with M. King. I feel "la cas" to write to B. and tell him a few home truths, so think I will accordingly. I wonder what will happen, quite exciting.

Didn't write to B. but phoned him up and told him not to take me for granted. He was very upset. Well so was I. I can't bear luke-warm love.

Wednesday 2nd December 1964

B. came in with a white face. I felt quite frightened. He's got into Barts! Hooray. We made it up over last night. I'm so glad it brought things to a head. Perhaps it will clear the air. We went down to the park and watched the ducks and were very sadly happy together. I apologised for nearly breaking off.

Thursday 3rd December 1964

Organic tests. 4/10. Not so good. Oh well! Decided to go to "Steak House" to celebrate B.'s success. What a laugh. I'll wear my silver dress I think. The chimney pots broken outside my room. Oh what a storm. The poor birds. Mummy's birthday. Daddy gave her a hoover!

Friday 4th December 1964

B. went to Kingston. We were friendly and determined to please each other. Sat in the park. Felt depressed when I saw him off on the train. Damnably depressed. Went to French then rehearsals. Got part in the skit. Maid. Type cast no doubt. Maurice very friendly. J and H gave me a lift down.

Sail On, Silvergirl, Sail On By

Saturday 5th December 1964

Went to Steak House with B. Quite delectable. Drank red wine and ate juicy steaks. Very awkward as we didn't know what to do most of the time. B. was very elated and yet I kept feeling that he had some bad news to impart. I gave him the ? a German nun had given me when I left the convent. I don't think he was very impressed. He was extremely amorous. Very nice. It's about a month since he was.

Sunday 6th December 1964

Did lots of homework (I hope). I do wish that reason ruled my actions instead of feelings. If only I could be kind and good and gay with B. as reason tells me instead of being uncertain and jealous all the time.

Sunday 7th December 1964

Had a boring chemistry morning, with old Robinson prancing around at the front. B. and I got in the first benches with Jimmy Lander and felt very diligent. In the evening stayed later to finish off on dogfish, thank goodness that's finished. I'm sure the lab assistant Judy thought we were mad staying on so late. Russell called, I was out conveniently.

Tuesday 8th December 1964

Went to French and then on to varsity match. Very boring but old B. was very sweet and kept explaining moves to me. Horrid Ann Skinner was there again with Lindsey. I do despise that skinny individual. Sat next to B. in the coach coming home munching peanuts, he kept holding my hand which I found rather embarrassing as people do stare and oh those vulgar songs.

Wednesday 9th December 1964

Oliver's in the morning for fillings. Ouch! Then into lunch with B. I must admit I was rather objectionable. However we made it up and he says only says mind, that he'll give me an umbrella for Christmas. We fed the ducks. I supplied the bread of course.

Thursday 10th December 1964

Nothing spectacular seems to happen in these days. We had another organic chemistry test. Got 1/10. Joy. Lindsey and Skinner completely ignored me. Oh well what do I care. I'm bored with life. The rain came down. I think I shall have to be a miser, as I'm absolutely skint. Lord, zoo is deadly sometimes.

Friday 11th December 1964

Had frightful emotional upheaval with B. I didn't mean to upset him and yet I did. Really it was because of Anne Skinner, oh she does make me depressed. I'm not such an ugly stupid thing as her looks imply. B. was wonderful lending me his hanky. We went up onto the downs and had a great reunion. Sounds melodramatic but I just don't know what I'd do without him. He sometimes says he will turn into a grumpy old man without me.

Saturday 12th December 1964

Martin's party. B. and I were very gay. Martin had too much to drink. Clive sat in a corner kissing a girl he'd only met ½ hour before. I had a lift home on B.'s scooter. Very illicit and rather chilly but fun.

13 Sunday December 1964

"What is this world so full of care we have no time to stand and stare." (*W. H. Davies*) I wonder. Great rows in the house. Oh well that's how wars start I suppose. I am becoming very wicked but the thought of church doesn't really appeal to me nowadays. End of term soon, hooray!

Monday 14th December 1964

Clive got pulled to bits about the party, so did B. and I but to not quite such devastating effect. Got a letter from the Polytechnic saying they will give me an interview. Joy. Had sandwich lunch. Boy, freezing and we didn't manage to get a drink.

Tuesday 15th December 1964

Had French. Then a chilly lunch with B. We spent the afternoon in the library. If I might venture so say so B. has very little of the organ of concentration left at 4.45. I went home with old Thorperite. Very sweet girl but too much in earnest. Brian didn't turn up to her party. Poor old Thorpes.

Wednesday 16th December 1964

Oliver's. My gods the apexectomy was hell. A dull nagging pain all the time as she hacked and drilled at my bone. Blood everywhere, on her face, my face, her overall, hands and floor. Awful, awful. I went into college afterwards but felt so giddy and light headed that I had to leave early.

Thursday 17th December 1964

Had lunch with B. in park, fed the ducks. He skipped physical organic. Everybody was very concerned about my tooth. Old Clive had the air of " and here is my prize specimen". Every time he explained to everyone what was wrong with me. Old B. was very concerned as well. Delectable.

Friday 18th December 1964

Everybody went mad. We went down to the Green Man first. I sat next to Clive. Then off in Bruce's car to the downs. The pub there was a mad house. Everyone drunk and kissing everyone else. I was revolted. Afterwards the concert was pretty foul. I didn't understand half the jokes as well I suppose. Bruce gave me a lift home.

Saturday 19th December 1964

B. came over looking very sad with some story about being glad to leave college, and wondering if he was glad to leave me. Of course, I was terrified that this was the beginning of the end and went onto my high horse. Rather unpleasant evening.

Sunday 20th December 1964

The other Gran came over. Pathetic little figure. She stayed until 6.15 pm. B. then arrived in a bad mood whisked me off to church. I hated every minute of it if this going to be a truthful diary. It depressed me more than everything else. All churches depress me. So do people and so especially does B. Imagine being married to such a moron.

Monday 21st December 1964

Up to town. I thought I would be a twitching heap of insanity when I extricated myself from the crowds. B. was in a foul humour. He bought me an umbrella and pair of stockings. In the afternoon we went to the Black and White Minstrel show. Great!

Tuesday 22nd December 1964

I slept in this morning and missed my French. Oh well I did feel pretty rotten anyway. The morning was miserable. I did a launderette and then quickly made lunch as I thought the twins would be back from the dentist by 12 pm. No such luck, at 2 pm I was still solitary. With a hard lunch and in a very bad mood. Poor things they had lots of shopping.

December 1964

Wednesday 23rd December 1964

Today I was supposed to phone B. at 12. We went to Aunty Winnie's in the morning and got I got B's wallet. Real leather, very expensive. I did phone him in the evening although I was in a bad mood. Went to see Great Grandpa and Aunty Fanny. They all look so terribly old. "Do you want to be an actress?" Oh dear. It does give me such a complex.

Thursday 24th December 1964

Today I actually managed to do some work. Mummy got home early. A blessing. In the evening B. came over. At first he seemed frightfully pleased to see me, however, after a very little while we began to feel a bit uncomfortable together. He says he adores the wallet, I do hope so. A great compliment really as he is so hard to please.

Friday 25th December 1964

I went to the Midnight Mass. I can say it was very cold and a bit dismal. After breakfast we opened one or two presents and then went off to Church. Daddy was in good mood and we drank wine with lunch, with lashings of turkey and white sauce. M and D gave me a beautiful dissecting set and marked " in love". [There were giggles when I opened it.]

Saturday 26th December 1964

Another excuse for gorging ourselves. B. was full of his Christmas day experiences at 12 pm on the phone. "Mornings at 7" is it. Evidently I have been missing that phenomena for years now! Wow I feel so damnably lethargic and depressed. Strange as I should be happy. I get such dreams nowadays though.

Sunday 27th December 1964

I didn't go to church in the morning; but had a bath. Desperate was my attempt to work in the afternoon and foul was my temper in the evening. Well, I did try to feel religious with B. but it was too much. We sat in the R.P. Hotel and reminisced, which I found morally bad both for him and myself as he appears to be living on the gems of the past and not preparing any for the future.

Monday 28th December 1964

Rehearsals. Oh boy. I had to do my Mothers union bit. Most embarrassing. Maurice sums up " perfect, perfect!" I had a bath and did very little work. Mummy was at home looking very tired. Oh dear, Christmas is a bit of a farce I suppose! Snow very cold. Brrr.

Sail On, Silvergirl, Sail On By

Tuesday 29th December 1964

Phoned B. at 12am. I'm frightful at talking on the phone as I always seem to rub peoples backs up the wrong way. Oh dear. Actually it gave me a very reassuring feeling to hear B.s voice again. Two days. Such a long time! The snow has settled and the sun is shining. Bliss. Pure and undiluted.

Wednesday 30th December 1964

Rehearsals again. Maurice was persuaded Pelham and I that we want to sing in the damn revue. Oh I nearly died with embarrassment. Old Maurice "flipped flopped" jumped out of bed. We kept giggling which I fear did not help matters much. Crawled back at 11.30 felt positively dead.

Thursday 31st December 1964

No work today. I'm too excited about going out with B. At first he was in a bad mood but that soon thawed out and we had a marvellous time. The poor man in the pub got his nose broken. But he did deserve it. We were very quiet after that but soon livened up. I felt positively exhilarated to be with B. on the last day of this year. Oh do wonder what the New Year holds in store for us.

> "Lord make me brave that I may stand protected by thy power.
> Before temptations burning flames made strong in needful hour.
> When comrades scoff let me not flinch
> but firm before the stand with inward prayer for help.
> Oh come uphold me by the hand.
> Teach to succour all the weak who fall on life's rough way,
> give me thy strength to speak the truth and serve the day by day"
>
> *(E A Vassie)*

> The year's at the spring
> And day's at the morn
> Mornings at seven.
> The hillsides dew peeled
> The larks on the wing
> The snails on the thorn
> God's in his heaven
> All's right with the world
>
> *(Browning)*

Diary 1965

In which Jenny finishes her A-levels and goes to university, and gets her own flat.

Friday 1st January 1965

But which part of the lavatory is the Izal? A howler by B. to start the new year. We had a very exciting evening as it was the social "Dood Dracious". But every one did laugh at the Mothers Union skit. Afterwards we sat on a gate on the commons and sang songs to the moon. Very romantic!

Saturday 2nd January 1965

I fear I would have liked to sleep in but I do think Grandpa comes first. The flowers looked simply lovely in the chapel. Poor Mummy was very unhappy today.

In the evening saw "South Pacific". Marvellous. Old B. squeezed my hand as "Once you have found her never let her go" throbbed out into the audience.

Sunday 3rd January 1965

We all curled up on the sofa and watched "Wuthering Heights". Not as good as the book. But entertaining anyway. College tomorrow. All the usual preparations. Baths and hair washing, fights and nerves, to bed late, nightdress, pillow slips away, blankets to come off, hot water bottle. Cold, worry, worry.

Monday 4th January 1965

Alarm! Brrrrrr. And then it wasn't so bad. B. was sweet and so was Clive. He asked me how my tooth was. Oh I'm flattered B. and I have been invited to his party and only 5 are being invited from the college. Wow oh Joy. Did 2 hours work to celebrate.

Tuesday 5th January 1965

I am putting such a curse on my father from this moment. Ignorant bullying swinish brute. How dare he say the hurtful mean unjust things he does. Alright I've had enough. So Uncle John says I've no "exceptional talents". Daddy says I'm a fool. I hereby vow to get grade "A"s in these damned A levels. Every time I stop work may I think of the hate and despair I feel when they begin to bully me. Of all my sorrow and agony at their injustice. Yes I shall climb above them, for then one day they can take back all their insults and jibes, and I shall kick and kick and kick them when they are down.

Thursday 7th January 1965

Had lunch with B. in the park and have decided that next week we are going to have cooked lunch! Worked in the library in the pm. Then organic chem. So hellishly boring. The goblin jumped around in a self satisfied manner. Sickening. And as usual for our homework I didn't do a stroke of work.

Friday 8th January 1965

Went to the Downs with B. and taught him Brahms's lullaby. He really is so in earnest to be able to sing. A few notes were correct but on the whole a bit wonkey. However I like to see old B. taken up with something like that. Went to rehearsals in the pm. Boring.

Saturday 9th January 1965

Clive's party. A dismal flop to say the least. I think I'm loosing my personality as nobody seems to take any notice of me now. Oh well. I have B. and perhaps I'd rather have him than anything else. Bart's — Oh that gloomy future. We went home on the back of the scooter. Bliss, I sang "The Lullaby" all the way home.

Sunday 10th January 1965

Went to St. Martins in the fields. Sang in Broadcast service. Then on to the other Granny's. Not very inspiring but then it never is. The pipes do gurgle so. We played lexicon and ate a literally mouldy cake. Poor G was very upset about it though.

Monday 11th January 1965

Clive was very quiet and said the party finished soon after we left. It poured with rain today. I should hate Poikitheria (?). Hibernation would I think be the only pleasant part of its life. Went home on the train with old L. Got an interview at the Northern Poly. 6 Feb. Sounds like fun!

Our paths finally start to cross! Obviously Northern Poly had been a possible from this point on for Jenny whereas for me it was a late choice after I didn't get high enough grades for Leicester University in my A levels. I was a year ahead and so at this time I was in second term of the first year of my chemistry degree.

Tuesday 12th January 1965

Had French lesson then cooked myself a smashing lunch. Only thing was I didn't do an awful lot of work. B. went to the boat show. Old Anne Marie called last night. I didn't go till after 11. Very bad. She is rather unhappy.

Wednesday 13th January 1965

Went in in the am to work in the library, then went for lunch with B. and into the pub. A pretty uninteresting day. Wrote to J.B. Wrote to Paddy and hated B. God knows why. I wish I could do something really worthwhile with my life. However to oneself perhaps ones own happiness is the only worthwhile thing. I wonder.

Thursday 14th January 1965

Anne S. has a new boyfriend. Good luck to her. Clive is ill and we have started frog dissections. The damn creature is so small.

Friday 15th January 1965

Maurice has given me the part of Margerite. Bliss! I had to fight for it though! We did a 3 hours dissection in the pm and then 2 hours of French. With D Ling of all people. He walked to the station with me. Of course we missed the train and had to sit for hours on the freezing platform.

Saturday 16th January 1965

Party (fancy dress) with J.B. Great fun at first. But depressing after a while. No matter what they say he's still in love with me. Conceit but I am convinced true. We talked about B. and almost got killed on the way back by driving on the wrong side of the road.

Sunday 17th January 1965

Went out with B. this evening. I was in a bad mood and he was jealous about last night's party! Joy. We stood in an archway in the pouring rain half way to Edge Hill and then steamed all way through the service. I of course felt damnably depressed and had a good wail on his shoulder. Poor old B. the things he puts up with!

Sunday 18th January 1965

Madly monotonous Monday chem. prac and zoo. We stayed behind and got our frogs finished. Wow am I grateful for that. My turn to bring in the soup. Actually I rather enjoy bringing in lunches now. Even if they are bringing me out in spots. Did a lot of French.

Tuesday 19th January 1965

French. The inevitable. Oh well. I suppose I'm learning something. Was supposed to be going up to town but nothing came of it. Mummy is still at home. We had a very cosy day and of course I didn't do any work. Poor old Daph. has started the curse. She has all my sympathy.

Wednesday 20th January 1965

Rushed into college and did a lot of work in the library. Saw B. in the break and almost had a row with him. We sat in the refectory after listening to the "flippin" little man yattering for an hour or so then and scooted off to a boring and uneventful evening among our books. Howling gale today.

Thursday 21st January 1965

The main topic of the today is org. chem. And zoo in the morning is a mere ride compared with organic. B. came by scooter, I do really hate meeting him first thing in the morning as I always look like the back of a bus and he always looks so positively handsome, sickening.

Friday 22nd January 1965

We did go up to the downs after all. The greenhouse was so hot or perhaps it was my disappointed face that made B. change his mind. Anyway I was grateful to him as I do so love to walk up there just chattering about anything that comes into our heads and feeling free as ——— – oh anything.

January 1965

Saturday 23rd January 1965

B. has a rugger match. So work to the fore to consol yourself Jenny. Mummy and the twins were very kind to me and I felt very touched when they insisted on my seeing the programs they like [even if I would rather have been working].

Sunday 24th January 1965

B. came over in the pm and we went to church then pub crawling, oh yes he was very happy tonight, v. amorous as well, I wonder why. Perhaps because he had an easy night last night. Oh stop your suspicious mind doubting him all the time.

Monday 25th January 1965

Great bold letters on the notice board "Miss Stephens is wanted at the college office", my knees always begin to tremble when I see that!

I interview with the principal. Suit and high heels to the fore again and here we go. Worked like a maniac at the French to take my mind off tomorrow.

Tuesday 26th January 1965

French. Then Buch, glowering from under his bushy eyebrows he fired questions at me from behind a rather suspicious outlook on life. I was very glad when it was over anyway. B. stayed in the library after all afternoon with me and I felt very happy with life.

Wednesday 27th January 1965

Didn't go in but stayed at home with Mummy. Went in in the pm and wasted my time in the pub with B. Next week I'm not coming in. I did a bit of work in the pm and attempted some tapestry. Seem to have got out of the hang of it lately and its very relaxing.

Thursday 28th January 1965

Got my money – Marg started putting her hair up and wearing eye makeup ahem. Dirty rotter making eyes at B. Luckily he didn't notice, but he might have done.

Snow, snow, snow, sickenly coldly, beautifully awful. Travelled home with Mr Quilty, he's awfully nice.

Sail On, Silvergirl, Sail On By

Friday 25th January 1965

L. in the morning and didn't learn a thing. He borrowed my book and butterflies and presses of flowers dropped out by the dozen. We went (B. and I) to little café afterwards and had cups of tea. Very cosy. Drama, yes Friday is rather an eventful day. Maurice's play is just like "Compact" (*British TV soap opera 1962–5*) and I can't act in it.

Saturday 30th January 1965

Went pub crawling with Brendan. W. Churchill's funeral was very moving and I felt frightfully sad. Mummy was most miserable.

Churchill died on the 24th January 1965. The news just prior had indicated that the end was nigh and a college friend had persuaded me to go with him and we sat on the steps of Churchill's house in London the day he died. Weird.

B. was very amorous and we talked of our friendship for each other, it seemed to jar on me to talk of it somehow. Better to let it be spontaneous.

Sunday 31st January 1965

Church with Margaret. She got drunk or something and I felt very ashamed of her.

Tuesday 2nd February 1965

Didn't go in in pm. Mummy's last day at home – we had a gorgeous lunch of chops.

Wednesday 3rd February 1965

By myself all day. B. came over at four saying I had promised to phone him, I'm afraid I wasn't very nice to him as I had just washed my hair, Oh dear.

Thursday 4th February 1965

Had zoo in the morning. Nearly everyone came in. B. wasn't very friendly and kept looking at the other girl's in the library which made me feel very hurt and unwelcome. B's scooter broken.

Friday 5th February 1965

Gorgeous day. B's scooter mended. Both in a good mood. Lawrence had a cold. We had slides in the pm. Then drama. S and H collected me and took me home. Sweet of them.

February 1965

Saturday 6th February 1965

Went for interview at Northern Poly. Very cosy. Got there 1hr to early so wandered around the market. It was frightfully sordid. Then Mr Etherington was deaf and I had to absolutely shout. Of course I made out I was brilliant which somehow I don't think he believed!

Sunday 7th February 1965

Tried to work today but afraid didn't get much done.

The catkins are out and its still light at 5 pm. Really the weather is just like summer! Seems strange not to have seen B. this weekend. Miss him quite a lot.

Monday 8th February 1965

1st Exam, chemistry wasn't too bad I suppose. Knowing Lawrence tho' I probably got low marks. Oh dear I keep thinking about Granny this time last year. Was her last evening on this earth. Oh and its such a lovely evening too with the rooks chattering overhead as I walked home in the dusk.

Tuesday 9th February 1965

My first thought this morning was of today 1 year ago. What ages it seems and yet what minutes. I went to French and didn't feel like it much. In the evening I phoned B. Poor old Daph was knocked over by a motor bike and was brought back by a man looking very white and shaky. Mummy was frightfully upset.

Wednesday 10th February 1965

Worked very little today as I was keeping Daph company most of the morning. The Dr came at about 12 and afterwards we ate one of Daddy's filthy lunches upstairs in the twins room. I felt frightfully depressed and as I couldn't do much work went down in the evening to see TV. A very creepy thriller "Ashes to Ashes". Cried myself to sleep.

Thursday 11th February 1965

Zoo exam. B. didn't look partic. pleased to see me and afterwards declared he was going to play rugger on Saturday. I'm afraid I just erupted and we had a hellish row standing besides the lockers positively hissing at each other. I felt so depressed and couldn't stop crying. In the pm mummy and I went and put flowers in the chapel. I could have died with sadness. We saw the "book".

Friday 12th February 1965

Made it up with B. Silly really all these rows. Feel tremendously happier. Perhaps it wasn't only B. making me nervous and on edge and really think perhaps it was all the memories of last year. We went into our bower in the pm after the chemistry exam and were very understanding to each other.

Saturday 13th February 1985

Went to Chinese restaurant with B. in the evening. It was marvellous with little waiters bobbing around steaming bowls of food. I ate piles and piles and was feeling positively ill when we stumbled out into the night again. We did a bit of a dance so B. could say he went to a dance and then talked leaning against the wall.

Sunday 14th February 1985

Went up to St Martins with Rosy. We walked through Trafalgar Square with the great fountains gushing and sparkling in the sunlight. The church smelt old as we quietly took our places in the pews and the lady besides me had a tickly fur on. I kept wanting to giggle as it was being broadcasted. We had a miserable Sunday lunch, as usual with gloomy daddy sitting at the head of the table.

Monday 15th February 1985

Zoo results. I just cannot explain my shame when I saw 36%. A hot needle seemed to be burning my soul and huge tears spilled over. The shame. And B. beat me by one mark. I could weep. In the evening I sat in the sitting room with Daph and did my French. Got Valentine from B.

Tuesday 16th February 1985

Had French with Mrs King and in the afternoon. Went swimming with Rosy. Gorgeous. The chlorine smell of the baths, the hard cold floor and the initial plunge when you're skin seems to contract to breaking point. At last I can swim 2 widths and I hope next week it will be 3. Wow I'm so stiff and I feel in a hellishly bad mood.

Wednesday 17th February 1985

I had lunch with B. We went for a walk round Ewell which was very exciting and climbed right up to the top of the railway bridge. Very cold though and I was, for once, glad to get back to the college. Warm, anyway. We spoke of the future and it seems so depressing I just can't bear to think about this time next year.

Thursday 18th February 1985

Organic again. I felt frightfully bored during the lecture. In the evening Mrs F. came up. Margarite has brought a holiday book so I think I'll write off for a job as a waitress. Mummy is of course dead against it. Never mind we can't all be right. Oh I feel in a bad mood.

Friday 19th February 1985

Went up onto downs with B. It was very lovely and I felt perfectly happy (a thing I rarely do). French in the pm. Wasn't very exciting. The boys are always mocking me but it shows I suppose that I must be popular. David slipped me a sly piece of chocolate on the way home in his car. I really was frightened as he's such a maniac.

Saturday 20th February 1985

B. et moi alous a le restaurant Chinese. Nous avous mange "bamboo shoots et chopped suey". Delicieuses! Apres, nous allous au la common et cessions a "The Fox and Grapes" Pur unpin our beaucoup? Ahem. Je le laissais a la porte et suit. Tres triste partir. A minuit et demie hous avons parle "Bon sonsee"

Sunday 21st February 1985

L' eglise! Mar. et moi marchions seules la colline. Le service etat tres borement. "Adam et Eve". Mummy et les twins retourne de St Martins et nous mangious le depuemer. La viande etait meuvais. J'ai mal aux dents et mal a la gorge et senti tres miserable.

Monday 22nd February 1985

La chimie. Lest resultats. 59% Tres bien. Je me pueus pas! Apre midi nous recievions les zoology resultats 36%. (oh dear). Si je ponvais je mouvirais a la s'il fait been temps demain je pause. Que je ferdi une neige avec Rosy. Brr Meis tres salubre. J'ai esperance. D. vondrait venire aussi mais elle me pent pas paree que Jane.

Tuesday 23rd February 1985

Francais en le matin. Je suis montee a Aunty Peggy's avec les vetemetns pour elle. Apres la dejeuner R et moi sommes sortee pour le bassine de nape. Il ayoit les froid et je me le resteries pas. En retournais j'ac achet de chocolat mm. Daphy a fait le the. Wow Je suis ripide meme maintenant Il fait tres froid auywdiane.

Wednesday 24th February 1965

I cannot write anymore in French. I am sick of it. We started doing our first questions on zoo today.

Good! I don't know French and coping with Jenny's handwriting and a language I do not know was doing my head in!

Thursday 25th February 1965

Went to see "Antigone" with B. (*Sophocles*) All in French!. We had a quiet supper in the refectory and then went dashing down to the pub for a quick drink before it started. Yes just like Saturday as B. remarked. The pub had charts all over the walls and lobster pots on the ceilings.

Friday 26th February 1965

Went up to the downs with B. Heaven! In the pm went up to Maurice's for great discussion. I'm afraid anything that I said wasn't very instructive. J and H drove me home felt tremendously tired.

Saturday 27th February 1965

Went out with B. in the evening to see "36 Hours". (*War film, James Garner starred.*) It was frightfully exciting and we both thoroughly enjoyed it. In the am Daph and I went to Dunmore Rd to do the garden. I planted some seeds. Later went to Smiths to get some rabbit food and a shelf load of tins fell about my ears. Ouch!

Sunday 28th February 1965

Went to church with Margaret. The others have gone to St Martins in the Fields. M. looked very bedraggled in the snow and my voice wasn't quite up to the mark. The others declared that they "loved" the service. I glad someone did. Ours was morbid. All about how God put a curse on Adam and Eve.

March 1965

Monday 1st March 1965

Marion called full of a boy called Brian. I wasn't really very interested but sat politely and listened for 1 – 2 – 3 hours. Almost asleep and worrying about tomorrows French. I at last threw manners to the winds and said I had a lot of work to do. In the end I had to see the dear girl home. Such is friendship.

Tuesday 2nd March 1965

Went to French. Then wandered around Sainsbury's and bought a job lot of tins and ate a really huge chunk of fish, some yoghurt. I felt a bit ill after it though. The twins were in a bad mood when they came back, which of course put me in one. Silly.

Wednesday 3rd March 1965

Slept in till 10.30. Oh well I can't usually sleep in on Saturdays. Trailed into college and ate the chicken I bought yesterday. It was rather "tasty". We gave each other back our questions. Huh, so he didn't like my style did he.

Thursday 4th March 1965

Down came the snow. And I was feeling in a very bad mood as well. We started dissection of the rat at about 11 o'clock as old Fluke's car got stuck. Poor old rats. Some of them had been returned as they were still alive. I felt almost like a cannibal as I pinned them down.

Friday 5th March 1965

We had a cold walk to college. Accosted by Anne Skinner. Stayed in all pm for dissections. French. Then Maurice. So the Pioneers have decided to desert us after all. I felt desperately sorry for Maurice. I do think he disserved a little more than this. We stayed up till after 11pm and I felt very sick and headache.

Saturday 6th March 1965

Wasn't at all well today but went to the Flicks with Brendan in the evening. It was all about this man who was dying, which in my present condition didn't help matters much. Margarite called conveniently at the same time as B. Ahem I wonder. She is always saying he looks manly.

Sunday 7th March 1965

Just worked like the blazes. Totally boring and uninspiring. It's like trying to learn a telephone directory.

Monday 8th March 1965

Mummy stayed at home. She wasn't at all well. I felt life too dull today. Mrs R gets on my nerves a bit and it's painfully obvious that B. is keen on her. Strange how I don't seem to be able to muster up enough jealousy. Sometimes I think what life be like without B. I would be nothing. Other people attract me but B. above everybody else makes me feel wanted, a person with a purpose. I can stand up to anything with B. by my side. If ever he was taken away I would die, literally and this I know for a fact of a broken heart.

Wednesday 10th March 1965

I stayed in bed all morning and then caught the train to Surbiton. Of course B. and I did the classic thing. We were supposed to be meeting at 1 o'clock but we both waited until 1.45 outside different entrances. Sailing although very cold is really rather glorious. We almost went over but B. had the presence of mind to keep the thing upright.

Thursday 11th March 1965

Oh the weather is glorious. Such a shame to be going into college. B. Clive and I stayed to a lecture on pest infestation. Quite interesting. The only thing is my eyes are really getting very bad.

Friday 12th March 1965

Went up to the downs with B. in the afternoon. He was frightfully amorous. And I must confess I was a little scared, as he kept on persisting that I take my coat off. It was the look in his eyes more than the rough hands that frightened me. Went to rehearsals in the pm with ? He reminds me of John Bryce. Went back for coffee later.

Saturday 13th March 1965

B. and I rushed along to the Chinese restaurant in the pm. The twins of course had a row while he was there. He kept saying how nice I looked. Gives me quite a kick. He bought a new tie – rugger one and looked very tired. Went onto the common afterwards and had heart to heart about morality. Thank God neither of us is licentious.

March 1965

Sunday 14th March 1965

Worked like the blazes today. Mummy was in a bad mood as Daddy wouldn't tell her where he was going. Unfortunately he came back for lunch. Yesterday I did so much gardening I felt positively exhausted.

Monday 15th March 1965

Daphy got tonsillitis so stayed home. Poor old thing. B. kept asking me whether I enjoyed Saturday. Probably I did more than him. However I didn't let on. We shall have to go back to the bower soon as our park is getting horribly full of those grotesque objects called people.

Tuesday 16th March 1965

Had a French check today. She says I can take the exam. Good! Daph is still at home. We had a good fry up of chicken and etc. Mrs Franklin came up to tea. I felt hopelessly depressed and didn't say much. Silly. Went to Kim's photo in the evening. I felt as doddery as everybody else by the time I got out.

Wednesday 17th March 1965

B. had an accident on his scooter and I felt like bursting into tears when I heard. Fool what good does that do anybody. Had a frightful shrieking match with Mummy and Rosy. Both are as mad as hatters if you ask me.

Thursday 18th March 1965

Great tension in our house after last night. Rosy and I had a fight. Rather melodramatic and got the best of it. Haven't had a fight like that for years, most exhilarating. B. kept finding fault with me today a thing I hate.

Friday 19th March 1965

Went up to the downs with B. Then to drama in the pm after French. We had a play reading and the things been cast. Whoopee I got the leading part. Went back for coffee with Ian and stayed a little too long for mummy who stormed round and dragged me home. Oh humiliation.

Sail On, Silvergirl, Sail On By

Saturday 20th March 1965

Robin's party – marvellous. B. and I had a great time and danced madly all evening. Tony was there which I don't think B. liked very much. I ate caviar and drank red wine. Unfortunately, owing to scooter troubles, B. had to leave early. In the long run he missed his train anyway and had to get a taxi. Crazy. The clocks went back today.

Sunday 21st March 1965

Phoned up B. to see if he got back alright. He was in a bad mood as I was. I felt utterly miserable and wanted to do anything, anything but work.

Monday 22nd March 1965

Felt very guilty about letting Tony kiss me goodbye on Sat. and wasn't a bit at ease with B. I think I would have left him if I'd been in his place. Oh well. When he goes to Barts I most probably will, so might as well have my fling whilst I can.

Tuesday 23rd March 1965

B. Got his scooter back today. It does look funny without the windscreen. We had lunch together then I worked in the library till 4. I happened to bump into him on the stairs so, like the chivalrous gent he is, he walked me to the station. I don't know why but it depresses me beyond all telling to be with B. at the moment.

Wednesday 24th March 1965

Went for a very cold sail. B. arrived on time so I was in a good mood. However he does tend to get so frightfully hysterical in the boat. This, I feel doesn't do anyone a lot of good; for as well as terrifying me, it is distracting from the main purpose – keeping the damned thing afloat.

Thursday 25th March 1965

Organic: The beastly man kept on asking me questions. Every time he asked me I had to put on my specs. Everyone laughed. My laugh of course being the loudest and most hysterical of the lot.

March – April 1965

Friday 26th March 1965

B. was very ill today and went home at lunchtime, somehow I was glad that he'd gone even tho' it did seem a bit strange without him. Drama in the evening and hard to be in by 11.30pm. Just had time for a quick coffee.

Saturday 27th March 1965

I phoned B. at 4 and he said that he was better. So I dashed home and with Daphy's help adjusted the pink dress. B. loved it and I was so pleased. We went to the Chinese restaurant and then onto the song club at the R. C. church. Some of the songs were very good, others highly boring.

Sunday 28th March 1965

Didn't feel too good myself today.

Monday 29th March 1965

Steve was really beastly to me and so was B. I don't know why but I just felt like curling up and dying. I walked off sadly to the station after college. Lo and behold B. was waiting near the station. I was very pleased to see him and of course had a good old sob on his shoulder.

Tuesday 30th March 1965

French. B. went to the dentist so I didn't go in until the pm. Phoned him at 8. We were both happy to speak to each other I think. Standing in a phone box is really a very uncomfortable experience.

Wednesday 31st March 1965

Went in in the pm. Mummy had an appointment at the eye hospital – I waited for her all morning. We had a meeting for sailing. Oh dear another damned girl has fallen for B. I don't really think I can go through all this mental agony. We sat on the field afterwards and it turned out B. had been "giving her the eye".

Thursday 1st April 1965

Last organic this term. B. and I had lunch in the bower, which, I might say I enjoyed immensely. He lent me his watch to wear in the library. I read The Times supplement, instead of doing any work. Wicked. Packed everything in the evening and Rosy mended my petticoat. Washed my hair and had a bath.

Friday 2nd April 1965

B. was terribly sweet. We went down to the Solent in Thomas's car. A great sweeping drive led up to a beautiful house. The dormitories were like a barracks, the beds had two blankets each and I disliked, <u>intensely</u>, the girl who kept making eyes at B. B. and I went for a walk before that last gunsmoke (cocoa).

Saturday 3rd April 1965

Hardly slept a wink and B. looked very unfriendly at breakfast. Went in the boat with awful girl and boy and felt wet and miserable and hated and loved B. alternately. Oh if only I was clever I wouldn't let him see that I feel jealous when he makes eyes at that damned girl. If he could see her at night I don't think he'd be quite so enamoured.

Sunday 4th April 1965

Gorgeous sail with Jill Bruce. B. was pleasanter but I still felt an atmosphere. I felt miserably unhappy on the way back as he kept grinning at the damned girl. It's so frustrating as you can't say "stop grinning, it makes me feel unwanted." It would sound ridiculous to say the least.

Monday 5th April 1965

Felt damnably ill. Slept all day was violently sick in the morning. Got up in the afternoon, Mummy went out to phone Mrs Kip and B. They were both sorry to hear about me. Ahem. B. kept saying "give her my love". That made me feel a million times better!

Tuesday 6th April 1965

B. rolled up at 10.45 and stayed until 12.45. Went into the dining room and listened to Gigi. I was wearing a blue skirt, blouse and B. kept saying how nice I looked. Quite frankly I thought I looked a wreck. He brought me a bunch of flowers. Daffodils. Gorgeous.

Wednesday 7th April 1965

Daph was ill with a sore throat. We slept in and then pottered around all day. In the pm I went out with B. and we had a simply marvellous time. Went to the Chinese place and then to our wall and I enjoyed every simple minute of it. Funny how well we click together. Perhaps we'd both got over our tiredness.

Thursday 8th April 1965

M. came round and was very sweet. I went to the opticians and got my specs. Daph and I didn't get into the kitchen until 3pm. Ghastly. And then I had to go out and get the lunch afterwards. Gorgeous day just like summer. Jumble collecting in the evening.

Friday 9th April 1965

Went in to Drama in the pm and decided to put a bit of make up on. My goodness what a difference, got a lot of attention for a change. Went back to Ian's afterwards and he put on "What beautiful brown eyes you have!" Ahem. I thought and beat a hasty retreat. Felt stupidly tired again and crawled into bed dying for sleep.

Saturday 10th April 1965

Uneventful. Went out with B. We sat for hours on the common and I made his face up. Rather silly, as he lost his temper. I felt more than usually small. Afterwards we went to the folksong place and I could feel my throat beginning to play up. Here we go for a really beautiful dose of laryngitis. Collected Jumble in Pelham's "Rolls".

Sunday 11th April 1965

B. mowed the lawn which was really nice of him. We went to church in the pm and could feel my throat getting steadily worse. After church I couldn't help thinking it was a little unfeeling of B. to drag me into a pub. I dropped thankfully into bed and then of course couldn't sleep. I tossed and turned all night.

Monday 12th April 1965

Got up at 5 and staggered into the twin's room for codeine. I had completely lost my voice and felt as sick as a dog. It was awful. The twins were really very sweet and hustled me into bed where I stayed all day. B. took his scooter test at 4.15 and passed. Hooray. Elizabeth phoned him to find out.

Tuesday 13th April 1965

I felt a bit better today but still v. throaty and didn't do a stroke of work. It was a heavenly day and I hated being ill. One of the guinea pigs had convulsions and bit Rosy. She was very upset. I stayed up as late as I could watching TV so I wouldn't toss and turn all night. Slept like a log.

Wednesday 14th April 1965

B. came over in the afternoon. I was v. pleased to see him again. However he was v. bossy which I pretended to find highly amusing. It did in fact leave a nasty taste in my mouth. He brought a crash helmet for me and we went up onto the common in the pouring rain. Didn't do my throat much good. The day of the holly bush and the white pants.

Wednesday 15th April 1965

Did a lot of revision. Mummy came home at lunchtime. I cleaned my room in the morning. It was a glorious day and I felt particularly on top of the world. Auntie Jean called in the evening. Mummy of course had to be at church. Most depressing woman A. J. Poor thing I think she's probably lonely.

Friday 16th April 1965

Saw a lot of Keith, Helen and John today. Had a marvellous time. I wonder if what Keith said is true. ... most people are keen on me ... Good for the moral anyway. Didn't get back until very late. They invited me down to Isle of Sheppey for the day. I don't think I'd like it though.

Saturday 17th April 1965

Slept in late and after doing 3 hours work gave it up and went out with B. at 3 o'clock. We went out onto the common. Found our holly bush and had a very good time. B. frightens me sometimes when he gets so amorous. However, the scooter broke down. Such as shame. We didn't go "folk singing" which was a relief. I of course always make out I love it. More fool I. B. bought me a beautiful card and 2 Easter eggs.

Sunday 18th April 1965

We had to get up early and go to church. J.B. was there with Bridget – didn't think much of her. However suits John. Looks submissive enough anyway. I felt completely exhausted. Phoned B. in the pm he sounded tired and irritable as well.

Got a large Easter egg from mummy and little ones from the twins.

April 1965

Monday 19th April 1965

There were frightful rows today. I hate v. intensely every living thing on this earth, except B. Mummy shouldn't tell malicious lies about me and seethe inside when she does. I loath Daddy, more in fact than words can tell. He no longer frightens me, I just feel contempt and disgust. Yes, he'd like to chuck me out.

Tuesday 20th April 1965

Went to Oliver's. Then over to B.s Had a pleasant afternoon at his house. And then went out to supper. At least he was sympathetic and I really couldn't bear to leave him when we said goodbye. I wore blue and he said I looked "lovely". Made me feel better anyway.

Wednesday 21st April 1965

Felt so depressed this morning I couldn't get out of bed. I made the lunch, worked for an hour or so, then gave up and watched TV. I phoned B. at 12 pm; somehow, although he's being frightfully kind I keep wanting to cry when I hear his voice. So silly. The weathers cheering up a bit.

Thursday 22nd April 1965

I phoned up B. again today and was very depressed again. We talked for an hour and my legs were aching by the time we said goodbye. The weather was glorious and I did a bit of gardening. Daph and I did a launderette.

Friday 23rd April 1965

Got up very v. late. Last day at home. What a foul thought. Oh well last day of making the lunches as well. One consolation Margaret came to rehearsals and as usual made a bit of a fool of herself. I made a hash of my speech. Brilliant. Ian took me home and lent me a copy of "The Art of Coarse Acting!"

Saturday 24th April 1965

Went out with B. and had an awful time. He brought some flowers over and we dug them in at no. 7. Then we went up onto the common for a picnic. Morbid. Then onto a party. The only enjoyable part of it was sitting on the stairs and confiding our depression to each other.

Sail On, Silvergirl, Sail On By

Sunday 25th April 1965

Preparing everything for college. I didn't think it was worth revising today so had a glorious day of freedom. I'm absolutely dreading tomorrow. Oh well can't be as bad as all that and as B. says, at least we'll see each other every day now. Joy!? I wonder.

Monday 26th April 1965

Horror. B. was in a bad mood. We just didn't click. He said that Lindsey looked very pretty. We had lunch in the rain and I was relieved to rush into the cloakroom away from him. B. gave me a lift down to the station.

Tuesday 27th April 1965

French. How I hate those lessons. I rushed home afterwards to be greeted by the unfriendly faces of the twins. In the pm I phoned B. He was terribly depressed as Finbar had just failed his driving test. Oh Dear. Worked v. late. I bleached my moustache. Very exciting.

Wednesday 28th April 1965

Went into college. B. was evidently worried about me. Can't understand it. We went up onto the downs and had a glorious time. B. was very quiet though. I really wonder why. Went home and didn't do any work. Went jumble collecting and cooked supper for Keith. Rather good.

Thursday 29th April 1965

What a terrible day this has been. I had a frightful scene with B. and told him I wanted to go home and that he did not love me and all sorts of awful things. It all started of course because I got jealous of that damned girl in the library yesterday. The he told me I should go and see a dentist as my abscess offended him. I just wanted to die.

Friday 30th April 1965

Made it up with B. and the abscess is better. We were very happy today. In the pm went to drama and ran through 2 scenes. Afterwards Pelham and I went to see Margaret. She wasn't at all pleased to see us. I had a frightful headache and couldn't sleep all night.

Saturday 1st May 1965

Did some gardening. B. came in the evening and mummy told him that I look ill and all sorts of silly things. Life is hateful at the moment. I know we shouldn't be going out on Sat. if we have an exam on Monday. Quite frankly, I think I am going mad.

Sunday 2nd May 1965

Today I worked like a Trojan and have decided to get up early tomorrow. I do believe that summer is here at last. I feel so, so depressed.

Monday 3rd May 1965

Got up at 6 am and did 2 hours work – organic. Sat in the exam room and felt those jolly old pains gnawing at my back and tummy. I just couldn't concentrate and felt very unhappy when I walked out. Stayed up late to do my French.

Tuesday 4th May 1965

Aches, pains, feeling sick. French was hellishly boring. The twins have gone back to school and I spent 3 hours searching for a pair of shoes. Eventually got a suede pair.

Wednesday 5th May 1965

I got up early and went in and worked. B. was pleased to see me. Went up onto the downs and ate ice lollies and then went up to the library to work. We were both in a good mood. Oh it's so hot I must wear something cool tomorrow.

Thursday 6th May 1965

Ironed my skirt (brown) and washed my hair. Major events. Unspectacular day. We lay in the field in the afternoon. It's really much too hot.

Friday 7th May 1965

No downs today. It was so hot. Lawrence was away and we had a tutorial. I felt v. irritable in the afternoon. Probably the heat. Margaret was at drama. She evidently cannot go to this holiday camp now! So Devon here I come.

Saturday 8th May 1965

"Jumbling" We marched through the streets in our sandwich boards. The sale wasn't very packed. I felt terribly tired. The party was a flop. I hate Keith. B. had supper at our house and D. made a fool of herself by forcing herself in on our conversation all the time.

Sunday 9th May 1965

Mummy and I went to church in the evening. The sermon was all about life and death. "There is no life after death only life instead of death" or so he said anyway. The weather is getting a bit colder and I feel rather depressed.

Monday 10th May 1965

Chemistry practical exam. I made a hash of everything and couldn't have cared less. B. was very sweet but Lindsey hovered over him all the exam which made my skin crawl. Men are such <u>fools</u>!

Tuesday 11th May 1965

French. Such a boring pattern of life, this is. I had an awful dream about Granny and Grandpa. How we all miss them. Subconsciously, rather than consciously, I think. I went in to do slides with B. He gave me a lift down to the station.

Wednesday 12th May 1965

Snuck in and felt simply awful as B. gave me an awful look. We went up to the library in the afternoon and just as I felt like working, B. had to introduce a blinking sailing book. So all afternoon was wasted in flipping through its boring pages.

Thursday 13th May 1965

Just a week to go. We went into the organic chemistry and were nearly killed by K.'s monotonous voice. How I hate it. B. and I didn't have much to say to each other afterwards – we were both nearly asleep and vowed not to go to another of his lectures!

Friday 14th May 1965

Only about a week to go to the zoo exam.

Saturday 15th May 1965

B. and I made a quick trip to the Zeta House in Putney. We made a beeline for a quiet, romantic corner and sat all evening in a howling gale. Pathetic. Afterwards we made a conducted tour of Putney. I was never so glad to get home!

May 1965

Sunday 16th May 1965

I feel unreligious and refuse to go to church. Dry old Bibles and prayer books. How simply awful. Something is going wrong between B. and I, and, quite frankly, I haven't the energy to stop it.

Monday 17th May 1965

It's the usual boring chemistry. I feel as if I'm going insane as I'm dying for B. to be nice to me and not cast sly looks at other girls, and yet all the time I'm making sarcastic remarks and appearing very hard and cold. Perhaps it's fear.

Tuesday 18th May 1965

I went to French and had a dictation in the p.m. I went into zoo to do some slides. Clive and Martin made some horrible comments about me and Lindsey. I hated them. God knows why, my feelings for B. are so mixed up nowadays.

Wednesday 19th May 1965

B. and I did slides all afternoon and, I hope, benefited from it. It was so cold in the lab. that I had to put B.'s jacket over my shoulders. Everyone thought it very funny. We found Clive at the station and I read over the notes. Frightful.

Thursday 20th May 1965

Went up for the zoo exam. It was frightful. We had a rabbit and an earthworm. The hall was vast and we each had our own section of bench, quite Dr Kilderish! Afterwards we went to the pub and Mike and Clive got drunk. On the train they started to sing dirty songs until B. stopped them. In the end it was quite a nice sing-song.

Friday 21st May 1965

Lawrence let us go up to the library, but I couldn't work. It was the relief after the end of the exams, I think. We went to the Bower afterwards and B. declared how pleased he was that we had met and meant so much to each other. I was thrilled.

Saturday 22nd May 1965

Went to Kingston and got very tired. Bought a new crotchet jumper. Wore it tonight.

Went on to the common and had a very boring evening. I felt depressed and hurt B. so terribly hard. I feel very ashamed of myself afterwards.

Sunday 23rd May 1965

Watched telly – "Tale of Two Cities" – and slept most of today. In the p.m. did some French. Otherwise very boring day.

Monday 24th May 1965

We spent most of the day in the library. As no more practical work until the exams. Dr F. offered me a lift this morning and I wore the white mac. I just love living at home.

Tuesday 25th May 1965

Had one of the most boring and lonely days I have ever had, as B. didn't want me to go in today. I spent my day in my room after French. And, like a silly and dutiful fool, phoned B. at 3.00 pm. He had some blood taken today.

Wednesday 26th May 1965

Had a very exciting day with B. and I laughed all the time. We had to rush back to the library afterwards because of the rain. On the whole, a very nice day.

Thursday 27th May 1965

Had an awful day. Zoo tutorial in the a.m. and then we went into Epsom in the afternoon. I felt almost like crying as B. suddenly said "We'd better go" and hustled me off on the train. I think that B. is becoming a bit too big for his boots. Perhaps we'd better have a little excitement soon.

28 Friday May 1965

B. and I are coming to a dismal and sticky end, I can see it coming. Ann told Terry that she didn't want to see him again. And B. and I had lately begun to hate each other.

Saturday 28th May 1965

We went onto the common and had a lovely time. No rows, no moods and a deeper understanding of each other. Bliss! Went to see Finbar's play. Very good.

May – June 1965

Sunday 30th May 1965

Felt very unreligious.

Monday 31st May 1965

Worked in the library with B. I usually work quite well. We made out a document for Ann S. to sign. It was rather crude, recommending B. as her lover. She was going around hand-in-hand with Terry still.

Tuesday 1st June 1965

French! Boring. I didn't go into the college but went to bed in the p.m. I felt very depressed: Mummy and Daddy are having such a lot of rows lately.

Wednesday 2nd June 1965

Derby Day. We just couldn't work in the library a minute longer. So went and sat in a field next to some pigs. Awful. B. says he's not coming in tomorrow – oh dear. On the way back we saw the Queen. She has a beautiful complexion.

Thursday 3rd June 1965

B. didn't come in today. I felt very lonely in the p.m. Went with Margaret to get my mac in Kingston. It's pale blue and cost £2.10d. Not bad. It was frightfully hot. I won 2 shillings and 4d on the Derby.

Friday June 4th 1965

Had a frightful time at drama. I just can't bear Keith. Iain was really very sweet. He drove me home and cruised around for about half an hour to enable me to " compose" myself. We bumped another car. No damage, thank goodness. Granny's birthday. We went up to the crematorium with some roses.

Saturday June 5th 1965

The fair's gone. We went to Aunty Winnie's for tea and said a sad farewell to Hazel and John. I rushed back to meet B. We were both a bit depressed. A ride to Putney on that scooter doesn't put everyone in the best of moods. We were back by 12.00 pm.

Sunday June 6th 1965

We went over to cut the lawn at Dunmore Road. In the afternoon. It was so hot. Tea was a picnic of banana sandwiches. We rushed up to church in the pm – a lovely service.

Monday 7th June 1965

Had an eventful day, weather very hot with a few showers.

Tuesday 8th June 1965

Went over to B.'s for lunch. We had a chicken and roast potatoes. Afterwards I had a bath and we watched his cine film. At tea time Finbar came back – funny chap. He drove me home at 7.00 pm. The twins and Mummy had rather a nice time at little Auntie Dee's.

Wednesday 9th June 1965

Rose's confirmation. She looked simply lovely in a blue frock. Victoria and Aunt Dee came. The latter gave R. seed pearls and amethysts – rather sweet! We had tea in the hall and Rosie spilt her cup.

Thursday 10th June 1965

Just revised solidly. I phoned up B. at 2.00 and got a very cold reception for being late. In the p.m. we watched a venture which was a rather boring rock-climbing exhibition. I went to bed at 12.00 pm. Mummy and Daddy had a row. Victoria came over. Mummy wrote Miss Clift a letter.

Friday 11th June 1965

B. and I went to work in Wimbledon library in the p.m. He came for lunch. We had pilchards. Afterwards we went to get his licence. The library was very hot and I didn't really do a lot of work. We went up onto the common afterwards for an hour. It was great fun.

Saturday 12th June 1965

I didn't go out this evening but did phone B. at 9.30 p.m. Really I wish I hadn't as he talked solidly for half an hour. Eventually I put the receiver down in sheer disgust. The twins went up to the fair. They had a very frightening time on the "whip".

June 1965

Sunday 13th June 1965

We went up to the 9.15 a.m. Rosie, Mummy and I went to communion. Poor old Daphs looked so forlorn. She certainly looks poor and old these days! Shuffling around, shoulders hunched, with an expression of ever-increasing self-pity on her poor pinched little face – my heart bleeds for her.

Monday 14th June 1965

This week our exams start – so depressing. Nobody at home is really much help, although Rosie is kind enough to test me on vocals. Sometimes Daphy's much too occupied with feeling sorry for herself, and Mummy and Daddy appear to enjoy fighting.

Tuesday 15th June 1965

French – a lesson on Saturday and then no more Mrs K. Thank goodness. I worked in my room all p.m. Very depressing. In the evening I phoned up B. to see how he got on with physics. Evidently it wasn't bad.

Wednesday 16th June 1965

We went to work in the library and got on very well with each other. Gosh, how I'm dreading tomorrow. Mummy and Daphy had another row tonight. It's really too bad and all Daphy's fault. Quite frankly, I think I've never met such a bad-tempered, spiteful creature as her!

Thursday 17th June 1965

Chemistry. It was foul. Afterwards I just sobbed and sobbed. We went to Darren's for lunch and then to look for Finbar's present. A girl took two of the guinea pigs. Daphy in a bad mood again – goodness!

Friday 18th June 1965

More exams. We worked not very hard, I'm afraid, in the afternoon in the library. It was very sultry. I went to French and then felt much too tired to go to Drama. French all evening. Daddy's been up to his nonsense with Miss Clift. This time it was a donkey.

Saturday 19th June 1965

French – a whole hour and a half. Frightful. She lent me a book. B. came over in the afternoon and we had tea. Smashing time on the common. Afterwards we went to the fair. A ride on the dodgems has, I think, earned me an aching kneecap for life.

Sunday 20th June 1965

I woke with a very stiff neck. Nobody was very sympathetic. Rosie started the curse – really she's a very brave person. D. always makes out that she's dying. It all adds to her general attitude of self-pity, I suppose.

Monday 21st June 1965

B. is very worried about these exams – he doesn't show much but, now and again, I catch him looking terribly sad. We've got zoo tomorrow and I'm dreading it. After library we had a swing in the kids' playground.

Tuesday 22nd June 1965

Zoo. A gorgeous paper. We stayed in the library afterwards to do some chem. for tomorrow. I have a sinking feeling it's going to be awful. Daph decided to disappear this evening and had everybody running around, looking for her. Sickening.

Wednesday 23rd June 1965

A bloody awful chem. exam. I was almost in tears when I saw all that maths on it gain. Damned examiners suddenly changing the style of questioning.

Thursday 24th June 1965

More exams today – zoo. Tomorrow isn't a very frightening prospect now. D. has to make sure that she howls for about two hours so that I don't do my revision. Really she's a little ...! Mummy and Rosie are being very kind about the exams.

Friday 25th June 1965

Zoo. A heavenly paper. Afterwards we went to the pub to celebrate. B. and I went for a long walk on the Downs. It was a shame that it was so cold. I feel as if a great weight is lifting off my brain, now that the exams are nearly over.

June – July 1965

Saturday 26th June 1965

Finbar's party. Everybody drank too much champagne. We sang a lot of songs and then got noisy and horrible. Mrs L. kept saying that she thought I was above the other girls in some things. Very embarrassing. I wore R.'s blue dress. B. took me home – kept declaiming how lovely I looked. I think he was almost frightened to kiss me goodnight "fine feathers …"!

Sunday 27th June 1965

Daphy showed herself in her true colours today. She rises beautifully, though, in an attempt to outdo me in Mummy's affections, she's absolutely doing anything for her. Let's hope that now she'll pull herself together.

Monday 28th June 1965

French tomorrow. Marvellous to get it all over with. Poor B. was left in the library whilst Endersby gave me a dictée. We had lunch in the park and then went onto the downs for an hour or two. It was heavenly. I did feel a bit guilty about French, but couldn't have done any work anyway.

Tuesday 29th June 1965

French. It was a frightful paper and we had a dictée at the end. It was just like an idiot blathering in the front. Oh well, one exam that I think that I've failed. Sod it.

Wednesday 30th June 1965

Chem. practical – I was a bundle of nerves. Made a complete mug of my titrations and I could have wept. We went to the downs, then the Green Men with the others. Afterwards we scooted to Reigate. A simply foul girl called Lynn was there – she was very cheap. I always did loathe Mike.

Thursday 1st July 1965

Sailing! Unfortunately, it wasn't a very good sail and we both stayed out too late in the evening. Exams are a bit of an anti-climax, really. There's nothing to do when they're over. One feels absolutely lost.

Sail On, Silvergirl, Sail On By

Friday 2nd July 1965

A picnic in Reigate and half way down a puncture. Typical. Still, B. was really very cool-headed and mended it inside half an hour. We had a drink in a little pub, found a shady dell and had our lunch, then scooted home. Every damn petrol station was stopped at on the way home. However, better safe than sorry, I suppose.

Saturday 3rd July 1965

A regatta. We scooted up and down between London Bridge and Putney, following the race, then went to Bernie's. The fish was absolutely heavenly. I could have eaten 6,000 of them. B. was in rather a bad mood – probably a bit tired.

Sunday 4th July 1965

Mummy and I went up to the crematorium for the special service. It was very beautiful. "Jesus loves, Jesus knows, Jesus cares" the main theme of the sermon. It's very true. We made cakes in the p.m. Medical student and fiancée came to see the flat.

Monday 5th July 1965

B. came over to take photos of us. With flashlight. Of course, the darn thing went wrong. I had an hour in which to ice the twins' cake – hell. I gave them a bottle of scent each.

Tuesday 6th July 1965

Sailing. Heaven on earth. Even if a bit cold and watery. I feel very proud at being able to take the helm. I think perhaps I spoilt it as I got very tired and, after two and a half hours, told B. we had better go in. B. really is very sweet, as not a grumble was uttered. A frightfully fat girl helped us with the boat.

Wednesday 7th July 1965

We went to Hampton Court Palace. It's really rather spooky; with all the dusty pictures gazing down at you. The vine is pathetic and I think that the kitchens are frightful. It simply poured with rain, which rather spoiled things.

Friday 9th July 1965

A glorious day for sailing – apart from the rain, that is. I took the helm and really enjoy

July 1965

sailing now. It's a marvellous feeling, turning the boat slightly into the wind and feeling it shudder and then leap forwards. Drama + B. in the p.m. Chronic! But fun.

Saturday 10th July 1965

I did a lot of shopping today. The wedding present. A handbag and gorgeous cheesecake. We went to Boney's in the p.m. I wore the new grey and white dress. Perhaps the front is a bit too low! Afterwards we went onto the common – it was a rash thing to do, after so much beer.

Sunday 11th July 1965

Rather a pleasant day. We went to 9.15 a.m. service and then for a walk on the common. Lunch was heavenly and I phoned B. (without Rose) at 4.30 p.m. A deep, foaming bath and then early to bed.

Monday 12th July 1965

It absolutely teemed down all day. B. was supposed to be coming over; however, getting wet is ample enough deterrence. We had a few, rather cold words over the phone. He'll probably come over tomorrow. I took Mummy to see 'The Ipcress File' *(Spy thriller with Michael Caine)* – it was very thrilling.

Tuesday 13th July 1965

Sailing. Speaks for itself. Of course, we had another damned puncture and B. got into a bad mood. I walked to the shops and got some chocolate for him. Gratitude isn't evidently one of his strong points.

14 Wednesday July 1965

We carried the lawn mower over to Dunmore Road. He cut the lawn. Afterwards we lay on Auntie Jean's lino and drank cups of tea supplied by Victoria. Of course, I have to lose the key. We went onto the common and I felt very close to B., both spiritually and physically.

Thursday 15th July 1965

Searched for hours for the damn key. We went sailing in the p.m. I felt lousy and had a frightful time helming. B. lost his temper. However, there was a touching reunion after the ensuing row. Mummy is very angry about my losing the key. I feel awful.

Friday 16th July 1965

Today we went on a sentimental journey, first to the Borough, then to the 'tec and finally through all our old haunts. Both of us were terribly unhappy at the thought of parting. In the p.m. we went to drama. I'm afraid I didn't do my best. Everyone was very sweet, wishing me a happy holiday, etc.

Saturday 17th July 1965

Last day. I feel like crying all the time, but must be brave. At 1.30 p.m. B. picked me up and we scooted down to Weybridge. I hated every minute of that fete; perhaps it was because all the time I was thinking of parting. A rather friendly, jolly meal at Zeta's was followed by a puncture. Tears, eventually B. rode home on my bike.

Sunday 18th July 1965

The terrible day has come. B. didn't turn up and I was frightened of missing my train. He saw me off at Paddington. We just stood and gazed at each other, tears running down our cheeks – it was very awful. The journey was a nightmare – I landed up in Plymouth. The first impression of the camp was terrifying. Loud music and hundreds of people.

Jenny had a summer job at Pontins Holiday camp in Devon.

According to the website "Butlins Memories" http://www.butlinsmemories.com/2/id184.htm.

> "A delightful full-board camp located high on the cliff top near Brixham. First opened in 1938 and used by Canadian servicemen during the war. Purchased by Pontins in the early 1960s and extensively rebuilt. Suffered a major fire in early 1991 and was not rebuilt. Currently lying closed and derelict."

Monday 19th July 1965

I was miserable and frightened the first day. Mummy phoned. I started work at 4.00 p.m. and went on 'til midnight. It's not that the work is hard, just tiring. I'm on the shift with Kate, Pat, Di, Ida, Marj and June. They all see quite nice.

July 1965

Tuesday 20th July 1965

Was thrilled to see absolutely gorgeous letters from B. and from Mummy. Di and I sunbathed on the beach – I must get a tan. June was in charge of the buffet tonight and reduced me to tears by her perpetual bossiness. John helped with the washing up.

Wednesday 21st July 1965

It was a gloriously hot, lazy day, and we spent most of the morning on the beach. This Ida woman keeps attaching herself to me. It's rather embarrassing as she's about fifty-odd.

Thursday 22nd July 1965

After the buffet work this evening, we all went down to Brixham. Quite horrid. John and I played table tennis. He was awfully sweet, letting me win every time I'm sure that he should have won. His talk is very immoral, though: all about V.D., etc.

Friday 23rd July 1965

Wrote to B. I was clearing the tables after having written to B. and washed my hair, when a rich, chestnut voice said "Jenny" and there was E. He looked very tired and asked about a camping site. I suggested up the hill.

Saturday 24th July 1965

I got up at 12.00 a.m., after sleeping rather later than intended. Met E. at 2.00 p.m. and we went for a walk over the cliffs. He was very charming. Nevertheless, we didn't get on very well. They've found a camping spot at the back of the camp. 4–12 shift.

Sunday 25th July 1965

Got up at 11.00 a.m. and had a rather embarrassing lunch with E., Alfred and Lisa Lottie and then we drove to Widdicombe and had a cream tea. Buckfast Abbey was splendid. I felt terribly car sick. I wish B. was here; it would be so gorgeous.

Monday 26th July 1965

So now I'm on the 9.00 'til 6.00 p.m. shift. Oh well, at least I can go out in the evening. We walked to Bury Head and then went back to the tent. E. told me all about his love life, I told him about B. It was rather strange, as I think he imagined we would start on the same footing.

Tuesday 27th July 1965

This evening we drove into Torquay. Looked at the lights, had a coffee and then drove back. Great fun; except the car makes me feel sick. We didn't get back until 12.30 p.m. Very bad.

Wednesday 28th July 1965

Had a terrible sore throat and hated everybody. I took Aspro all day. Thank God I've heard from B. at last. He leaves for Ireland tomorrow. I went to bed early. Eileen must have wondered what was the matter with me.

Thursday 29th July 1965

Wrote to B. Felt bloody awful all day. Went to rocks in the p.m. Thought of B. sailing the high seas.

Friday 30th July 1965

Went to the flicks with Ida – "Never Mind the World". Very good.

Saturday 31st July 1965

Sunbathed. Worked from 4.00 'til 12.00 shift – very tiring.

Sunday 1st August 1965

Day off – slept 'til 12.00. Went for long walk to Bury Head. Then to pub – drank one pint.

Monday 2nd August 1965

Very depressed. Rained all day. Went for walk in the p.m. Drank Hopkins in the lounge.

Tuesday 3rd August 1965

Went to Kingsmere by ferry. Great fun. Went into pub for pint. Visited the castle.

August 1965

Wednesday 4th August 1965

Wept almost all day. Very worried about B. not writing. Letter from home. Went to Torbay today.

Thursday 5th August 1965

Day off on beach in p.m. Shopping. Letter from B. Thank God! He does so sound as if he's enjoying himself.

Friday 6th August 1965

9.00 'til 6.00 – very long day. Went with D. to the cliffs

Saturday 7th August 1965

Interesting day. Went to work at Wool Park in the p.m. with Kate. Mummy and the twins arrived – they phoned.

Sunday 8th August 1965

9.00 'til 6.00 p.m. Hurried over to see the family.

Monday 9th August 1965

Awful day. It went so damn slowly. Went out with D. Wrote letters.

Tuesday 10th August 1965

Only four of us. Hectic.

Wednesday 11th August 1965

Got the shock of my life as Mummy and the twins arrived at the camp. Got a letter from B. asking why I hadn't written. Cheek.

Thursday 12th August 1965

Went over to Torquay after dentist. Sunbathed all day, went to dinner in the p.m. at Mrs. Goodman's.

Friday 13th August 1965

Usual boring day. Went dancing in the p.m. To bed too late!

Saturday 14th August 1965

Met B. E. introduced me. Drank too much. Only slept for about two hours – very hot night.

Sunday 15th August 1965

Fagged out. Slept only hours. Went bowling with B. Marvellous.

Monday 16th August 1965

Dead! Slept for an hour, then went to the beach with B. Had party in our room. Great.

Tuesday 17th August 1965

B. went.

Wednesday 18th August 1965

Washed hair. Nothing spectacular.

Thursday 19th August 1965

Mummy came over. Went to concert with D.

Friday 20th August 1965

Lesley left. Last day on days. Joy. Went to the fair.

Saturday 21st August 1965

First night on nights. Sold hot-dogs. M. phoned.

Sunday 22nd August 1965

Went into Brixham in the morning. Rain. Very tiring work.

August 1965

Monday 23rd August 1965

D. and I went onto the beach. Did my travelling expenses. Letter from B. Did hot-dogs.

Tuesday 24th August 1965

B.'s passed his exams. Thank God. One step on the way. On nights.

Wednesday 25th August 1965

Letter from M. She arrived safely, thank God. No results. I think I shall go mad.

Thursday 26th August 1965

Last night in the buffet – blessed relief. Walked down with Doreen.

Friday 27th August 1965

Went to Bury Head with D. then took the boat over to Torquay. Saw Lily and co. Party in the p.m.

Saturday 28th August 1965

Returned – absolutely thrilled to see B., who met me at the station. Went to the steak house. Great fun.

Sunday 29th August 1965

Saw B. in the p.m. Something seems a bit wrong between us, though I can't tell what.

Monday 30th August 1965

Saw B. in the p.m. Mummy wasn't home all day. B. and I have hardly anything to say to each other now. Silly.

Tuesday 31st August 1965

Went sailing – behaved very badly. B. is rather cold towards me. I feel very, very unhappy.

Wednesday 1st September 1965

J. and H. wedding. B. and I had a terrible heart-to-heart. I almost fainted with shock. I didn't know that he was loathing me.

Thursday 2nd September 1965

I am so fed up with being lonely and unwanted. This morning I went into Kingston with the twins. I bought a black jumper and lots of frilly underwear. I wrote B. a very cold note, saying "drama off, sorry". Wish I hadn't, now. I cried and cried over B. today.

Friday 3rd September 1965

It came down in sheets today. At 6.45 p.m. B. phoned to say that he'd got my letter and wasn't coming anyway. I felt very hurt and angry. Although it was a filthy night, I went out for a long walk up to the common.

Saturday 4th September 1965

Tonight I spent hours making myself up and trying to look nice, so that B. would appreciate me again. I wore the new jumper. Thank God he made a great fuss of me and was absolutely wonderful. I, in return, though, was slightly off. Perhaps I did the wrong thing.

Sunday 5th September 1965

I went to Dr. Pritchard on Friday and he gave me some Vitamin B. pills. Went up to St. Martin's and had a very pleasant service. Later, we walked over Waterloo Bridge. Phoned B. in the p.m. Rows, I'm so tired of all this.

Monday 6th September 1965

I got up at 10.30 today and was supposed to be at the hospital at 11.00 a.m. Instead, however, I phoned up and cancelled the job. After all, I've got all my damn botany to do. I got my passport photos taken. B. was in a very good mood in the p.m. on the phone.

Tuesday 7th September 1965

The twins went back to school today. There were black looks at tea time and I don't think they had a very good day. I got a letter and photo from Eileen. In the p.m. went bowling with Steve, Martin and Brenda. Great fun. I came second – just a fluke, though!

September 1965

Wednesday 8th September 1965

At 4.00 p.m. I suddenly woke up with a start. My God – sleeping in all day! Mummy and I went up to the television studios. It was interesting, but not as good as I had expected. Still, at least we got a free biro. We had a very bumpy train journey home.

Thursday 9th September 1965

Ann-Marie turned up. I suppose it was nice to see her – she definitely has a lot of troubles, poor thing. B. and I were going to the folk club; however, four shillings each is rather a lot of money. Instead, saw Von Ryan's Express – rather horrifying. (*War escape film with Frank Sinatra.*) B. swore that the usherette was a lesbian and was trying to get off with me. Gave me the creeps!

Friday 10th September 1965

Oh dear, it's rather difficult to tell B. that there's no drama when he's specially changed his babysitting to Wednesday. He came over and we went to the Dog and Fox. We were in deep harmony again. Wonderful. Wendy's disappeared.

Saturday 11th September 1965

A supper of celebration was the bill for tonight. Yes, I suppose it was lovely. B. was very, very tired, though, and rather irritable. We drank rosé – Heaven on earth. Well, had a loving greeting and then we charged off on our chief stop.

Sunday 12th September 1965

I had a frightful row with Mummy and the twins and stormed out of the churchyard. We had a dismal lunch, and I phoned B. in the p.m. He's got a lovely job – working in the theatre, watching people being cut up.

Monday 13th September 1965

So it's "bowling again". Actually, it was great fun. Clive came this time and was as sarcastically cutting as usual. B. was sweet and very attentive. Of course, I couldn't do it tonight and kept scoring nil. We sang as we drove home on Archie.

Tuesday 14th September 1965

Visited great-grandpa this evening. He was 96 years old. Incredible. Letty and Nina and all those were making nasty remarks about Vivvy going to Oxford and my going to "some tec". After all, what's wrong with a tec? I tell you, I'll get that degree if it kills me.

Wednesday 15th September 1965

Had a frightfully lonely day. Ann-Marie came and unburdened herself on me in the p.m. and I must confess I was in a flaming mood by the time B. came for me at 7.30 p.m. We chugged off to the folk club. It is six shillings each to get in! Very good songs, though!

Thursday 16th September 1965

Another appallingly lonely day. I wish now that I had taken a job. Botany is hellishly boring. I get so bloody depressed by myself all day. Phoned B. in the p.m. He sounded pleased to hear me and so was I, until he went on and on and on. I put the phone down with a curt "goodbye".

Friday 17th September 1965

I got up very early and tidied my room. My packing took only a few minutes and by 5.00 p.m. I was all ready. B. turned up at the college at 6.10 p.m. and we set off for Botley in the pouring rain. I was in the Mini and B. in the Volkswagen. We were both a bit upset at being parted.

Saturday 18th September 1965

A beautiful day but rather windy. We went for a lovely walk in the country. Supper at 6.00 p.m. and then on to the pub. B., of course, drank too much. He's been in a funny mood today – I think I'm getting on his nerves. Anyway, he was very ashamed of drinking too much.

Sunday 19th September 1965

We were up at 7.30 a.m., breakfast at 8.00. A glorious sail with B. and Jack and then, after supper, home to dreary room. Drove back with Jane and Mike. Drank a bottle of Merrydown on the way. B. then drove me from his house. I felt very depressed at saying goodbye. Silly.

Monday 20th September 1965

I feel so diabolically depressed; I just don't know what to do with myself. I lay on bed as long as possible and then just mooned around all day on the sofa and cried. I keep thinking of B. It's almost an obsession between wanting to talk to him and never wanting to see him again.

Tuesday 21st September 1965

Felt much better today, perhaps because I'm going to see B. tonight. Bowling was quite a success, I suppose. Pam turned up. She was very charming but we didn't get on. B. was very, very attentive – I just couldn't understand it.

Wednesday 22nd September 1965

Didn't go out – very lonely day.

Thursday 23rd September 1965

Went to the folk bar. It was rather terrifyingly jolly.

Friday 24th September 1965

Drama.

Saturday 25th September 1965

Very depressed as it's our last night out. I, of course, burst into tears. Luckily, it was raining.

Monday 27th September 1965

First day – most of the time was spent talking and filling in forms – I just don't get on with any of the people in my class. They are very unfriendly. Especially that Sheila. Phoned B. in the p.m. I was almost in tears, I felt so miserable. B. started at Barts.

Jenny enrols at the Northern Polytechnic and starts her Botany and Zoology degree.

Tuesday 28th September 1965

Botany practical all day. B. came over. I was very pleased to see him but, of course, was in too much of a hysterical state to show it.

Wednesday 29th September 1965

Another horrid day. Hate this place.

Sail On, Silvergirl, Sail On By

1 Friday 1st October 1965

Week too early. Went up for the induction course. It was very frightening and I hate the place. In the p.m. we watched a film. I went along with a married man called John. I just got back in time for drama. Everyone was sweet. New bloke – Geoffrey.

This entry does not seem to fit in correctly but to avoid more confusion I have left it where it is.

Saturday 2nd October 1965

Went to the game. Out to dance in the p.m. – Patrick plus. Quite fun.

Sunday 3rd October 1965

Moved into flat.

Tuesday 5th October 1965

Went to Hanley Woods, I felt awful in the p.m. as we had three hours chemistry and then that long walk afterwards. Ian waited for me at the station. We get on quite well. Talked with Maria for hours.

Maria Paley was an interesting character. I had always fancied her from when I started at the Northern Polytechnic to do Chemistry the year before. She completed her Chemistry degree although her main interest actually was ballet. She said that she wanted a useful qualification because ballet was such an uncertain business.

About 6 months after Jenny's death Maria contacted me and we started seeing each other. The affair was not consummated and she had a horror of falling pregnant. An attempted seduction (I was living in Cricklewood in a shared flat) failed when my flatmates returned home unexpectedly one evening. Things fizzled out after an incident. I had invited her out for a meal with my parents, after my Ph. D. presentation ceremony. She met us at a tube station, refused to meet my parents, (but gave me some flowers for my mother), and darted off. She must have thought that I was getting too serious!

Wednesday 6th October 1965

Met J.B. on the train. We had a good chat. Zoo was hellishly boring today. Didn't phone B. Watched "Jeeves". Very funny.

October 1965

Thursday 7th October 1965

See back a week only. Two more days of this travelling. We've got a flat, I'm sharing with a girl called Maria. She's very quiet – French, I think.

Again this entry seems out of sequence.

Friday 8th October 1965

Drama after a hectic day at college. I loathe chem. practical. Especially with Ian, who makes me look so damn stupid. B. was in a bad mood.

Saturday 9th October 1965

Went to see "The Student Prince" with B. It was magnificent. We got on very well at the beginning of the evening but he seemed rather glad to say adieu at the end. Brought me some apples.

Sunday 10th October 1965

Back to the digs. Out with A.

Monday 11th October 1965

Chemistry prac. this afternoon – found out that doing it with Adrian. There was an explosion in the lab. – awful. Anyway, we were let out a bit earlier.

I vaguely remember an explosion in one of the research labs in which one of the Ph. D. students – a very striking and attractive Jamaican girl – was blinded in one eye. This may have been a later and separate incident.

Tuesday 12th October 1965

Went to Box Hill. I talked to David. I think he's smashing. We had a picnic on the top of Box Hill. Chemistry in the p.m. David Fisher looked at me very coyly and said " Oh I'll leave this place for Mrs Lordship".

Wednesday 13th October 1965

B. came over for lunch, it was lovely to see him. Took an hour off from 3.00 – I think they were rather annoyed.

Thursday 14th October 1965

Half day – bliss. Worked in library with Maria. Adrian took me out in the p.m. to the Victoria – I was exhilarated. It absolutely came down in buckets this afternoon and evening.

Friday 15th October 1965

Drama. B. came and looked as bored as hell. It was awful.

Saturday 16th October 1965

Had a rotten time with B. We had a great scene on the common and almost broke it off. However, both agreed that we couldn't live without each other. Anyway, in the end we decided "this is it". We're so much closer now than we were before. I hope so.

Sunday 17th October 1965

Had the usual "churching" Sunday. Out with A. in the p.m. Why he sleeps at King's Cross is beyond me. He's rather a boring little fellow, really. Of course, we went to Trafalgar Square.

Monday 18th October 1965

Did judo for the first time. It was absolutely fantastic fun. At least I've learnt how to fall. I phoned J.B. He has invited me out next Monday – joy. Met a funny little Italian bloke, rather sweet.

He is subsequently referred to as E (Enzo).

Tuesday 19th October 1965

Woe, am I stiff – no trouble today, thank God. We did horrible slides and I had a frightful headache – chemistry in the p.m. didn't help.

Wednesday 20th October 1965

Brendan went sailing today. The weather was glorious, I did envy him. We did horrid preps of okeha. Awful. I still can't get on with everyone in my class – silly, I suppose, but true, awfully true.

October 1965

Thursday 21st October 1965

Horrid day: I went over for lunch with B. He, of course, was beastly. Then I met Mummy – that was very, very pleasant. He showed me the actors' church and John Betjeman's house. In the p.m. I went to the Christian Union and met quite a few "nice" people.

Friday 22nd October 1965

Drama really held some drama this evening. Maurice phoned up B. and now the latter has the part of "Nicky" in the play. It's rather ironical, really, as Keith is going to Capri or somewhere.

Saturday 23rd October 1965

I thought B. wouldn't come today, he had a wedding. However, 8.30 p.m. a ring at the door and there he was, I wasn't even ready. The party was really great fun; I'm glad we went. As the others had gone, we helped them clear up, and left at 1.30 a.m. The clocks went back.

Sunday 24th October 1965

Felt very, very bad. A. took me out in the p.m. and we looked for the Cheshire Cheese – not finding it, we had a gorgeous drink, meat pie outside a dirty old tavern. Poor A. is so sweet.

Monday 25th October 1965

Awful phys. chem. lecture. Can't stand that man. J.B. took me out in the p.m. He, of course, drank too much. Wow, was he amorous – I'm sure it was merely the drink though! Got home at 2.15 – Maria was still up.

Tuesday 26th October 1965

Horrible day of botany. Ian turned up in the afternoon. I felt absolutely out of it, everyone was talking gaily and I just sat there, nobody saying a word to me. Only now I wish B. was here; I keep wanting to talk to him.

Wednesday 27th October 1965

B. called over for lunch. I was so very, very pleased to see him and took him back to my digs afterwards. I don't think that he liked them all that much. I was told off for missing the first hour in zoology. B.'s going sailing this week. Strangely, I'm rather relieved.

Thursday 28th October 1965

Afternoon off. How I hate being so alone in this place. Having lunch with Adrian, then just being alone all afternoon, with nobody to talk to. Just having to sit in the library and try and look as if I'm doing some work. I miss Brendan. Went to the C.U. and then to the chemical lecture.

October 29th Friday 1965

Felt very depressed. Had lunch with Ian and supper. We went to work in the library for half an hour and he looked a bit upset when I left! Drama in the p.m. First night with P. I suppose it works all right, although the poor thing was scared stiff of me.

Saturday 30th October 1965

Went to see Auntie Winnie and Uncle Howard. After a good tea of bread and cakes, and then drank out of Chinese cups. In the p.m. "La Belle Helène" with J.B. It was, I suppose, "fun". He looked frightfully handsome and was very friendly. His part couldn't be smaller, fortunately.

Sunday 31st October 1965

Went back to go out with A. Quite good fun. Didn't make a cake.

Monday 1st November 1965

Period and, of course, I did my judo like a fool.

Tuesday 2nd November 1965

Botany. Seemed to feel a bit like the old way with the class today. About time. Met E. in the p.m. He saw me home again. B. kept phoning, poor Maria was sick of it.

November 1965

Wednesday 3rd November 1965

B. came over. We had lunch and went to the pub. I'm afraid it was a bit of an anti-climax. I felt so, so sad to see him go. Silly. Harry gave me supper – great fun.

Thursday 4th November 1965

Horrible day. Went home and did six hours' zoology. At least I've learnt embryology.

Friday 5th November 1965

Met Dr. Swallow – I almost fell over with delight. Drama, B. is absolutely useless, poor chap. John got a new car. Auntie Winnie and Uncle Howard left for Canada.

Saturday 6th November 1965

Firework display. The bonfire was quite fantastic, then "Zulu" (*Battle of Rorke's drift with Michael Caine*) – a very frightening film – then on to Raynes Park, oh gosh.

Sunday 7th November 1965

Awfully depressed, don't know why. Perhaps it's the thought of going back.

Monday 8th November 1965

Judo again. E. saw me home. My God, was I stiff. We went to do the statement – He kept kicking me under the table because I couldn't stop laughing.

Tuesday 9th November 1965

Chem. in the p.m. E. saw me home. It's getting a bit much of a good thing! Phoned B. – he has to go into hospital to have his wisdom teeth out – poor B.

Wednesday 10th November 1965

Cooked supper for E. God knows what he felt. Then on to finish the statement. The people were very nice.

Sail On, Silvergirl, Sail On By

Thursday 11th November 1965

E. saw me home again. I did quite a lot of work in the p.m. B. sold Archie for £40.

Friday 12th November 1965

Drama: Harry's going to do B.'s part. Went to the pub with John afterwards.

Saturday 20th November 1965

B. came over in his new car. I tried to look as enthusiastic as possible, but he seemed to rather hate me. We pub crawled and then went for a drive. He had to be back by 10.00 p.m. as Mummy worries so!

Saturday 27th November 1965

The car's broken down.

Monday 29th November 1965

Didn't do judo. He was v. pleased.

Tuesday 30th November 1965

Didn't go in, felt pretty awful – went in to see E. after tea. Glad I did as he was very nice.

Wednesday 1st December 1965

B. came for lunch. He looked ghastly. I took the afternoon off. Of course he had to go back to Barts. It makes me a bit suspicious.

Friday 3rd December 1965

Didn't go back but went to Senate House with Maria to study. Mummy's birthday – gave her a manicure set. We didn't get back 'til about 10.00 p.m. Still, one can really work there.

Saturday 4th December 1965

Came home. Had birthday tea. B. came in his brother's scooter as the car's broken down. Back axle is still broken.

Sunday 5th December 1965

Went up to try and study for my exam tomorrow. Of course Maria didn't turn up. I hate sleeping there by myself. The landlady is ill and was very rude to me.

Monday 6th December 1965

Stinking phys. chem. over exam. E. came into the library to find out how I got on. He is very sweet.

Tuesday 7th December 1965

Botany exam all day. Frightful. We had a beastly seaweed as our main question. I. walked me home, blessed relief after all that work. Went to study in the library with Paul and I. 'til 9.00 p.m.

Wednesday 8th December 1965

Zoo exam. Had the afternoon off. Went out with B. in the p.m. Didn't get back 'til 1.00 a.m. I must be mad, as I've got my chem. tomorrow.

Thursday 9th December 1965

Awful chem. exam. Phoned B. – he was horrid. How I hate phoning from that smelly phone box and then being told all about those girls at Barts.

Friday 10th December 1965

Last rehearsal before the play. We had our chem. exam – organic – frightful. I skived off at lunch time. Maurice, of course, has now discovered that we have no-one for Mickey – but a John Thornton. He's better than anyone we've had so far.

Saturday 11th December 1965

Went to Barts! dance with B. It was great fun. I met some of his friends. None of them really seem like him. Poor thing. He got lost, of course, on the way up, which rather put a damper on the evening.

Sunday 12th December 1965

B. went into hospital. I went to see him and tried to be very jolly. Of course he couldn't get rid of me quick enough and I was in tears as I left. Oh I loathe hospitals. Went back to the digs. Maria's mother stayed the night. My God, it was awful – I liked her very much, though.

Monday 13th December 1965

Went to judo in the p.m. B. didn't turn up but Mr. Davy was marvellous, rather embarrassing. Met B. at 8. After a shower he had a very nice evening. But I must get on early every night before the play – by the way, we first had a terrible row.

Tuesday 14th December 1965

Got into botany a little late. Skipped off to see "The Glory Girls" with B. in the afternoon, then back to chem. in the p.m. Met B. at 9.00. We went to the Wimpy Bar, it is a frightful place.

Wednesday 15th December 1965

Got our results on zoo. Passed, thank God – about 42%. Met B. in the p.m. after paying my deposit for the botany trip. Said goodbye to B. for a week – very sad. He gave me a gorgeous box of chocs for passing my exams.

Thursday 16th December 1965

Dress rehearsal of the play: frightful, really chronic. I just didn't know my lines. Didn't go back to town – the Marlborough Hall is hopeless to act in. I felt completely lost on a stage after having rehearsed in a room all these months.

Friday 17th December 1965

First night – only 26 people turned up. Shocking. I just couldn't act. The twins did the profiteroles and Mummy helped with the teas. I just couldn't have given a damn. I felt so tired.

Saturday 18th December 1965

B. came at 6.00, Mummy did the teas – she was very upset about a Mrs. Doswell. About 80 people turned up, so did the Press. Afterwards went to a boring party at Maurice's – Aunt Eileen turned up, gate-crashed. We left at 2.00 a.m.

Sunday 19th December 1965

Slept like a log.

Monday 20th December 1965

Went up to town with B. Met Clive after B. had had his stitches out. Clive bought a suit. We had lunch in The Golden Egg. Clive left after we'd had tea at my flat. There B. met Maria. They weren't very impressed with each other. Lost Clive, ended up in the Western Bar, then home. B. drove me in the car. We were very tired.

Tuesday 21st December 1965

Slept most of the day. I hate being alone in this house. Went carol-singing with B. and drama in the p.m. We made quite a lot of money. Collected in the pub afterwards and made about £1. B. was in a bad mood.

Wednesday 22nd December 1965

Went bowling in the p.m. with Clive, his girlfriend Viv – awful – and Peter, "a friend of Clive's". B. and I were so tired we both got irritable. Left at 12.30 – we must be mad.

Thursday 23rd December 1965

B. turned up on time. We went shopping and he bought me a gorgeous scarf and a box of chocolates. We had a marvellous lunch. Then went up to Soho to do some more shopping. Afterwards, to B.'s friends' – they were very friendly and insisted on my tasting their favourite wine. Revolting! Still, I grinned and bore it.

Friday 24th December 1965

Came home at 3.00 p.m. B. came at 6.00. We went to see Brian, his nephew, then met Martin. B. looked very well. Clive invited us back to his house for a coffee and we met his father. B. got terribly jealous as Martin put his arm around me. B. gave me a marvellous present of talcum powder, scent, bath salts, etc.

Saturday 25th December 1965

Didn't get to bed 'til 1.30 a.m. Went to church – quite a moving service. Mummy gave me a gorgeous dress – Daph a pair of false eyelashes and Rosie bath salts. It was a very quiet day and we all ate too much. Watched "Moby Dick", then went to bed early.

Sunday 26th December 1965

All got up late. Rosie and I cleared out the animals. Their water was frozen. Phoned B. at 3.00 p.m. He's going to take me to a party at the Rowans. He didn't turn up until 9.10 p.m. The party was frightful, we just sat and I wished that I was anywhere but there. B. was hateful and I loathed those Collins girls.

Monday 27th December 1965

Slept in very late and, after much thought, decided to phone B. in the p.m. He was very sweet. Mummy at home all day, she's very hysterical these days – I really don't know why. Wish I didn't feel so damn tired all the time. Watched "Toulouse Lautrec" – marvellous, poor little man.

Tuesday 28th December 1965

Went out with B. We got on very well and, after wandering around looking for the folk club, eventually ended up in the cinema. Saw "Shenandoah" – it was really great. He was rather quiet on the way home; really, I don't understand him sometimes. One thing I know, though: he's very, very selfish – whatever he wants, we do.

Wednesday 29th December 1965

Went up to town. I felt awful as E. had prepared spaghetti and chops and all sorts of things for us and, of course, I didn't turn up yesterday. We went out for a walk in the evening and he was very annoyed at my phoning – well, I just couldn't let B. down. After getting on so well with him last night, perhaps I was a fool to always give in to B.

Thursday 30th December 1965

Had lunch with (rest of sentence crossed out). Went out with B., Clive, Steve, Dave – oh bowling – Rotten. B. was foul; so was Clive.

Friday 31st December 1965

Went to Trafalgar Square with B. First, though, we had a terrible scene. I was very unhappy that he said something was wrong and that he was going to Ireland. Oh – after all our plans, how hurt I was. Anyway, we both wept a lot and I thought I'd made a fool of myself. After a while I uttered those apparently unforgettable words "one must give and take in every relationship". He was all over me after that, as he'd got his own way, as

December 1965

usual. I was pleased, though, when he said that he could only love me, whatever happened. Trafalgar Square was chaos; I really thought that I was going to be crushed to death. We got lost on the way back, eventually arriving home at 3.30 a.m. My God – what a way to start the New Year.

Diary 1966

In which Jenny settles into college life and meets Bill.

Saturday 1st January 1966

The first hours of the new year. Phoned B. and I'm marching down the Strand underneath a dripping umbrella. All around us people were hurrying to get home. On the way we stopped in for a meal at the Golden Egg.

I slept most of the day and in the p.m. went to see "Once a Thief" (*A gangster movie with Jack Palance et al*) with B. Although I was at first loath to go, it was very good.

Sunday 2nd January 1966

Mummy and Daph weren't feeling very well – so Rosie and I went to church. We, however, favoured a walk over the common more than a dismal church service. It was a really beautiful day, apart from golfers beckoning at us and angry roars – one of the most enjoyable walks I've ever had.

Monday 3rd January 1966

What a lovely feeling, to be able to lie in bed and think – I can stay here all day if I want to! Mummy was still not very well today, so I thought that I'd better not go up to town. The weather was beautiful – and I sat down to some serious study, however, 6.30 p.m. heralded B. As usual we had a bit of nastiness and a bit of niceness. Thank God he said that he didn't really mean what he had said about my letter-writing. "Mutiny on the Bounty" was, in feeble terms, fantastic. We drove home in a very bumpy fashion and I had a splitting headache.

Sail On, Silvergirl, Sail On By

Tuesday 4th January 1966

Mummy still ill. The twins went to the dentist and, at 4.15 p.m., I was on the train, travelling up to town. 5.15 p.m. found me hanging around suspiciously outside the Poly, waiting for E. We had a marvellous evening, with, unfortunately, liver and bacon for supper – ugh! Maria has gone youth hostelling. Seeing the Poly again was very disturbing; I am absolutely dreading going back. Oh well, that's life, I suppose.

Wednesday 5th January 1966

Woke up in the room – it was a funny sensation, not to be at home. After a hurried breakfast I met E. for lunch – we had a Chinese in a restaurant. It wasn't exactly delicious, but very filling. Saying goodbye to E. was very peculiar – the way that he looked at me. I spent about four hours looking for a coat and eventually bought a marvellous black and white fitted one. B. rolled up late. We went to the folk club in Surbiton. Quite honestly, he was like a spoilt brat – refusing to clap when they didn't sing his favourite songs. We got back at 12.05.

Thursday 6th January 1966

First thing – did the laundrette, really I don't mind doing it if only the others wouldn't pretend it was they who had done it (got very confused). It was a very lazy day and most of the evening was spent watching T.V. Victoria came over at about 8.30 p.m. My goodness, she's changed. Her voice was very high and nasal and cockney. I just couldn't believe that it was Victoria. Poor old Daph lost Ian – quite honestly, I always thought that she was too good for him anyway. She was very upset. I had a bath and went to bed by 11.30.

Friday 7th January 1966

A really beautiful day – I set off to buy my bag and came back with a beauty – soft, light brown leather, £4.4.00 is rather a lot to pay though. B. came in the p.m. and we went pub crawling; of course, in the brewery tap, who should we meet but our dear friend Rodney Rye, Brian and David Sherwin. Rodney and Brian are "engaged" (not to each other!). I wore my muff and, of course, caused a sensation (mild). Gosh, I think it's going to snow. The car is named "Liverpool Lou" – rather appropriate, as the damn thing will never start.

Saturday 8th January 1966

B. and I went to John and Helen's party – it was great fun. I felt rather embarrassed at meeting them all after that light-up. As B. said, the party was a mixture of everything:

singing, dancing, talking, laughing. Beryl had a little too much to drink, I fear, she's funny up to a point, but when she started flinging her arms around B., that was the last straw. Talk about Stephens jealousy.

Sunday 9th January 1966

Got up very early and did the botany essays. I went up to town about 7.00 p.m. Gill's had a boy. I was very pleased to see Maria again. We talked far too late in the night, though.

Monday 10th January 1966

Back to college. Actually wasn't too bad after all. Everybody seemed pleased to see everybody else. I went to judo in the evening, only four of us turned up, so I had Mr. Daly as my partner – he thought I was hopeless. Unfortunately, he was right! E. met me at 8 o'clock and we had a smashing supper. I told Maria that it would be only one night out this week – I really must stick to that. Getting a grant and being completely self-supporting is a fantastic feeling – unfortunately, I feel terribly guilty if I'm not working. I found out that Tony Webb has a girlfriend already. Thank God?

Tuesday 11th January 1966

Perhaps a diary should be about the weather and the faces of the people one meets, and all sorts of silly irrelevant things. I don't know. We did botany all day and I could have cheerfully wrung Ethel's neck, and then chemistry in the p.m. Loathsome. Tony had a stinking cold. I spent a whole evening preparing solutions and then got them muddled up, so consequently had to throw them away. Then I prepared them again and knocked them over. My hair was virtually standing on end by the end of the evening! E. and I went for a walk to the top of the hill, it was a gloriously ghastly night.

Wednesday 12th January 1966

Poor old Dr Terry wasn't very well today. She rambled on about the crayfish – I really could have screamed. In the afternoon Etherington gave us each a three-minute viva – luckily I managed to photograph them in my mind long enough to remember them from my questions. The dogfish is a boring animal, though. E. met me at 8.30 p.m., after I'd had the most marvellous shower in the gym. He was in a funny mood. I really don't think that I like him much, he's frightfully egoistical and know-it-all. B. went to the boat show today.

Thursday 13th January 1966

A rather awful day. We had inorganic chem. and botany in the morning, both of which were as boring as well. In the afternoon I decided to go home and work, only succeeding in the end to do a very little work. Maria's book, "Brad Kaner", is rather melodramatic, but very moreish. After holding it off as long as possible, I eventually phoned B. He was very polite but not terribly welcome, or is it just because of his family down about his ears. Probably he's behaving just the same and it is I that have changed. Didn't see E. tonight.

Friday 14th January 1966

The first of our chemistry tutorials – it was terrifying. Martin is a funny chap – I think he was horrid to me before because he was a bit frightened of me. Met E. in the refectory at 5.30 p.m. He was very nice – very cold and yet very flattering. E.'s going dancing tonight. I met Maria at 9.50 p.m. – thank goodness she waited for me. I felt a bit dingy in my old brown dress but managed to make quite a hit. I don't really like posh people, though. We danced those Polish dances and drank rather a lot – the chap Volshky (or whatever it was) was very attractive but had rather a weak, dissipated face. Maria and I were thankful to crawl into bed at 6.30 on Saturday morning.

Saturday 15th January 1966

Woke up at 3.45 and almost had a blue fit. I just prayed it was supper that we had been invited to at Alex's – unfortunately, it wasn't and the others had already gone. I felt terrible. The evening was quiet and I had a bath and went to bed – only to fall asleep straight away – I don't know what's the matter with me.

Sunday 16th January 1966

B. came over at 4.00 p.m. Evidently he had a good time last night. We went for a walk on the common, in the snow – it was marvellous, so clean and cool. Afterwards we roasted in the Dog and Fox and eventually said "au revoir" at 9.30 p.m. A very, very pleasant evening.

Monday 17th January 1966

Judo was a bit of a farce ce soir. I'm really very bad at it. Tumbling around on the mat and pretending to enjoy it. The only thing is perhaps it keeps me healthy. Kirsteen is a funny creature, terribly ungainly and loud-mouthed, yet really rather nice. Mind you, she calls a spade a spade, and no bones about it. Adrian is supposed to be taking her out at the moment. They make a nice couple, both speaking broad Yorkshire: "eeh by gum"!

Tuesday 18th January 1966

Great drama befell me today for, whilst gazing into Tony's eyes, I managed to ram a thermometer into my hand and was rushed off to hospital as I thought I'd done something awful because of the bleeding. The nurse was very scathing and the doctor glanced at it and said no stitches, just bandage it up". A bit of an anti-climax. Kathy took me down in the car. Of course, I came back and finished my chem. practice – like a martyr.

Wednesday 19th January 1966

Brendan had his biochem exam today. I do hope that he does well. Maria phoned him up last night, to tell him about my hand. Anyway, he didn't seem very worried.

Thursday 20th January 1966

B. went folk singing with Terry, etc.

Friday 21st January 1966

This evening I decided to dye my hair. What a waste of money it turned out to be. Celia did it for me and, by some odd fluke, I think that I must have bought the same colour as my hair – because nothing happened. Most disappointing. E. took me to the West End and we had a glorious meal of chicken "bonne femme" with lashings of mushrooms, etc. Unfortunately, the evening wasn't too happy – I was supposed to phone B. and I felt terribly guilty about it. (However, I later learned that B. had been in a very bad mood that evening anyway.)

Saturday 22nd January 1966

B. and I went to a dance at some teacher's training college. It wasn't really very good as, as usual, B. was in a filthy mood and, as usual, we got lost on the way home. The car is very good nowadays. Yes, I suppose the name "Liverpool Lou" was a bit cruel. B.'s got a new pair of trousers – they're awful.

Wednesday 26th January 1966

Disaster, but at least it brought me to my senses. E. insisted on following me to the station, as I was going to meet B. for lunch – I almost had heart failure when they met. Of course, B.'s too big-headed to realise anything. He just took my arm and gave me a filthy look, told me off for not greeting him properly and said that if E. didn't stop following us, he'd tell him off.

Thursday 27th January 1966

Had lunch with Adrian.

Saturday 29th January 1966

Went home at one o'clock and after rows all day, went out to a mad party with B. in the p.m. It was given by Viv, a girlfriend of Clive's! B. wasn't in a very good mood and my back was aching. However, we sang and danced and drank a lot. I was horrified at the morality of the people there. Got back in the early hours of the morning.

Wednesday 30th January 1966

Maria and I gave our famous tea. Enzo and Bill turned up and we gave them popcorn and Martini. I loved the folk singing club. Bill was very wicked and kept wanting to hold first my hand and then Maria's.

There is a section crossed out here which is undecipherable.

Well I don't remember the holding hands episode! I think that I was accompanying Maria and Jenny was with Enzo but by the end of the evening we had swapped over! But this is how we came to start seeing each other.

Monday 31st January 1966

Told E. that I didn't want to see him any more. It was a really glorious feeling of relief as now I can sleep better at nights and get a lot more work done. Chris and Brian did judo for the first time today – I haven't laughed so much for years. Even Daly laughed. I really felt a bit of a cad about E. But it's his own fault, he shouldn't have behaved so badly. Went to bed early.

Unfortunately I don't know what Enzo did to cause Jenny to dump him.

Tuesday 1st February 1966

Chemistry after six hours of botany is just about the last straw – of course, I burnt my hand with acid. As Tony (demonstrator) said, I'm "accident" prone. Phoned B. in the p.m. He was very nice. The day was beautiful – like Spring. Sitting on those hard stools in botany is just about more than I can stand on such a lovely day. It reminds me of the time B. and I used to walk along the Downs – of course, like a fool, I said that to E. this evening, twice. Each time he pretended not to hear. He went home early; I saw him skulk out of the labs and felt a bit awful.

Wednesday 2nd February 1966

The anniversary of Granny's death. It all seems so long ago and yet, when I think straight back through time – just a minute and Granny is back at Dunmore road again. Death is inevitable, yet we won't face it. Merciful, yet we won't admit it. I wish Granny was alive for Mummy's sake; she really is unhappy without her. I've tried to talk to Mummy, yet she's always lost. Perhaps it is myself on the defensive. I understand words turning into bitter ones. Hard to understand her. There will always, however, be the feeling of mother and daughter relationship at points of divided opinion. She unconsciously adopts the attitude that the mother is right automatically. I, of course, am usually equally as stubborn. I do think, however, that, apart from anything else, it is good manners to apologise when proven wrong. However, the mother/daughter attitude still persists. I love Mummy very much, though, and do hate to hurt her – stupid pride.

Friday 4th February 1966

Felt lousy, so went home. I met Bill on the way; he was very flirtatious – I think that he's almost as bad as I am. Went to bed and slept all afternoon. Felt much better by the time Maria got back.

Saturday 5th February 1966

Went out with B.

Sunday 6th February 1966

Bill, Maria, the Greek and I went to the folk club again. I went to tea with Bill. At first it was rather strained, but the folk club was very good. We went for a kebab – the Greek's idea – afterwards. My God, what a loathsome dish.

Monday 7th February 1966

Met Bill by accident – he saw me home after judo.

Tuesday 8th February 1966

Saw Bill this evening – what a funny chap. Still, he's good fun to be with. At least I laugh a bit with him each time; he really couldn't break anybody's heart. He saw me home again and insisted in stopping in a pub, of course, I met E. and he mocked me, saying was I going around with that "monk". I loathe E. so very much. He was literally like a bad dream. However, the food he gave me sometimes at the restaurant made it worth listening to all his stupid ramblings. I don't know how he managed a first degree.

Wednesday 9th February 1966

What a day – first Bantock having a marvellous time flirting with all the girls in the 3.00 p.m. practice, and then Bill and I went to the cemetery and had a shopping session – really, that's the only word to describe it. His method of kissing is very powerful, though. It's like a full-scale attack. Oh well, he's actually kissed me now – not a peck on the cheek like I liked. Strange feeling.

Thursday 10th February 1966

Bill is going home tomorrow. Strange, I'll miss him – I would have liked to have gone with him, but afraid he'll never be serious about me, so why annoy a lot of other people.

Friday 11th February 1966

Bill went home today, to Bedford. 10, Greenacres, Bedford, Beds. I, of course, also scooted home to see B. Martin – the obnoxious beast – said that he was looking forward to seeing me at Ian's party – he'll be lucky.

Saturday 12th February 1966

Went to the pub with B. He very coyly told me that he'd sent me a Valentine. He went to some boat show today, I think.

Sunday 13th February 1966

Bill came back and we met up in town and went to see "Life at the Top". *(Film with Lawrence Harvey and Jean Simmons.)* It was very funny and very sad – pathos. Bill did look scruffy – something will have to be done about that.

February 1966

Monday 14th February 1966

Valentine's day. Was very upset at B.'s card.

Friday 18th February 1966

Went to some medic's party – awful.

Saturday 19th February 1966

Had lunch with B. Stew – then went to Dave and Martin's party. Had a big row with B. He bought me a large bunch of daffodils and two pounds of sweets.

Sunday 20th February 1966

B. had a chicken lunch – it was very delicious, at least I thought so!

Monday 21st February 1966

Felt ghastly – with a hellish sore throat – feverishness. B. saw me home, then made me supper – he stayed until Maria came home – very sweet of him.

Tuesday 22nd February 1966

Slept 'til lunch time and had almost got up when who should come through the door but Bill and Maria. I felt so embarrassed. B. made lunch and stayed all afternoon. I was terribly thrilled at their kindness – it's really not many people who would do that.

Wednesday 23rd February 1966

B. came over for lunch – it was rather a dismal affair. Bill put on the hurt little boy act and I was fed up.

Thursday 24th February 1966

Didn't do a stroke of work as it is the big debating union dinner. The debate, "one green field is much like another", was very funny. The dinner was really rather embarrassing and we sat opposite Mr. Griffiths – the only sensual pleasure left in his life is eating. Of course, B. phoned and I wasn't there.

I had been involved with the college debating society since going there and at this time I was President of Debates. I think that Griffiths was a lawyer giving some of the courses at the college.

Friday 25th February 1966

A very eventful day. Mummy came to the poly and had supper. Bill hung around and we gave her a conducted tour of the building. Off to visit Annette who, by the way, is a spoilt brat – but very pretty. B. came for me at 8.30 p.m. and we buzzed off to the party – thank God I felt ill – I met B.'s great Welsh girlfriend, Gill.

Saturday 26th February 1966

Had my hair cut at Charles' and set it. Was a frightful experience – poor Mummy, I felt a bit awful when told her, she was so proud. Went to B.'s party and acted as hostess. It was a simply fantastic feeling. The party was a roaring success. Of course, I felt really ill and had to go and lie on B.'s bed.

Sunday 27th February 1966

Went to lunch with Bill. It was very relaxing in the p.m. I made a revolting mushroom sauce. Eventually got home at 11.30 p.m.

Monday 28th February 1966

Ian said blasphemous things about my morals – there was an almighty and melodramatic scene in the library – all conducted in heated whispers – with much marching around the tables and sitting down and standing up again, and eventually running from the library in black despair. Poor Ian was terribly upset, though, with great tearful eyes. I felt very guilty.

Nowadays this will seem a funny thing to get upset about. Ian had said to me that Jenny definitely wasn't a virgin and when I had passed this on to her the above scene had occurred.

Tuesday 1st March 1966

Big row with Bill over nothing at all. Phoned B. – had an interesting chat, as he puts it. Evidently he went drinking in the lunch hour. Bill has a frightful inferiority complex;

although flirty and cheeky, he has a very good heart – one hopes! Weighing 12 stone, with a 36" waist, specs perched on the end of his supercilious nose, he gives the world the impression of rather a benign owl – deceptive.

Wednesday 2nd March 1966

Dissected a rat. B. didn't come over. Sheila and Kirsteen didn't feel too good, so went home.

Friday 4th March 1966

Went to see "La Belle Hélène" with Bill. He stayed the night. Of course there have to be great rows. He slept in the sitting room. Davy was very, very good – lovely voice, but overacted a bit. He certainly has a smashing physique.

Saturday 5th March 1966

B. came over. He hurt his leg sailing and has to limp in a melodramatic fashion. We went to see "La Belle Hélène". Poor old Rice almost had a blue fit when he saw me in the front row a second time.

Monday 7th March 1966

Did judo. Did me – would be perhaps a more appropriate expression. Falling is a horrid sensation – even when does break fall. Bill always chucks me onto the ground – usually so hard that my neck clicks alarmingly. Ground work is the best, I think, rolling around on the floor, fighting for mastery. It's the most glorious feeling when you get some large bloke in a good grip and all his muscle power won't get him out of it, even from weak little me!

Tuesday 8th March 1966

Just as, for the first time in my life, I felt like doing botany practical, Kirsteen gets ill and I have to take her home.

Friday 11th March 1966

Went out with B. but can't remember where.

Saturday 12th March 1966

Bill proposed to me on bended knee. Very exciting. After much thought, I said "yes". We're both very happy.

Well that was pretty quick work.

Sunday 13th March 1966

Bill and I went for a long walk on the downs of Alexandra Park. Gorgeous.

Monday 14th March 1966

Was told that I'd got a part in the rep company's play. Oh gosh — just as exams come up as well. Still, I'll take it. Phoned Mummy up to tell her about Bill and I. She was very pleased, yet rather sceptical. Judo.

Tuesday 15th March 1966

First rehearsal's rather exciting, but very nerve-wracking.

Wednesday 16th March 1966

Bill and I spend rather a lot of our time in that damned union office. His great friend, El Bizri "the orange" haunts it, though — and they have a lot of typing and secret documents to compile in association with the debating society. It really is rather difficult to imagine Bill as President of Debates — however, he is a damned good President! — He takes with gown and glasses — such a comical sight.

Khaled El Bizri was a very short, smart Arab with a moustache, who had a great anarchic sense of humour that needed to be reined in sometimes. He studied mathematics. Recently (2007) getting in touch with him via the Internet his English is still as fractured as before. He married an English girl and has had a varied career in the UK and USA in computing.

Thursday 17th March 1966

Today I was elected Treasurer of the judo club — I'm very afraid that I'll do something wrong. We all sat on stools and looked suitably solemn and proposed and accepted nominations. Being the only girl is rather exciting, especially when they make a great fuss of me. There was a debate this evening.

March 1966

Saturday 19th March 1966

Stayed up in town and with Bill. We were a very lazy pair, really. Anyway, as we are engaged, I supposed that it didn't matter that I stayed the night. I must confess I felt a little guilty. Hardly slept at all; the bed was frightfully uncomfortable.

Sunday 20th March 1966

Woke up at 12.00 p.m. and rolled out of bed to get lunch. We went for a long walk in the afternoon.

Monday 21st March 1966

Exams have begun. A three-hour chemistry paper practically finished me. Judo was great fun, but I really shouldn't have gone.

Tuesday 22nd March 1966

Botany – all day. Oh, it was ghastly. I felt like bursting into tears the whole time.

Wednesday 23rd March 1966

Zoology exam theory. Bill had a one-hour practical.

Thursday 24th March 1966

Chemistry exam. Another one that I've failed. Worked with Bill in the library all afternoon, then the rehearsals in the evening.

Friday 25th March 1966

Had our last exam. It was a zoology practical. Frightful as we had to display the anatomy of the hind leg of the frog. Went to rehearsals in the p.m. and then studied in the common room with Bill. When I arrived home, Mummy was ill. Bought a new skirt in the afternoon.

Saturday 26th March 1966

Bill came over to ask Daddy if he could marry me. It was a frightful interview, in which Daddy said Bill had to be confirmed first. He also made some sly hints as to our being committed. Ugh!

Sail On, Silvergirl, Sail On By

At the time I was living in Crouch End and I attended classes at Christ Church on Crouch End Hill. I had a single room bedsit and it was there that we first made love – first time for both of us.

Sunday 27th March 1966

Met Bill for lunch at his place. Rehearsals, six hours of them. There was a great wind today – I could hardly stand against it.

Monday 28th March 1966

Six hours chemistry practical – ghastly thought. In fact, it was worse than the thought ever aspired to be. At first the time went so slowly and I kept thinking, "my God, another six hours, five hours, four hours – and then, suddenly, there was only half an hour and I still had a whole question to do. An absolute nightmare. Afterwards I had to rush up and act on stage for the dress rehearsal – quite honestly, I don't know where I got the energy from.

Tuesday 29th March 1966

Another dress rehearsal this evening. The producer is really excellent, even though a bit of a slave driver. Acting is the most rewarding feeling, I think. With the lights and the glamour. Dear old Bill waited for me 'til 10.00 p.m. He and El Bizri are a pair. They get so fiery over these silly debates. And El Bizri shouts and waves his arms about, whilst Bill's glasses almost fall from the end of his little nose – quite a spectacle.

Wednesday 30th March 1966

First performance. I have awful nerves. Bill has been trying to calm me down all day – but it's no good. We went to the social in the common room first. It was there that I met El Bizri – a stroke of luck, as he's decided to attend the play with Bill. "Brush with a Body" wasn't uproarious, but it was a success. I felt exhausted afterwards, however, but obliged to go with Bill and El Bizri for a drink at the Vic. I crawled into bed at 1.00 p.m. and slept and slept. Bill was to arrive at 10.00 a.m. tomorrow.

The play was "Brush with a Body" (*Maurice McLoughlin*). It had been directed and produced by John Woodnutt. He appeared on TV in later years as a character actor. I remember being at rehearsals and how he ordered the actors about. Jenny had a small part in this period (30's) drama. I remember that she had a line "What? Am I a leper or something?" which we used to trot out later whenever she we felt we were being ignored in a conversation. See the play bill later.

March – April 1966

John Woodnutt died January 2nd 2006 and had an obituary in the "Observer":

http://news.independent.co.uk/people/obituaries/article342104.ece

Thursday 31st March 1966

Breakfast in bed, the first order of the day. It was glorious. Bill was kind. He's terribly het up about the debates, though. We arrived at college at 1.00 p.m. and had lunch with Sue and Maria. We discussed Bill. They say that he's immature. Perhaps, in a way, he is – but aren't we all? The twins came to see the play – went up to Waterloo to see them off and to fetch them. Bill took them to the play – he was very kind and actually offered to pay. Poor old thing, he had to walk home after seeing the twins off with me.

Sue Ellis and I had gone out briefly the year before but it hadn't gone very far. Notably we went to see the film "The Collector" and she had not been impressed. It featured Terence Stamp who kidnaps and then murders an art student.

Friday 1st April 1966

Maria and the landlady are coming to see the play – they enjoyed it. B. was supposed to be coming, but didn't turn up. Bill had waited for me in the common room – so we went for a meal in the Indian restaurant. Smashing! I felt frightfully guilty, though, as the landlady gave me dirty looks for being back so late. We went to a dance in the afternoon with Maria and Bill. I thought that there was going to be a row. Breakfast in bed again – luxury.

Saturday 2nd April 1966

Last night of the play. I felt terribly on edge as both B. and Bill were to meet me after the performance. Oh well, having two escorts wasn't such a nightmare as I had thought. B. and I had a good talk about Bill. B. told me he thought that I was too immature for marriage – I suppose that he knows me as well as anyone ever will do.

Sunday 3rd April 1966

Stayed with Bill, B. having gone off in a huff last night. I really feel upset, as today Bill went back to Bedford – he was so sweet, standing at the gate until I'd disappeared around the corner. My God, my tummy is aching.

This is a distant memory for me too! Jenny in her blue mini skirt walking up the street and disappearing round the corner.

Monday 4th April 1966

Got up at 11.00 p.m., just in time for the library. Maria and I went for lunch at 12.30 p.m. – the café was filthy. However, I rather like places like that. B. came for me at 6.00 p.m. I was so pleased to see him. We sat and talked for hours and then went out for a meal. I was very touched to notice that he still keeps my photos in his wallet. Went back to an empty room. Maria has gone out with the Greek.

Tuesday 5th April 1966

Got up very late and spent most of today making posters for the judo club with Tika Singh. He's a sweet little fellow, really, and does karate. The posters weren't too good, however, we did stick photos onto them, which gave them quite a professional finish. Maria and I had a glorious fry-up in the p.m., with chicken and red cabbage – sounds ghastly but it actually was absolutely delicious.

Wednesday 6th April 1966

Worked in the library with M. all day. We went to Berts for lunch – a scruffy little café but great fun eating there in the pm. The Greek took us to ULU (University of London Union). We had a delicious meal and then studied for two hours. Afterwards we went to play table tennis – guess who should be there, but E. We went on for drinks afterwards. It was quite fun, but not really gay. I wish to God that I had never met E. He's really a dangerous person.

Thursday 7th April 1966

We worked in the library all day and then packed up all our things and set off for home. I arrived home at about 9.30 p.m. It was a funny feeling, arriving in the rain. The bed was gorgeously soft, though. Mummy looks better.

Friday 8th April 1966

Good Friday. We all got up at 10.00 and had a good breakfast. It still feels funny to be home. In the afternoon we went to the three-hour service. It really was rather boring – even Mummy agreed. I phoned up B. but he was beastly.

I found the following letter from this date which I think is interesting:

April 1966

12 Amity Grove
Raynes Park
SW20 London

Saturday
8th April, 9.00 a.m.

Darling Bill,

Thank you so much for your letter, which I received about 10 minutes ago, just as I was sitting down to write to you again. How are you? You don't sound too cheerful, from your letter – only we know though. Thank goodness. Quite honestly, this has been one of the slowest weeks of my life, perhaps next week will go a bit quicker.

Yes, there are a lot of ifs in everything – another name for fate, really. I sat up most of last night, reading (*Requiem for a Nun*). It is really a powerful little book and, perhaps, relevant to our "ifs", in that Stevens says " the past is never dead, it is part of the present and the future". Although not wholly agreeing with this, it is true to some extent and here come our ifs again – a vicious circle.

Concerning Brendan – I really wish sometimes that we had never met. Please don't worry about it Bill, that part of the past will not affect our future in any way at all. How foolish to let a mistake haunt and ruin our relationship. I have made it quite clear to B. that he is honest enough with himself to accept it. I have pointed out to him our (yours and my) compatibility in so many respects that were lacking in his and my relationship, also the fact that you are and I am more deeply in love than he and I ever were. So now we surely can forget Brendan and be happy together.

I have just read the above over and it's absolute chaos, grammatically – however, it's the thought that counts.

I feel terrible at turning your sister out of her room Bill, Thursday, and then to the digs. They're going to arrive later. Please tell me which day I'm expected. It would be horrid to arrive on the wrong one. Bad luck about those physics papers – would you like me to nip along to your room and get them – I'm sure the landlady wouldn't mind. Look after yourself – write soon, please.

All my love,

Your Jenny

Saturday 9th April 1966

A quiet day and evening. I'm having a rest for three days and then starting work again on Monday. I phoned Bill this evening – his mother answered at first and, of course, Bill was out. She was really very sweet. I waited in the phone box for half an hour. He didn't sound too pleased to hear me when he eventually did phone. However, he's not very demonstrative. I'm sure he was actually thrilled to bits!

Sunday 10th April 1966

Easter Day – not horribly exciting, but very relaxing: church, lunch, presents and then a walk on the common with Daphie. We were very lazy in the p.m. and watched T.V.

Monday 11th April 1966

We spent a quiet day at home. Victoria came over – she was very scathing about my engagement – I suppose that she thinks herself as an old married woman, or something.

Wednesday 13th April 1966

Went bowling with B., Clive, Martin and Steve. It really was great fun, although B. was rather spitefully triumphant – declaring that he had no feelings for me at all. I felt a little lost and bewildered when the thought actually went home. However, I always felt a little too dependent on B. – it will probably do me good to stand on my own legs for a bit. I find it hard to believe that the warm and passionate love of his could suddenly change into cold indifference. Human nature.

Thursday 14th April 1966

Mummy went back to work. She was terrified at the thought. However, she enjoyed it, I think, and managed to wheedle a lift home and arrived home at 4.30. Daphne's friend Denise called round.

Saturday 16th April 1966

Set off for Bill's. It was a hellish journey. And, of course, when I arrived: no Bill – I could have wept. Eventually he turned up, though his parents are very nice and really I think they were more embarrassed than I was. I'm sleeping in his sister's bedroom; it's rather spooky.

April 1966

Sunday 17th April 1966

We got up at 8.30 a.m. – nearly killed me – and had a day in Cambridge. It was heavenly – even though we had a bit of a row. His parents are very much against September.

We had quite naïvely assumed that we should get married at the beginning of the next term – I had a further year to run and Jenny had two. My parents wanted us to wait until I had finished my degree. Of course they worried about us starting a family too early and me getting distracted. In the end we agreed to leave it for a further year.

Looking back it was a mistake because we endured some very unpleasant lodgings for the year, and we were already lovers anyway! The landlady was quite literally mad and would stand at the bottom of the stairs shouting up about some supposed infraction or other. Somehow I managed to break the toilet seat and when I told her she took it very calmly. We had rooms on the top floor of three stories. The building shook each time a bus went past. I had a single room and Maria and Jenny shared the other. Our kitchen and bathroom were down one flight shared with other lodgers.

We had a happy time in the next place we lived after getting married the following year so it was a pity we lost that time.

Saturday 23rd April 1966

Came back from Bill's home – we came by car and I felt very queasy by the end of it. In the evening we had supper (soup) and talked and talked in Bill's room. I just caught the last train home.

Sunday 24th April 1966

Went over to Bill's. We went for a long walk in Highgate woods afterwards and fed the squirrels. A dear old lady came up to me and said "may you always go through life hand in hand and be as happy as you are today." We were very touched.

This is a very distinct memory for me. We were shocked at the time at these words from a stranger.

Monday 25th April 1966

Back to college. Bill has his exams next Monday, so has to work hard this week. Judo was very exciting: we had five new attendees – of course, none of them were girls. The boys (new ones) were rather scathing in their criticism of me. However, I managed a few not-too-hard throws. We bought the ring today and spent an hour choosing it. A real beauty. It's second-hand, but very good value for £21.

Tuesday 26th April 1966

I showed off the ring and everybody rendered polite congratulations. Botany was hellish.

Thursday 28th April 1966

Mummy rang up this morning. She was thrilled to hear about the ring. The great Annual General Meeting of debates took place. Bill was very brave but, to my eyes, it was a losing battle. I felt a bit of a cad, really, as I didn't have the moral courage to say anything. A very personal remark was made by that David Dewar, though: " when are you getting married, Mr President?" I could have slid off the chair!

This was the occasion when I was unseated as President of Debates in a kind of coup! Quite upsetting at the time but perhaps I had been spending too much time on it. The reason for the coup – I still don't really know – but it was the kind of thing that students get up to! (and then they go into politics.)

Friday 13th May 1966

Mummy brought up my silver dress and gave it to me. We met at Oldsgate. Afterwards going to a horrible Italian restaurant. My clothes have come from Halford's.

Saturday 14th May 1966

We went to Chantale's 21st. It was great. Dr. Bartok was there and I got drunk.

Jenny had kept the following letter from her mother:

12 Amity Grove
W. Wimbledon
SW 20

14—5-66

Dear Jenny

    I was very upset when I phoned your flat to hear that you had not returned there last night. What conclusion am I to draw from this?

    You remember that daddy and I were both anxious for you to live in a hostel (mainly so that you would have some supervision) and that we would know that you were safe.

May 1966

However you insisted on going into digs and we trusted you – are you honouring that trust Jenny?

I have given you repeated warnings as to the unhappiness a few minutes of selfish pleasure can bring. Think Jenny what you are doing – I have done all I can for you to make you happy. Don't you think that you have a few obligations too?

I await your reply and I want the <u>truth</u> and depending on what it contains I shall see what actions I shall take.

I am very against you and Bill going away on your own in the holidays and shall talk to you about that sometime. You are still under 21 don't forget.

I can only repeat how very upset and unhappy I was to hear about your not going back to your flat last night.

I have always trusted you. please do not let down that trust.

Expecting to hear from you by return –

If you saw my black bag or took it with you by mistake please let me know.

With love

From Mummy

Saturday 21st May 1966

I didn't go home – instead, Bill came over for lunch and tea. It was a rather dull and boring day – we worked in the evening at chemistry.

Sunday 22nd May 1966

I did a huge washing, with Bill's help.

Tuesday 24th May 1966

Botany consisted of a refresher course. It was really very helpful. We worked in the library all p.m.

Wednesday 25th May 1966

Went home to see Daphne confirmed. Victoria and John were there. They make rather a nice couple. Vic has, of course, to tell Daph that she didn't enjoy the service. Bill and I spent the night at home – he slept on the sofa.

Thursday 26th May 1966

Bill's final debate. It was a very amusing debate – Suki and Roger Clamp won it. We all went for drinks to the Vic afterwards. Dick Assing asked M. out.

Friday 27th May 1966

In the evening went to the Chinese restaurant. Of course they brought the wrong meal, and there was a lot of unpleasantness. To crown it all, they overcharged us. Really, I don't want to go there again.

Rather bizarre in that I remember that we ordered a Chinese meal and then after that was served they turned up with something like chicken and chips from the English menu!

Saturday 28th May 1966

Worked all day. Terribly depressing. I went out for three or four walks to relieve the monotony.

Sunday 29th May 1966

Went to Bill's for lunch. He's an excellent cook!

Monday 30th May 1966

I worked in my room, sitting on the window sill. Bill came over for lunch at 2.45 – a bit late, I thought. Anyway, the lunch wasn't too bad and he brought some beer to go with it. Maria went to Dick Whittington park. Poor thing: it was absolutely miles away. She was in a very bad mood when she got back.

Friday 3rd June 1966

Day of the chem. exam. What a filthy first paper!

10 Friday 10th June 1966

Bill's chem. exam. Meal for Bill.

Saturday 11th June 1966

Rejoiced, went home. Auntie Alex.

June 1966

Sunday 12th June 1966

Came back in p.m. Missed last bus.

Saturday 18th June 1966

My birthday. Bill gave me a gorgeous gold St. Christopher's medallion and gold chain.

Sunday 19th June 1966

A big night.

Tuesday 21st June 1966

Bill started work at Jones Brothers. He quite likes it.

Jones Brothers was a department store, part of the John Lewis Partnership just up the Holloway Road from the Northern Polytechnic. I worked in the lighting department at first and then was transferred to the crockery and gifts section. The building still exists but is no longer a store.

Thursday 23rd June 1966

My botany tomorrow. I met Roy in the buffet and managed to extract some hints about the botany practical. I dashed off to the library and worked like mad. Bill came for lunch. He was in a bit of a bad mood as he has to work late tonight. I went back to the library after lunch. Dick Assing and I had coffee in the tea break. In the end, Bill didn't work late. We had an uninspiring evening doing nothing at all.

Friday 24th June 1966

My botany practical. I worked in the library all morning, had an easy lunch and then set off. Of course, I was destined to get lost and just arrived in time. It wasn't a bad exam, however, I didn't finish the middle question. It was a photosynthesis experiment. I went back to Bill's room. It's his birthday. I gave him a wallet thing with a leaf for holding keys – think that he liked it. We had a curry for supper.

Saturday 25th June 1966

Hellish day. I met Bill for lunch and went shopping. The Holloway Road was packed with busy shoppers and the pavements littered with the suitcases of cheap salesmen. I went to

Bill's room, did his laundrette shopping and my legs. He came back and was in a bad mood. We went out to the pub in the p.m., then to bed.

Sunday 26th June 1966

We set off early for Epping Forest. Before we left, there was a very tearful scene with Bill – it gave me quite a shock. Eventually, after three different bus journeys, we arrived at the forest and had a glorious day in the sun – laughing and eating spam sandwiches – Lord, did my feet ache. Bill was very happy and so was I.

Monday 27th June 1966

We had a lazy day. In the p.m. we went in for judo – of course, there wasn't any. Anyway, I had a shower and washed my hair. Bill had a shower as well. He washed his hair this morning – praise be. We went for a walk this morning and felt very strange and told him that I wanted to be by myself. Of course, I didn't, really. He was very sweet and understanding.

Tuesday 28th June 1966

Worked in the labs with Suki, etc. It wasn't a very inspiring day: lunch with Bill, as usual. He's on lampshades still. We watched "The Devils" on T.V., a science-fiction thriller. My God, it was frightful. Martin Hems was quite nice to me today – I almost fainted.

Wednesday 29th June 1966

Worked in the chem. lab all day. Bill came for lunch. We went to get the passport form. It was so hot. I had a hearty cry ce soir – over what, I don't know. I met Bridie, the girl that Bill is working with. She looked very sweet. Bill looked ghastly – I really would have liked to have seen him home.

Monday 4th July 1966

Chemistry practical exam. It was, I think, one of the worst experiences of my life. I went wrong with titration, couldn't find the substances in the spot and altogether made a filthy mess of the whole thing. Afterwards, went back to meet Bill at college. We went out for a Chinese supper. I went to spend the evening with Bill and it turned out to be the whole evening.

July 1966

Tuesday 5th July 1966

I went home after having lunch with Bill. We were both terribly relieved and are better friends again. Bridie is a very sweet girl, although I never talk to her. Bill does look funny with a greatcoat on, grinning amongst the lampshades. I had an eye appointment with Pitman. The twins' birthday was rather sweet. I gave them each six shilling record tokens and D. earrings and R. a vanity bag.

Wednesday 6th July 1966

I had my photo taken and then met Bill for lunch. Evidently, he'd been asleep when I phoned last night. I was wearing a lot of make-up – I don't think he really approved. In the p.m. we watched T.V. and afterwards had an awful row. I always thing that we're better friends after we've had a row, though. M. was in a terrible state, as she thought I'd been murdered or something.

Thursday 7th July 1966

Usual routine. I can't bear the thought of Bill going on Sunday. Oh well, it will only be for three weeks. I think that he's dying to finish at Jones Brothers so it's a sort of split thing for him.

The following section covers our continental trip of that year. I had a summer job in the analytical laboratory of George Fischer AG in Schaffhausen, Switzerland, which had been arranged by my father who worked for their UK company in Bedford. Jenny was to join me for the last couple of weeks and then we were going hitchhiking. I visited Schaffhausen again in 2006 partly inspired by the trip we had taken and followed the rest of the itinerary as far as I could recall it. GF still exist but the big foundry and factories seem to have more or less closed. Of course in 2006 we drove rather than hitchhiked!

Jenny drove to Schaffhausen with my father and a colleague of his.

Sunday 31st July 1966

Doctor Dittmer and myself met at Marble Arch at 13.00 hours. We had a rather nerve-wracking drive down to Dover, where, at 16.00 hours, we deposited the car and had a coffee. The boat was due to leave at 17.00 hours and crawled painfully out of the harbour. The day was a beauty and after we went out on deck. I had never seen the sea look so fresh. In the middle of the channel le Capitan announced that we would now see both the white cliffs of Dover and those of France, and indeed we could – it was a splendid sight. The crossing took about an hour and a half. France seemed very flat somehow and the Customs were very inefficient.

Dittmer was driving and Mr. U. was having 40 blue fits. I expected I would feel the same if somebody drove my car is such an erratic manner! So far, France was just like England, except for the French signs, flat countryside and shuttered windows. We drove up to Ostend (which I thought had a melancholy pseudo-Brighton look) and, from there, to Brussels. The city is large, with huge neon lights and dirty streets. There are no narrow streets, as in London, though – and everybody drives on the right. The drivers really are dangerous. They suddenly appear out of side streets or put on their brakes. Toute de suite – very alarming.

We registered at our hotel in Brussels, changed and then went out for a meal. The Chinese restaurant that we went to was exquisite and waiters spoke German, French and English (and, obviously, Chinese). After the meal, we went for a drink in a beer house. I declined anything, as I felt quite tipsy already. At 1.00 a.m. I toppled into bed.

Monday 1st August 1966

At 7.30 a.m. I was woken by the shrilling of the telephone beside my bed. Allo allo, click. It was supposed to be a polite way of saying "get up, or else". I bathed in the huge bath. We had the most miserable breakfast of a cup of lukewarm tea and half a stale roll. By 9.30 we were on the road. All I can remember of that terrible journey is that we came via Liege but, on the way, we stopped at a café along the autobahn. Dittmer was driving. No wonder there are so many crashes along the autobahn (we've seen about half a dozen, one involving five cars). The drivers all turn into little maniacs and toot and screech along, vying to see who can get there first.

We stopped at Heidelberg on the way. It is magnificent. Even though it was bombed in the war and one can still see its splendour, even in the ruins. And the sunlight crowding hundreds of years of history through the stained glass windows. The flower festival was on, with over a million flowers on display. We went out onto the battlements and Mr. U. took a photo of us.

Tuesday 2nd August 1966

I woke up at 6.00 a.m., whipped up the blinds in real film star fashion. The bed was most uncomfortable and the Swiss have a large eiderdown affair instead of blankets. Mr. U. knocked consciously on the door at 8.30 a.m. and we had breakfast: an egg and a cup of tea. This time there was no Dittmer to make things run smoothly and the air was a little tense between Mr. U. and myself. The drive to Schaffhausen today took longer than we had expected. On the way, we picked up a French boy. I felt most odd and a bit shaky when we reached Schaffhausen. It was probably the rich food we had had at the hunting lodge the night before. Mr. U. deposited me at a corner and went burning off to see if he could find Bill. I waited and waited. At last, in the distance, two little figures emerged from a large building. Bill looked very healthy. It was lovely to see him again.

Mr. U. and I then disappeared to have a meal, after much procrastination we eventually decided upon a restaurant and had a huge lunch. I felt ill. At 3.30 p.m. I met Bill and was taken up to the labs, where I met his boss. All afternoon I sat in the labs – just waiting. Eventually Mr. U. arrived and whisked us off to my digs, and then to the first class restaurant to have another slap-up meal. Bill and I walked up from the station (bahnhof). Mr. U. came to say goodbye at 9.30 p.m. My room is in a wooden house. The house is in the valley of Fire . The floor creaks when I walk on it and I feel rather homesick. By 10.00 p.m. I was asleep.

Wednesday 3rd August 1966

6.00 a.m. and already I was awake. Somebody next door was snoring loudly. Breakfast time – a long dreaded moment – was a frightful ordeal. My watch went wrong and I was 20 minutes early. They were all setting the table as I fell into the room. First I sat in the wrong place, then ensconced in the right one, made every mistake under the sun – they were very patient, though, and, at one point, the woman flung her arms around me, cooing "little Englesie".

All morning I wandered around in the town. At 12.00 I met Bill, we had lunch, he disappeared and I, again, just wandered around the town. We saw Bill's father off at 12.00 o'clock. Supper consisted of rolls, cheese and fruit. We ate it beside the river.

Thursday, Friday – the days followed the same pattern, except for different things for supper and lunch, which we now eat in the canteen.

Saturday 6th August 1966

A beautiful day. We met at 10.15 and decided to go down the Rhine to Lake Constance. All morning we sat beside the river. At 1.15 p.m. we set off. Instead of going all the way to Constance, we alighted at a place called Stein-am-Rhein. It's a very pretty little town. For most of the afternoon we sat beside the river and lazily watched the water lapping the shore and the odd boat go past.

6.00 p.m. found us in a little café, eating the eternal chips. It was quite a pleasant little place. At 7.30 p.m. the boat left. We boarded it and sat below deck. On the way, herons peered at us out of the trees flanking the river. Half way home we changed boats and were forced to go out on deck, into the cold night air. Schaffhausen seemed somehow like "home" when we alighted at the quay.

Sunday 7th August 1966

We visited the Rhein falls. A tram took us to the top of the hill and then we walked down into the falls. One could hear the water booming minutes before actually reaching the falls. We went out onto a platform, with the water roaring and falling a few feet above us. Terrifying. Lunch was taken in the café overlooking the falls. We sat outside and ate it.

In the afternoon we lay on a bank for about an hour and then went back to B.'s room, where we had tea. We eventually arrived at my place and I fell into bed.

Monday 8th August / Tuesday 9th August 1966

Both followed the same pattern as recent days; with lunch in the canteen, a dismal afternoon as supper either beside the river or on the castle battlements. On Monday it rained and we were forced to eat our tea outside on a bench, as B.'s landlady has taken a dislike to me and doesn't want me in house. Later that evening we went to a café for coffee.

Wednesday 10th August 1966

I went up to the swimming baths and Bill was to meet me at 3.30 p.m. Something went wrong somehow, and we didn't. There was rather a terrible scene. The weather is stifling.

Thursday 11th August 1966

I went for a long walk in the forest. It was beautiful. In the p.m. I went swimming. B. joined me later in the afternoon. It was absolutely boiling.

Friday 12th August 1966

Swimming again. Bill had to check in at the police station. We ate our tea on a bench in the square. I received a letter from Mummy.

Sunday 14th August 1966

After a foul breakfast and a frantic packing session, Bill and I eventually bid the Baumans and Emile farewell and set off. The time was 11.00 a.m.

August 1966

We staggered down the road and stood for 15 minutes on the road above the bridge. Two Italians gave us a lift. They looked pretty lecherous, however. We lurched in the back and they deposited us, in fact, at Winterthur. I felt lousy and we still had to walk out of the town. Our lift to Zurich was quite an experience. A little old man drew up at the side of the road. Poor thing, he looked very ill and very ancient; I was rather uneasy. Zurich station is filthy. We made the mistake of eating at the second class restaurant. I ate two mouthfuls and then pushed the plate away in disgust. It was that hateful sausage; and such a shame, as we had proudly marched into the place with five pounds' worth of new Swiss Francs in our pockets, which we had just changed at the station "money house".

Luckily, after setting out to walk out of Zurich, we managed to get a lift from three young people obviously trying to kill an afternoon – they took us all the way to Zug. We sat beside the lake and watched the dinghies. Bill then set off with gallant determination to find that youth hostel. We found it: a little shed, stuck out in the wilds. 7 o'clock found us beside the lake again, this time eating our tea. We had a row, made it up "that's the best part" and went back to that shed. The beds consist of one long board with six or seven pillows on it. Bliss!

Monday 15th August 1966

(Note the entries for 15th –16th were by myself.)

Bill got up at 6.40 and went out to wash in the trough provided. He then sat down to wait (as usual) for Jenny. Promptly at 7.10 she came out and told the most awful tale: the night before she had been in a bed next to a woman who snored and had only gone to sleep at 5 o'clock. After Jenny had washed, they set off, walking by the lake to the road for the Gotthard and Schwyz. Jenny remarked that she couldn't go any further without breakfast. Bill asked a passer-by and was told that Monday was closing day. At this news, Jenny nearly collapsed. They walked to a café that was just opening and asked whether they could buy milk. After being told "no", they collapsed by the roadside. At this moment, a roadside kiosk opened and Bill went across and bought two peaches. On seeing Jenny, the woman reached behind the counter and pulled out two other peaches that were slightly bruised and handed them to Bill. These the loving couple ate and, being fortified, started hitching.

They waited 15 minutes and then, surprise, a vast American car pulled up. Inside were two Swiss, who looked, to the nearest approximation, like a gangster and his moll. However, this lift took them to Gösenen by several beautiful lakes. Jenny felt rather queasy after the trip and they retired into a restaurant. Then they went for a walk through the town, followed by dinner at the bahnhof buffet. When they came out, it had started to rain and the mist was closing in. They stood by the road, hitching with the rain beating down until a little Volkswagen stopped. This lift was quite eventful: first to Andermat, where there was a great hold-up. The driver, after getting through the jam, decided to take the Oberalp pass but turned back when he found the way too tough. He then took the Gotthard, which was officially closed because of a landslide. He took them to the heights above Airolo. But, again, the road was blocked and Jenny and Bill set off on foot. After three quarters of an hour they reached Airolo, only to be told that they had to walk back some way and then turn off the main road to go to the youth hostel. This they did and, in an exhausted state, they arrived. They then had a good meal of soup, cheese, bread and peaches, wrote the diary and went to bed!

Tuesday 16th August 1966

The wind howled all night and the rain beat down. We were up at 7.00 a.m. to greet a clear day. After a peculiar breakfast of cheese, toast and hot water, we set off. At 8.30 a.m. we were in Airolo village and at 9.00 we were still standing beside the road – were we really hitching? Yes. I was at one end of the road and Bill at the other. A fiendish row was in progress. Reconciled in the vegetable van which picked us up, we were in Bellinzona. We walked out of the town for about half an hour. Eventually a very sweet couple picked us up and took us all the way to the youth hostel at Ascona. The place was filthy. We went swimming in the Lago Maggiore and then fell into bed.

Wednesday 17th August 1966

They rose at 6.40, at breakfast: a crust of bread and a milk chocolate drink, walked a few hundred yards down the road and started hitching. The first lift took us to Brissago, we walked through the town and got another lift, which took us to the Italian border. We walked over the border. It was dangerous walking because the road was narrow, with walls either side. We eventually got a lift off a Spaniard who worked in Exeter, who took us to Cannobio. The next lift was off a man going to Stresa. We had a good view of the lake. He took us all the way to Feriolo, where we stayed. We looked round and decided that we'd be very good to buy presents here. We bought bread, butter, cheese, a tomato and a bottle of wine, and had a good supper. We had a good night.

Strange how memory can play tricks on you! On a recent trip (2006) I stayed in Pallanza on Lago Maggiore on the main water taxi route because that was the name I remembered. However it did not look familiar (and the roads and buildings by the lake were certainly quite old). It was only when I found this travel diary that I found that it referred to Feriolo which is further round the lake towards Stresa.

August 1966

Thursday 18th August 1966

We were up at 7.00 a.m. and sitting beside the road, hitching, by 8.30 a.m. Gravelona was gained by means of a lift from a young couple. We changed one of our traveller's cheques into Italian money. From there, it was easy going: we were picked up by a jolly-looking old farmer in a grey car. He spoke French and German. We were thrilled. B. sat in front and this very singular gentleman cracked jokes, waved his hands about and pointed to the back of the car, where I was sitting on a kind of shelf. We all laughed. I laughed loudest of all – we didn't understand what he was saying. The drive was magnificent through the Simplon Pass. It was very cold at the top and we stopped for a cup of coffee. Our friend insisted on paying. He gave us his name and address on a very smart-looking black and white card. Bill suddenly gulped – our very extraordinary friend was an undertaker. His previous jokes referred to a body in the back. We arrived at the youth hostel at Visp. He took us all the way. The beds were on the floor; it was very cold.

Friday 19th August 1966

They rose, as usual, at 7.00 a.m. They had coffee and bread for breakfast. Bill asked the girl in charge if they could buy butter. The girl gave him some butter and some jam and wouldn't take any money. They walked a few hundred yards and started hitching. They got a lift in a Volkswagen van to St. Niklaus. The driver also picked up a couple of English hitchers. From St. Niklaus they walked, taking five hours to do 16 miles. Jenny almost dropped dead on the way but Bill often carried her duffel bag. They find the youth hostel and cooked a meal of macaroni and tomato soup. They staggered to bed at 9.00 p.m.

Saturday 20th August 1966

Jenny almost strangled herself with her cross and chain in the night. We ate a good breakfast of stale bread and cold coffee. Bill then decided that it was about time for another of those walks. We staggered out, bought out lunch and set off up the mountainside. Two dogs unashamedly acted out a love scene in front of us. The lunch was eaten on the top of a hillside and a nest of ants – delicious. We rested on a hilltop. A perilous walk around the edge of a precipice – Jenny's knees were knocking – Bill was very cheerful, but was it a façade, one wonders? Supper was taken at the youth hostel. It was sausage. After supper we went out to the pub. At one point a woman stood up with an angry expression and asked us to leave by 8.30 p.m. We were furious. However, in the end it turned out that the table had been reserved for two women musicians. What a hell of a noise it was, too.

Sail On, Silvergirl, Sail On By

Sunday 21st August 1966

9.30 train to St. Niklaus. Hitched a lift to Visp. They left their luggage at the youth hostel. They went in, started up the stairs and were startled by a loud cackle of laughter. On looking up, they saw the warden and her daughter leaning over the edge, greatly amused by the man with glasses pitched on the end of his nose. They left their packs and started down. Bill slipped, nearly breaking his leg, much to the amusement of the warden and daughter. They went to a restaurant and had fondue and a litre of white wine. At first they liked it, but they soon got drunk. It was two hours before they left, leaving behind quite a bit of fondue. They walked up to the hillside and fell asleep. At 4.30 they walked down to the town and had a drink. At this point they decided to get off the following day for Nice. Then they went back to the hostel, washed and ate supper.

I don't think it was part of our original plan to go to the South of France and I suspect I was the main instigator. However we had been able to travel quite easily and quickly through Italy and Switzerland and find accommodation.

22 Monday 22nd August 1966

We ate breakfast at 7.30 a.m. and were on the road by 8.15. Aunty Jean's lighter was purchased at a little shop beside the railway. Farther down the road, we began to hitch. A very large car stopped. It had an Italian driver. We drove very fast and very dangerously to Sion, where he dropped us. There was a magnificent castle there. We drank grapefruit juice and then managed to get a lift to the top of the entrance to the St. Bernard pass. After lunch we stood beside the road for well over an hour before we were picked by a van of English boy scouts — a stupid move as they were overloaded already. We were stopped at the customs for about an hour and so forth. Eventually, by 6.30, we were still over 40 miles from Torino. We had a meal of chicken and soup. As we came into Italy, we managed to lose an hour: it was 4 o'clock in Italy and 3 everywhere else. We found room in a little village and went to bed after a good wash.

Tuesday 23rd August 1966

We got up late, about 9.00 a.m. and went to the bathroom to wash. When we got back into the room, there was a knock at the door. The old woman asked if we wanted breakfast. We said "yes". It came about 15 minutes later and was really delicious.

Another strong memory — crispy toasted slices of baguette style bread with real coffee, butter and plum jam eaten in bed. I also remember the breakfasts while lodging in Schaffhausen — they would put a large freshly baked loaf, a pat of butter, dish of jam, jug of fresh coffee and hot milk on the table — and most days I would end up eating half a loaf! I think that before that I had only ever had instant coffee!

August 1966

The rest of the morning we spent searching for presents to take home. After three hours of this, we decided that everything was far too expensive and set off to walk out of the town. Half an hour later we managed to get a lift from a crazy Italian and his son. An English couple were in the car. They were so scruffy and the girl told me they had slept in the field. We were dropped at Torino, where the famous shroud is, and eventually caught a bus into the centre. Lunch was eaten at the station restaurant and we were late in the afternoon before we started hitching again. We caught a bus out of town and onto the main highway. The first lift was from an Italian, a second also Italian and a third a Swiss, who took us all the way to the youth hostel. He was a medical student and spoke English. The youth hostel is a sort of chalet affair. I was the only girl and had to sleep all by myself in the chalet. We had a meal and they charged us an exorbitant price. By 10 o'clock we were in bed. We were at Cuneo.

The main square of Cuneo with its arcades was a short walk from the Youth Hostel. Now it is more touristy but I remember that we saw some rough men in the square with a large live turtle which was on its back and destined for the pot.

Wednesday 24th August 1966

We spent a long time searching for presents. Bought a mug and then set off, taking a few photos on the way. We arranged quite a few lifts, between which, though, there was a long wait. Eventually a lorry driver took us over the pass (Colle di Tende), a cheese wagon down the road and another lorry driver all the way to Nice. The latter going so slowly that I thought we would never get there.

The next few days are missing from the diary. I think that we had expected to stay a day in Nice and then get to Paris in a day or two. However it became very difficult to get lifts and it took us three days just to get to Avignon. Our money was starting to run out and we decided to use up what we had for a train to Paris where Jenny would be able to draw some money out of an account to get us home. We were so short of money that we ate very little on these days and Jenny became quite ill.

Sunday 28th August 1966

We travelled all night from Avignon to Paris. I felt really ill on the journey.

Monday 29th August 1966

We were still in Paris for, after that frightful journey and nothing to eat, the banks are closed in England. It's bank holiday. I could have wept. We went back to the youth hostel, dumped our stuff and then for a walk beside the river. I felt so depressed and so did Bill. We both had awful tummy trouble.

Sail On, Silvergirl, Sail On By

Tuesday 30th August 1966

We caught the train at Gare du Nord and at last were on our way home. From Boulogne the boat took us to Folkestone. My God, what a crossing and no food inside us either. I said goodbye to Bill at Victoria and caught the train home. They were very pleased to see me and I was even more pleased to see them.

Wednesday 31st August 1966

It felt funny to be home at last. I do hope that the twins and Mummy and Daddy liked our presents. I wouldn't dream of telling them that we almost fainted due to lack of food so that we could buy them presents. I am so glad to be home, though.

Friday 2nd September 1966

I just sat around, recovering from that trip. We did a few laundrettes and some shopping.

Saturday 3rd September 1966

Mummy and I went to see Jorrock. It was really worthwhile and I enjoyed every minute of it. Poor Mummy, I do think she's very lonely at times.

Sunday 4th September 1966

We went to church – had the usual Sunday lunch. Watched T.V. and went to bed. A typical Sunday.

Monday 5th September 1966

At last I set off for Bill's. The twins go back to school tomorrow, so I don't really feel too bad about going. Bill met me at the station. I was absolutely thrilled to see him again. And meeting his parents wasn't too bad, really. I settled down into Bill's room.

Tuesday 6th September 1966

This morning heralded bright sunshine and the call of the big outdoors – so we jumped onto our bikes and rode over the hills and far away. I don't think I've enjoyed a cycle ride so much for years.

Wednesday 7th September 1966

We both felt very stiff after yesterday's cycle ride and just lazed about today.

September 1966

Thursday 8th September 1966

I discovered something very exciting today – I can row! Exciting because every time I've handled a boat before, I've made an utter fool of myself. This time I told myself that I was going to row, and I did – after catching a few crabs, I just sailed away.

Friday 9th September 1966

We decided that it was too late to go out so we just stayed in and were very bored. Bill was in a bad mood and, therefore, so was I before very long.

Saturday 10th September 1966

The great meeting of parents today. Of course, the Unsworths were late and I felt cross with them. Mummy really is a good actress; she carried it off perfectly in the Strand Palace Hotel. Bill, Marie and I then went off in search of digs. We found an attic room with Bill's next door.

Sunday 11th September 1966

Went back with the Unsworths.

Monday 12th September 1966

We went to see "Alfie" (*Film starring Michael Caine remade in 2004*) this evening and I really wished that we hadn't, as it's put me off having babies for life, I think. But perhaps it hasn't. Afterwards we went to a café and met one of Bill's old friends.

Tuesday 13th September 1966

We spent the day sadly, somehow. It will seem a long time 'til Saturday week, when Bill comes. In the p.m. we went out to a Chinese restaurant, but it was the same one as we were in this time last week.

Wednesday 14th September 1966

I'm going today. I've rather mixed feelings, I must confess. I don't want to say goodbye to Bill but I want to see Mummy and the twins again. We sorrowfully said goodbye. Mummy and I went to great grandpa's birthday tea. He's 97 – fantastic. John and Victoria took us in their car.

Thursday 15th September 1966

Today I took the ring to be changed.

Friday 16th September 1966

I spent the day cleaning, washing and ironing.

Saturday 24th September 1966

We came up for the Fresher's Tea. I met Bill at St. Pancras station and we set off for the poly. Of course, I felt disillusioned as well, when I got there, as everybody kept crying "hello Bill …" I was completely ignored. Bill had to keep saying "Remember Jenny?" and I'd get a fleeting nod.

Sunday 25th September 1966

Bill stayed the night. We started the day with church. I suppose really that is a good way to begin the term. At 2.00 we had lunch and, around 3.30, we were up in town, meeting Bill's father. He brought up all Bill's stuff. We settled in okay at 109 Stroud Green Road not far from Finsbury Park.

Monday 26th September 1966

The first day back at college was taken up with filling in forms, etc. Mrs E. gave us a botany practical and we have moved into the tower block. The lifts are awful. Really, if it wasn't such an effort, I think that I'd walk up those stairs. In the afternoon we were supposed to go and listen to a meeting of the union, or something – I was so bored. We had our supper at college and went to judo in the p.m. It was great fun. A new girl, called Mary, attended.

Tuesday 27th September 1966

Etherington has decided that we can have this morning off. Thank God, as I was very late. In the afternoon we had a biology lecture with Etherington. He really is a good lecturer. Bill has decided to cook supper at home. The trouble with the kitchen is that the others never do their washing up. Also, whenever one wants to sit down and have a meal, one has to wait until the others have finished. Maria and I don't really get on with the other girl, Mary – although Bill appears to be his usual pleasant self to her.

September – October 1966

Wednesday 28th September 1966

Botany lecture with Mrs. E. Again, I was late. It seems to be a regular thing now! I think that part 2 really is going to be difficult. I hope that I can keep up with the others. I like this year's lot, especially the part-timers who have now become full time. We worked in the library.

Thursday 29th September 1966

Terry spouting away on hemicorda. I felt very depressed today. Mrs. E. gave me a nerve-wracking tutorial in the p.m. Evidently we have to write an essay on instrumentation. Bill and I went to a debate in the p.m. It was "This house believes that familiarity breeds". It wasn't as good as the title implied and I was really shocked by Suki's speech. My God, fancy giving a speech about electronically tested S.T.s. We ate sweet corn for supper.

Friday 30th September 1966

I woke early this morning, feeling like nothing on earth. I went downstairs and was sick. Bill came scurrying in and made me breakfast. I just couldn't keep it down. Eventually they left me in bed all day. The worst day of my life. I just lay there, vomiting and feeling awful and extremely sorry for myself. At last Bill came back – I was so pleased to see him. The end of a long day.

Saturday 1st October 1966

Bill was marvellous. He really would make a splendid nurse. I got up today and pottered around. It rained cats and dogs. At 9.00 p.m. I went back to bed and slept like a log.

Sunday 2nd October 1966

Bill is ill today. I kept him in bed and gave him a light lunch of chicken. He was back in bed very early – after getting up at 6.00 and asleep by 9.00. Poor old Bill, he did look an awful colour.

Monday 3rd October 1966

Another long week. We had an awful experiment to do in botany. I got so confused and, in the end, had to copy it up from Kirsteen. Zoo in the afternoon was very exciting, as we got a new demonstrator.

Tuesday 4th October 1966

I always feel like lying in today, as we don't have to go in 'til the afternoon. However, Bill has to be there at 9.00, so up I get and drag him out. Really, I'm becoming quite a little matron as I tap him sharply on the head and shriek "time to get up, lazybones". Quite amazing.

Wednesday 5th October 1966

We went sailing – the one and only time we go, I hope. It was absolutely awful. Taking us two hours to get there, we eventually persuaded them to give us a boat between us – whereupon we got stuck in the rushes. Most humiliating. The two hours journey home seemed like ten hours. What a day. And Mummy was supposed to be coming as well.

Thursday 6th October 1966

Today was frightfully boring, as we had most of it off.

Friday 7th October 1966

Practical all day. We had some filthy experiment and had to keep rushing around, testing colour samples all morning. In the p.m. we were each given a sea squirt – I shared one with David – we had to keep prodding the poor creature and noting its reaction.

Saturday 8th October 1966

Mummy and Daphie came up to see the digs. They were pleasantly surprised, I think. Bill did the launderette – I did the ironing – and then we went to bed. It's funny: I just live for the weekends, and then they go so quickly and it's Friday again.

Sunday 9th October 1966

We slept in 'til 12.00 and had lunch at 3.00 – a wasted day. I did a little work; so did Bill.

Monday 10th October 1966

Judo is really the obsession of Mondays. After a whole day of practical, I sometimes think it's the end! Of course, I had to put up with all the beginners. Very humiliating. We had showers and then went home to bed. Blissful to get an early night for a change.

Tuesday 11th October 1966

I have this morning off – I went to do some work and somehow didn't do any at all – old Etherington gave us a theory tutorial. Thank God he didn't ask me anything.

12 Wednesday 12th October 1966

Drew £30 out of the bank. Bill and I went to a debating meeting. Madam Suki is now President of Debates – sickening! Afterwards we went to buy my skirt and shoes. The former was a hopeless failure and I'm to take it back tomorrow.

Thursday 13th October 1966

Dr. Terry's lecture on sea squirts. I suppose it was quite interesting – she also gave a tutorial on the coelivertebrate. Mrs. E. in the p.m. was in a good mood. We had a tutorial on enzymes – I really didn't know much about them. In the p.m. Bill and I went up to be in a T.V. programme. I can't really say that I enjoyed it – but it wasn't bad. The train got stuck in the tunnel.

Friday 14th October 1966

I went home after a hectic day at college. Bill looked very sad to see me go and Mummy looked very pleased to see me, so life isn't so bad.

Saturday 15th October 1966

I went to Oliver's and had two fillings. Agony. Also went to the Swiss patisserie and enquired about wedding reception. In the p.m. I scuttled back to the digs. Bill, like an angel, had done all the washing and ironing. I felt rotten and have got an awful pain in my chest. Terry came in the evening, and we went pub crawling. It was enjoyable. He's going to be our best man.

Terry Lander was a friend of mine from secondary school – Biggleswade Technical Grammar I think it was called at the time. I had shared a flat with him at the Oval before meeting Jenny. He studied dentistry and subsequently emigrated to South Africa and then to Australia.

Sunday 16th October 1966

We spent the day quietly. Maria has gone home. Bill made stew and we left it cooking for about two hours, while we went out to Finsbury Park. Bill managed to catch a leaf, so it should be a lucky year for him. The park looked so lovely, with the leaves all turning reds and browns.

Saturday 22nd October 1966

I decided that we must have a night out, so we went all the way to town. I spent £1.10.00 and we ate the most horrible Chinese meal, after finding that all the cinemas were booked. Afterwards we came home and I slept on the floor in B.'s room, as I was too frightened to go into my own room.

Sunday 23rd October 1966

Just a lazy day: nothing ventured and, consequently, nothing gained.

Monday 24th October 1966

Judo in the gym in the p.m. The instructor is certainly getting very bossy, even to Mr. Jim Daly. I think that I'm getting on better with the people in my class. They are a much nicer lot this year.

Daly (mentioned previously of course) was a lecturer in the chemistry department.

Saturday 29th October 1966

We went home and didn't arrive until one o'clock. They were all a bit annoyed. After supper, we went to the theatre and saw a rather pathetic (in the true sense of pathos) comedy. Mummy was very sweet and gave us the money for the theatre. Bill slept on the divan, which Daddy brought over from Dunmore Road. I think that he likes Bill.

Sunday 30th October 1966

Mummy got me up and I got Bill up (rather like the house that Jack built). We sat through a rather boring service and then saw the "vicar". We made an appointment to see him. Auntie W. and Uncle M. came over at 4.00. They were very sweet. Mummy had prepared a gorgeous tea for them. We left early as we had to go back to the confirmation class – Bill's first.

Monday 31st October 1966

We have botany practical and then zoo practical. I think a whole day of it is too long. The new labs are rather impersonal, although, with time, they seem to be gaining a little character. One has either to go by lift or climb hundreds of stairs every morning – I

October – November 1966

don't know which is preferable, really. The lifts are usually full and one sails in, eyeing the others in the lift anxiously. The doors close and, with a horrid shudder, the awful contraption creaks its way up the thirteen floors.

This was in the tower block at the poly. Apparently overhead in the street one day "Nice building but I wouldn't want to live there"!

Wednesday 2nd November 1966

The debate at Q.E.C. I was the only one of the audience from the poly, and felt pretty stupid. I arrived late and, from there, everything seemed to go wrong. The motion was "if given the opportunity, this house shouldn't". Both sides spoke rather weakly and, at the end, although I had said that I would make a speech supporting the poly, I couldn't, in all seriousness. They were furious and Suki said that I looked silly! I probably did as well!

Thursday 3rd November 1966

I didn't go in today at all – neither did Bill. We came home in the p.m. after lunch and just sat around.

Friday 4th November 1966

We've decided to go home and see Bill's family. In zoo we dissected the salamander. It's such a waste of time, looking up all its anatomy first. If only they'd tell us what we're doing.

Saturday 5th November 1966

We set off at 11.30 a.m. and were earnestly hitching on the M1 by 12.00 noon. It was very cold and we eventually arrived at about 2.30 and ate a big lunch of chips and mince. In the p.m. all the neighbours' kids came in and let off their fireworks in the garden. The bonfire was a great blaze and hot cocoa and sausage rolls were had by all. Bill slept in the sitting room, on the camp bed, and I slept in his room. The radiators were on.

Bonfire night was always a great event at the Unsworth household and as a child I think I found it more exciting than Christmas.

Sunday 6th November 1966

We got up at 10.00 and had an awful heavy breakfast of fried bacon, etc. We watched a film in the afternoon and then left on the ten to eight bus. It was an awful journey.

Monday 7th November 1966

We made our first studies from the micrometer today.

Tuesday 8th November 1966

Mrs. H. caught me this morning – I'm a fool, really, as I just stand there as she goes on and on. A chair was broken in the kitchen and, of course, there was a long moan about that and then her back. And everything else. At last I managed to get away and get to college. Ethington's lectures in the p.m. have a peculiar soporific effect – and it's no use because I don't find them interesting. I felt terribly depressed today and had frightful tummy ache. I had my hair cut.

Wednesday 9th November 1966

A hateful day. I went to the library and worked, and crept back to bed in the p.m. with a hot water bottle. And many miserable memories. Maria's in the same predicament and we both couldn't sleep. We got up about midnight and did exercises to "relieve tension". It gets rid of the pains, anyway.

Thursday 10th November 1966

Took £30 out of the bank. Put £14 cheque in.

Saturday 12th November 1966

Bob's party. I was looking forward to it all day and managed to get terribly excited when we were dressing up. Then it really was awful. Bill was very sweet to John, and then got a bit drunk and behaved objectionably to most people. We left early on. I can't say that I was sorry. We had Sue Ellis on the train coming back and I felt terribly sorry for her. For many reasons – the first being that she looked so alone. Poor Sue.

Sunday 13th November 1966

Sunday was a very quiet day. Some bloke has invited Maria out next weekend.

Monday 14th November 1966

There's such a lot of work to be done and so little time. We worked for three hours – Bill doing his posters and I doing chick reconstruction drawing. Then I did the ironing and went to bed in a filthy mood. It was terribly cold that night, even with a hot water bottle.

Wednesday 16th November 1966

We had Noddy for botany and, really, he is boring. In the p.m. I went to judo. What fun – I just sat on the edge of the mat and did nothing. Two black belts gave a demonstration; they were very, very, very good. It gives one great aspirations to greatness.

Thursday 17th November 1966

I didn't go to the intercollegiate. Bill's hair is getting much too long. Soon it will be on his shoulders, like that objectionable brute, Price. I wrote home and to the Unsworths.

Friday 18th November 1966

Bill was speaking in a debate " and NATO has outlived its usefulness". He spoke very well and I felt quite proud. In zoo we went on dissecting the lizard.

Saturday 19th November 1966

We didn't go out at all and, yet, somehow this was the nicest weekend I can remember so far in this place. Maria went home and we were left alone. Bill made a scrumptious curry and I baked a cake and some scones. It just shows how well we can get on when nobody else is around.

Sunday 20th November 1966

We prepared our reception. It was a very imposing list but I think it will be fun. Poor Maria: she got all ready this evening to go out with some bloke – John Higglesden – and then he didn't turn up.

Monday 21st November 1966

What a foul day – I have been shanghaied by El Bizri to speak in a bloody debate. Then, to crown it all, an idiot called Kath yelled at me when I got back to the digs. Thank God "he" gave us a sense of humour. I hate bullies.

Tuesday 22nd November 1966

I debated today. God, was I nervous. Perhaps nobody – least of all myself – will understand why I made such an awful mess of that speech – last night had a lot to do with shattering of any self-confidence I may have – but why? The fear – feeling of guilt – as I got up and spoke – and the awful compulsion to lose control and scream at those ugly faces sitting there, looking so bored – that's why.

Wednesday 23rd November 1966

Today wasn't so bad, although I hardly slept last night. Chris and I did judo and suddenly everything clicked and I found myself really doing judo. I think it's all due to that little man – Bert. He really managed to give one confidence.

Thursday 24th November 1966

I was so bored in Terry's lecture and did not go to the intercollegiate. I stayed in the library and worked in the p.m. with Maria. She tried to phone up John Higglesden, with no success. I didn't get to bed until 11.45 and felt very irritable, as I couldn't sleep.

Friday 25th November 1966

Bill was in a bad mood today. Maria is going to the 'Miss Poly' dance with Mary and I dissected the snake. Ray Khan showed up in his true colours. He was really nasty to me, so Bill came up and shouted "you bum", whereupon Ray lashed out – unfortunately, just to add humour to the situation, a blow hit me instead and I got a glassful of milk all over my new skirt – no good crying over spilt milk? I wonder.

Ever the gentleman – that's me. I remember the incident but not what it had been about. Khan had been a friend previously and, for example, helped me move digs on one occasion because he had a car.

Saturday 26th November 1966

We didn't go out 'til the evening. In the darkness of the smoky cinema, and munching "Mintoes", we watched the most ghastly horror film and then a tragic film, "This Property is Condemned". Natalie Wood starred in it – I think that she is going to be fat, like Liz Taylor. I brought my mattress to Bill's room; I felt so frightened in mine.

November 1966

Sunday 27th November 1966

We did tons of work and the rain beat down outside. It was so gorgeously cosy inside. Unfortunately, we didn't go to church.

The diaries stop here. Perhaps life was just getting two busy. We did marry the following year after I had finished my degree, and Jenny completed her degree the year after.

Diary 1969

In which Jenny is diagnosed with Leukaemia.

Sunday 26th July 1969

Life during the past month has been fraught with misery, fear and misgivings. Almost four weeks to the day I accidentally discovered that I had Leukaemia. My reaction has been one of numbness – a feeling that this couldn't happen; isn't happening to me.

I spend three weeks in hospital having tests and treatment. Three ghastly weeks of entertaining visitors, agony of mind and isolation from the normal sane world. Bill was marvellous, so cheerful. He would roll up every afternoon with flowers, sweets, ice creams, the lot. I would count the hours until he came and weep each time he left.

Mummy was a great comfort and also tried to be cheerful. What a failure her children seem to have been; especially me with my perpetual ill health.

Last week I was discharged. I felt and looked dreadful. Somehow I have managed to slot back into flat life though. Bill has started his research again and we are making a pretence that life is back to normal.

I was frightfully impressed with the Apollo 11 moon shot. It seems quite unreal especially as the TV pictures give an almost ghost like quality to the whole thing.

There is now a break in the diary until September. You can read later in the book the autobiography that she started but unfortunately didn't finish. I have tried to fill in what I know of her early life there.

We had finished our degrees in the gap prior to the events covered here. She had obtained her Botany and Zoology degree at the end of 1968 and I had finished a year earlier. I had then gone on to do research for a Ph. D. in chemistry and the final period of that is covered later in her diary. There are references to various job applications I made during the subsequent entries.

She had got her first job at Davies Tutorial College, near to Victoria Station in London and after getting married in 1967 we had a flat in Muswell Hill. I was doing my research at the college where we had met and done our degrees – Northern Polytechnic (now University of North London) in Holloway Road. I suppose she had always been someone prone to illness although I am sure we never thought anything of it particularly. After a bad day she would go to bed, for example, and I suppose whilst a student she was able to be more flexible in coping with things. But really there was nothing to lead me to suspect a serious illness building up.

However she had as a child had a number of tropical diseases – Filaria is one that was mentioned. Filaria is associated with the disease of Elephantiasis and is common in West Africa where she had lived. It is transmitted by mosquitoes. Victoria recalls that Jenny had a serious operation to remove a lump from her neck that was dangerously close to her spine that was related to the tropical disease. I think that Jenny told me she had a lump removed from her neck that contained teeth and hair and that was thought to be an undeveloped twin.

She found it increasingly difficult to cope with working at Davies' (i.e. with a full-time job it was necessary to go in everyday even if you were feeling under the weather and holidays were of course only a couple of weeks a year) and was visiting the doctor regularly with colds, coughs and sore throats that would not clear up. Eventually the doctor decided to refer her to the Hospital for Tropical Diseases in London for tests to see if she was still suffering from the childhood illnesses. Blood tests were taken and when she went back for the results her curiosity got the better of her. The doctor had left the room for a moment and she looked over and read his notes. On the margin the doctor had written "Leukaemia?" So she received a dreadful tentative diagnosis without any preparation. She had rushed out of the hospital and phoned me at work and in a tearful hysterical phone call had asked me to come over immediately to the hospital. They were in a flap also given the casual and unfeeling way they had behaved and there were more tears before things were calmed down. Jenny had been interested in becoming a doctor earlier and so she had already some knowledge of the disease and its prognosis. She says later in the diary that she wished she had never gone and read up more about it as it meant that she was aware of the various stages of the disease as it took its toll on her.

Although her later treatment was at University College Hospital in Gower Street in London I seem to recall that the initial period of treatment was at St Bartholomew's hospital in the City of London where of course Brendan O'Farrel had gone to study medicine although there is nothing to indicate they were in touch again.

September 1969

Monday 15th September 1969

What a crazy life! Switch time back 6 months and there I am fighting for a cause – I never defined it – even though I felt lousy life had some meaning. Now – what? Whenever I attempt anything, be it a friendship or German grammar I think – "what the hell" the effort isn't worth it. What are we all killing ourselves for?

And yet. Life is such a wonderful gift

A newspaper clipping about Jenny's great grandfather is included in the diary here:

Celebrating a hundred active years

One of the few remaining officers to hold a commission from the reign of Queen Victoria celebrated his 100th birthday at his home in Wimbledon on Sunday.

Lieut. Col. Francis Watling, is one of the oldest doctors in Britain and an honorary president of Edinburgh University.

During his career as an Army doctor Col. Watling survived the 1900 Boxer rebellion in China and was mentioned in despatches for gallantry in action in Mesopotamia during the first world war.

Born in India Col. Watling returned there after graduating from Edinburgh and receiving his commission.

His service took him to the famous North West Frontier and he took part in the relief of Chitral and the Afghan war.

Even at 100 Col. Watling remembers much of his youth and service in India.

"Once when I was a student, I had a drink too much and managed to enlist in the Army," he said with a laugh. "My mother had to buy me out in the end!"

One of his fondest memories is of an Afghan tribesman who offered him his daughter as a gift after he had cured the tribesman's son.

"A little red-haired girl she was a pretty little thing, but I told him I could not take her – I was married already."

His recipe for 100 years of active life? "We must all have a little fun in life – life is far to serious without making it more so."

On Sunday, Lt. Col. Watling celebrated with his family at a party at his home. He has four children, 11 grandchildren and three great grand children.

October 1969

Note by Jenny:

New Scientist

Chronic Myeloid Leukaemia

Half long arm of chromosome G^1 missing in some myelocytes and some leukocytes. Thought to normally be non-inheritable. CML normally seen in adults only; Abnormal G^1 chromosome seen sometimes before clinical symptoms become apparent.

Chronic Lymphocyte Leukaemia

Chromosome abnormality is passed from one generation to the next i.e. is inheritable. [Traced through family in New Zealand. The member usually contract the disease late in life and live long enough to pass on the abnormal chromosomes to their offspring]

I met an old friend – Anne Marie at the beginning of the month. She has the most adorable little girl of 11 months. What a relief it is to have someone to talk to during the day. She pops over here every so often and we have a good natter over cups of my dreadful dishwater tea.

Bill has applied to the Open University for the post of lecturer. I do hope that he gets it. It would be an excellent outlet for his creative energy.

I went up to the hospital for another check-up. Souhami has left and a rather nervous Dr Simmons has taken his place. He didn't seem to know what he was doing. I can't bear these incompetent people. My blood count has dropped to 10,000 which is normal, as far as I am concerned anyway.

Wednesday 22nd October 1969

Today Victoria (*cousin*) and Sammy came up to see me. That baby is growing. At 8 months she is already standing and talking! (well the odd gurgle which could be mistaken for Mummy). We had a very relaxing day with steak for lunch and a delicious treacle pudding.

Crane came out of hospital this morning – poor old thing he does look old and shaky. It must be dreadful to grow old, at least I shall be spared all that. I keep wondering when we will adopt a baby – I think that I would prefer a boy – they seem to be so much easier to control than girls. It would be wonderful to have something to love.

October 1969

Reginald Crane owned the house in 22 Tetherdown, Muswell Hill and we rented the top floor off him. It was an unconverted house and we had a large bedroom and sitting room on the second floor and a kitchen and bathroom halfway down the stairs. Crane still had a sign up outside saying "Commissioner for Oaths" although we were not aware of his getting any business. He must have been in his 70s or even older at the time and he died a couple of years after we left. We had moved there after getting married and had had a happy time.

Crane was a good landlord but in failing health really. He tended to forget things and one day there was a dreadful smell. I went down to investigate and found that he had put an egg on to boil, forgot it, and it had boiled dry! He had a horrible cat that brought him gifts and so we found dead maggoty birds when we had gone down to his flat to check things when he had been ill. His garden at the back was completely neglected and we had hacked out a small patch to try and grow some vegetables such as runner beans. He had a formidable sister who came to visit every so often. He said that he had never married although he had got close but the girl's father "in the motor trade" had disapproved and it had never gone ahead.

The flat was drafty, with sash windows, and we had bought a few items of furniture such as an easy chair from Heals in Tottenham Court Road. The basic accommodation did not really bother us. There was no central heating of course and the only heating we had was an electric fire in the sitting room. I remember we went to the cinema on the corner of Fortis Green road one dry and cold breezy winter evening. When we came out all was still and it had snowed quite heavily. Back at the flat in our living room the snow had blown through the gaps in the windows and was all over the window sill and floor of the sitting room – and it was not melting.

We bought our first car from the garage near the cinema in Fortis Green Road – a grey and purple Ford Consul which had a column gear shift and bench front seat – for £70. We sold it later for £75! Jenny never learned to drive although I did give her driving lessons while we lived in Bedford. I think that she drove my father's car into a ditch one night under my tuition and we pretty well stopped the attempt then.

I am sure that it was around this time that Jenny read Rachel Carson's book *Silent Spring* (published 1962, which is said to have triggered the whole environmental movement). She certainly wondered what had caused her illness and whether it was genetic or down to exposure to carcinogens in the environment.

I have decided to have my front tooth out and have a plate with a false one stuck on it instead. I think that the initial discomfort of the plate will outweigh this dreadful incessant toothache. Six years is quite enough.

She attributed this injury to her father and there is documentary evidence to support this. She had had her nose broken whilst trying to protect her mother from her father. Previously whilst at Ewell Tech she reports numerous visits to the dentist – Oliver's.

Thursday 23rd October 1969

Crane has been impossible since he came home. I have cooked all his meals as he is far too ill to do them himself. The trouble is he knows in his heart that he is dying and he is taking out his rage and fears on all around him viz me. I must confess that I wept a few very bitter tears this morning at the irony of the situation – two walking corpses.

Yesterday we went to the Dairy show. (The Chemistry department at the Northern Polytechnic had for some reason the job of analysing the milk for the purposes of awards at the show and all staff were roped in including research students – Bill included.) I felt awfully peculiar and light headed at first but this wore off as the afternoon progressed and I found myself really enjoying the outing by the time evening fell.

Newspaper clipping included in diary dated August 5th 1967:

Polytechnic students marry at Wimbledon

Two students at the Northern Polytechnic in London, Miss Jennifer Holly Stephens and Mr. William David Unsworth were married at Christ Church, Wimbledon on Saturday.

Mr. Unsworth is the eldest son of Mr. and Mrs. F. Unsworth of 10 Greenacres, Bedford. He is a former pupil of Stratton school and Newnham. He has just obtained an honours degree in chemistry at London University, from the Northern Polytechnic, and is now commencing further studies leading to a Ph.D in chemistry.

His bride, the eldest daughter of Mr and Mrs D. R. Stephens, of Wimbledon, is just commencing the final year of the course of a London University general degree in Biology at the Polytechnic.

She wore a slimline dress in lace with a three-tier train. Her white tulle veil was secured by a coronet of orange blossom and she carried a bouquet of pink roses and white carnations.

Bridesmaids were the Misses Daphne and Rosemary Stephens, brides sisters and Miss Margaret Unsworth, the bridegrooms sister. The best man was Mr T. Lander, bridegrooms friend.

After the ceremony, conducted by the Rev. Mr. Smith and a reception at the Wimbledon Hill Hotel, the couple left for a honeymoon touring Wales. They will live in London.

November 1969

The best thing that ever happened to me!

Thursday 6th November 1969

Had my front tooth out. It fractured and he had to dig out the root.

Tuesday 11th November 1969

Moved from Tetherdown. What a day! I really couldn't believe that we had accumulated so much stuff, we piled it in the hall downstairs and it covered every inch of available space. At one point I thought that we wouldn't get it all into the van we had hired, eventually we did though but not before much insulting language had enriched the air!

I had a comfy seat in the back amongst the packing cases. Just before we bade our last farewells Bill and I went into the garden to get the washing line and also to have a last look. There were tears in our eyes as we walked back. It is somehow the end of an epoch in our lives. I wonder what the future holds.

Jenny had given up work after being diagnosed with her illness. She became increasingly isolated being in the flat all day and not going out. My parents had offered to let us live with them whilst I finished my Ph.D. They had a house in Greenacres, Putnoe, Bedford, where they had lived since the mid 50's, which had central heating! I had gone to the local school – Newnham Secondary Modern, and later after "O" levels to Stratton School in Biggleswade where I had got "A" levels in maths, physics and chemistry. We sold our car (probably a mistake in retrospect because it would have probably given good service for a number of years). We had one room and so a lot of our stuff went into the loft. I commuted every day to London St. Pancras where I took the tube to Holloway Road. In the diaries to follow there is reference to the U's – collective for Unsworths, M and D for Mum and Dad (although Jenny's mother Cynthia is sometimes referred to as M also), and to my brothers and sister Andrew, Martin and Margaret. The neighbour – Valerie – is referred to, as are the neighbours on the other side – the "Ganys", Betty and Stephan. He was a Polish doctor who worked at Bedford Hospital and had settled in the UK after the war.

Saturday (mid November) 1969

Bills mum had pains in the night and went to the Doctor. Started on her diet. Mummy and Daphne ill with flu and I also had flu myself.

Monday 24th November 1969

Went to UCH. My blood count has gone up from 4000 to 12000. I could weep.

Mummy and I went to Schmidt's for lunch. (A German restaurant in Goodge St) Afterwards we went to Bourn and Hollingsworth and M. bought me a new coat £20. I felt very guilty but it will certainly last me a long time (will in fact almost certainly "outlive" use). I am very grateful.

Felt very ill on returning home.

Sunday 7th December 1969

Fed up with this bloody house. Am on completely different wavelength to them. Absolutely the wrong idea to come here – moans – TV turned off when I am in the middle of watching a program (no "are you watching this?"). Shouting. Never seeing Bill. Must find some friends or will go mad.

Monday 8th December 1969

Have just found out that I have <u>acute myeloid leukaemia</u> not chronic. What a fool I was to read that book. I had every symptom – sore throat, fever, bruising haemorrhage. All one gets with the chronic form is sore throat and tiredness and they treat that with X-rays. Of course looking back on it I now realise that Prankerd had known all along but had put down chronic to keep one from knowing.

I am not going to tell anyone, least of all Bill, poor thing. What a life I have led him. Perhaps it will be for the best if I don't wake up after this abortion. That's another thing to look forward to. Oh how I wish I believed in God.

Actually this explains a lot. I knew that she had leukaemia of course but had not read up on it as she had. I knew it could kill her but I really did not accept that she would die until the very end. I encouraged her to follow the doctor's advice and take the treatment that they offered. The reference earlier to adoption also makes more sense in the light of this passage. Nowadays there is much more discussion of choice for patients – including the choice of refusing treatment if its outcome is likely to be to prolong suffering and not significantly extend life.

Presumably the reference above is to TAJ Prankerd who worked at University College Hospital at the correct time. A search with Google lists hundreds of papers by him in blood disease related areas.

Also found:

http://www.ucl.ac.uk/current-students/financial-support/scholarships/alpha-list/fund/?fundcode=MCLIPHIB7

this is a link to a page giving details of prizes offered by the college:

December 1969

"The Prankerd-Jones Memorial Prizes were founded in 1983 by the subscribers to the Prankerd-Jones Memorial Fund, in memory of Nicola Prankerd (a former student of University College Hospital School of Medicine, 1976–1982), her brother, Richard Prankerd, and Alison Jones (a former student of the Slade School of Fine Art, 1976–1980), all of whom were murdered in Zimbabwe in 1982. The fund was subscribed to by their families and relatives, the Sir Jules Thorn Charitable Trust, the "Friends of University College" and many other benefactors. The Austin Heady Prize in Biometry was founded at the Royal Free Hospital School of Medicine in 1983 by Gerry W. Fenn in honour of Austin Heady."

Given the same, unusual surname, we have to assume they were related to Professor Prankerd.

Tuesday 9th December 1969

Cycled down to the hospital this morning to deliver the wine sample for the pregnancy test. It is a lovely fresh day today and it feels good to be alive. I have decided to forget that I have leukaemia – if I have acute L. then I have only a little time to live but it might as well be a happy time. I feel so <u>well</u> today, it's a <u>wonderful</u> feeling to be alive.

Wednesday 10th December 1969

Was busily typing out a letter to Mummy when the phone rang. Mum answered it and as she called out "it's Dr Murdy for you Jenny" a horrible cold hand clutched at my innards and I <u>knew</u> what it was about. After he had told me I felt numb – pregnant; what a turmoil of feeling then broke loose. I don't want to loose it, I don't want to have it, is it murder to have and abortion, will it be a boy or girl, I want to <u>live</u>. I don't want to give up all I have fought for during these past months. Margaret and Mum were very kind. I phoned up Prankerd and then Bill. I like to think that Bill didn't really take in the magnitude of what I was saying as all I heard was a non-committal "oh" on the other end of the line.

I suppose I shall have to loose it. My god how I'd love a baby, a child. The thought of anaesthetics and death are fast obsessing me.

Although it really was not a dilemma – whether to have a baby or not – it created much sadness. We did discuss it but decided that it would only exacerbate her condition and probably lead to her death sooner rather than later. Certainly we were aware that life expectancy was likely to be drastically curtailed even in the most probable outcome.

Thursday 11th December 1969

Bill decided to stay at home with me. Poor thing he does look tired. We had a late breakfast and then caught the bus into town. The shops were gay and reached out warm fingers into the street as we stood peering in through the misty windows. First to the bank where we collected £13 – a fortune. Then on to Roses, the big store in town. We bought some marvellous perfumed talc for Daphne and Margaret, also some eye make up remover. By the time that had been bought, a pad for Martin and game for Andrew – we were thoroughly exhausted. As we waited for the lift to take us down to the street I suddenly had the most violent pain in my tummy. It was so sharp I felt as if someone had stabbed me. I just said "Ouch" and Bill said "Oh what's the matter <u>now</u>" in a tired sort of voice. Some sympathy!

We had a gorgeous Chinese meal and I had a few more stabs. We walked home. I had lost a little blood and hoped, feared etc – am I having a miscarriage?

Monday 15th December 1969

Well as it turned out I lost a lot of blood but didn't in fact abort. This morning we caught the 8.05 train to town and I went to the hospital. I felt terribly sick and dizzy. I had a blood test then went to see Dr Prankerd. He told me the blood count was "ok" and felt my tum. "Gynaecologist this pm for you my girl". I phoned Bill and he came over for lunch. In the pm waited for hours to see a certain Dr Holmes (Mr H actually so he must be a surgeon). Tall bad tempered man. 7 weeks pregnant. Have to have an abortion. Somehow I felt relieved.

Tuesday 16th December 1969

Sore throat for the past 6 weeks has now got much worse. Pains in my bones again, feel sick.

Thursday 18th December 1969

Went shopping. Bill getting on well with his thesis.

Friday 19th December 1969

Opticians – have to have new glasses. In the pm walked to the shops. Burr – it was cold, as I came out of the butchers twilight had descended, the street lamps came on and a gentle fall of snow was beginning. Perfect Bliss!! I walked happily homeward watching the flakes falling and how good it is to be <u>alive</u>!

December 1969

Wednesday 24th December 1969

Mummy and Daphne came to see us last Saturday. I was pleased to see them. We had prepared a fish casserole and an apple crumble for lunch. I think that they were enjoyed by all.

After lunch Mrs U. went up for a rest and left us to our own devices. We listened to records and drank tea. I think M. was anxious to be off as she kept saying "What is the time?" We drove them down to the station.

Thursday 25th December 1969 – Christmas Day

One of the happiest I have had for a long time. Martin (aged 12 then) woke up at 5 am and has successfully routed everyone out by 6. We went down and opened our presents. I gave M, Daphne a waistcoat, Bill a record token and chocs, Martin a sketch pad (9/-) and Andrew a Jack Straws (which he loathes!) I opened my present from Bill, it was the most beautiful fur cap – just what I wanted. Mummy and Daphne gave me scent, makeup and socks – lovely.

Delicious Christmas dinner – got a bit tipsy. Games in pm and watched TV.

Boxing Day

Same as Christmas day.

Saturday 27th December 1969

We went round to Valerie Wiles. Delicious tea – although I thought that the salad could have been cleaner!

Monday 28th December 1969

Valerie and her Dad came round here. I did a huge washing and ironing. Felt very ill in pm. Dizzy and twitchy – couldn't breathe.

Tuesday 29th December 1969

Packed. Felt very light headed – probably nerves.

Wednesday 31st December 1969

Dread days. Had an awful night and woke with a splitting headache after having rammed my head up against the board at the top of the bed. Felt sick at breakfast. Thick snow – waited for hours at the bus stop eventually someone gave us a lift. Cold station, nausea in buffet.

Eventually arrived at hospital. Horrible medicinal smell, fear in the pit of my stomach, awful feeling that I'm going to cry. Fill in forms, shown to my bed " Get undressed Mrs Unsworth". Bill leaves quietly – sudden feeling of terror and loneliness. Undress and climb into hard high hospital bed. Blood test, lunch, feel sick and can't eat. Afternoon sleep.

Victoria comes, looking so well, chat for 20 minutes. Mummy and Daphne come, both look worried. I feel that I have to make conversation – oh weary hospital life. I have a vision of myself perpetually holding forth among the " woman's" and grapes. They leave. I feel very lonely and wish that Bill would come.

Night – sleep well, horrid draught from bedside window.

Diary 1970

In which Jenny gets her own home.

Thursday 1st January 1970

What a way to greet the New Year, starving for an op. I think back to all the previous New Years I have spent. They all seem so happy in comparison. Parties, people, happiness, laughter, <u>life</u>.

Lunchtime – my stomach is complaining bitterly, I feel very light headed. In order to keep my mind off it I talk to the girl in the next bed. Well I never lives in Muswell Hill, goes to the same doctor as me and is a student at Davies'. What a small world!

Premedication. Sinking feeling as I have the injection. Then horrid feeling in throat and mouth. Wheeled up to theatre needle in vein. I can feel the cold anaesthetic creep up my arm – 10, 9, 8, 7, nothing – I start again 10, 9,

Having this "dream" about being crushed, can't move a limb, cannot open my eyes, can't breath, terrible croaking noise – open my eyes after superhuman effort. Scream – nothing – lights, voices, terrible pain in throat and chest. "Sorry dear – we didn't find a baby".

All night long I cried and was sick. In the morning they gave me an injection to stop me retching. In the pm they sent me home. I felt dreadful. Journey home a nightmare. Spent the next few days in bed, lost a lot of blood and felt very ill.

Saturday 10th January 1970

Should have gone to John and Helen's party today but didn't feel well enough to go. It is a miserable day anyway. We went shopping in the morning and I bought a gorgeous purse with wallet attached (37/6 with the gift vouchers we were given). I also bought a pen which on trying out at home was found to be broken. Dad and Mum are going out to Valerie's this pm so that we will be left with the kids. Yesterday Bill's "Chemistry in

Britain" came. It dealt with cancer and of course I read the article. This awful compulsion to read the worst is a nightmare. Planted Zea maize. Golden Bantam (F, hybrid).

John and Helen Doswell were friends of Jenny's from her time in Wimbledon and had been involved in amateur dramatics with her (see earlier entries).

Tuesday 13th January 1970

Uneventful past few days. I have continued with my typing and can now plonk along at quite a speed. Yesterday I made what is known as Apple Blossom pie, evidently it is the national dish in Australia. It was very tasty, but I don't think that I would have the strength to make it every day. In the afternoon we went for a walk up to the shops and after buying a few "edibles" set off at a tangent to look at a new estate of houses. I can't say that I thought much of them. Horrid square boxes. This morning I received my pills from the hospital (no stamp on them, I honestly don't know how they arrived). I also received a letter from Anne Maria and one from Rosy. It was nice to hear from them both even if the letters were rather uninspiring.

Bones aching and terrible full feeling. Bill's spots a bit better.

Thursday 15th January 1970

Feeling very well and happy (apart from headaches). At last the weather is taking a change for the better. It is becoming warmer and the sun actually peeps out from behind the clouds every so often. Bill is looking tired but denies feeling unwell at all. The spots have coalesced on his neck and he now appears to have a very healthy looking sun tan. This morning I received letters from Jill and Annette and one from Mummy. Jill's husband Barry has just lost his job. Understandably they are both very upset.

Mummy says that Daphne is being rather troublesome. I expect that it is a bit of exam nerves. Poor thing. It does seem a long time since I went through all that.

Wednesday 21st January 1970

This morning there was great excitement as a letter came for Bill from Adams. The gist of it was that Adams is very optimistic about Bill's chances of landing the job with Coderg and that he is to go for an interview with the Managing Director in Paris. I do hope that I will be able to go with him.

D M Adams was a lecturer at Leicester University. I had come across him when using equipment for my Ph.D, "Low frequency vibrational spectra of metal halide-pyrazine complexes and related compounds", University of London 1970. He knew my

January 1970

supervisor Michael Goldstein well and they had produced joint papers (I think) previously. Adams had got involved in the commercial side after purchasing a Laser Raman spectrometer from a French firm called Coderg. They had indicated that they wanted representation in the UK after selling a number of instruments (actually including Kroto at Sussex University later famous as the discoverer of so called "Buckyballs"). Adams had suggested to them that I would be suitable although to be honest I had no commercial experience whatsoever at that time. However this did eventually much later lead to my employment at Hilger and Watts, a scientific instrument manufacturer, who gained the agency for Coderg. This then launched me on my early career in sales and marketing of scientific instruments.

The last few days have been rather unspectacular. On Friday we went to see "Lady Precious Stream" at Martin's school. The scenery was very colourful, so were the costumes. The plot was good, but my god, the players managed nevertheless to ruin it. Why oh why do the performers in school plays have to say all their lines in a flat monotone.

On Saturday Bill and I went to see " Gone with the Wind"! The cinema was packed and we were lucky to get seats even if they were at the front. I thought Clark Gable fantastically good looking and such a natural actor. Vivienne Leigh was excellent as well, although I thought at times that she was merely playing herself. On Sunday two yellow green shoots of Zea maize showed themselves.

Monday and Tuesday. Blood count felt as if it was falling- giddiness. Sweet taste in mouth, black tongue, ulcers. Made an appointment at UCH for next Monday. Wrote to Rosy, Kev, and Kirstie. Received a letter from M and one from Daph.

Made cheese straws and chocolate shells during the week.

Feel very guilty about not writing up my diary for so long. I went up to UCH on the 26th February, saw Prankerd for a few minutes. He said that as my blood count was perfectly normal 7,000 I could come off the pills. I felt incredibly relieved. – (like the last day at school with the whole holiday ahead)). He has put me onto a month's trial. Met Mummy – she was pleased to hear the good news. We had lunch in a little Italian restaurant and then went to an exhibition of Polish art. I enjoyed looking at the paintings and weird sculptures. I caught the 4.20 train home and was met at the station by Mr U. Next week spent at home reading, playing, chess and typing out Bill's notes. Thursday the 5th of February we went to a slide show. I felt dreadfully ill as we hurried to find out seats. My pelvic bones felt as if they were cracking and the room started to go round. The show was fairly entertaining – but went on far too long. I was glad to get home and watch the last episode of Henry VIII. Saturday Bill had wisdom teeth out. Went for an exhilarating walk to the woods (Sandy) on Sunday 8th. Monday 9th an exciting phone call from Paris. Coderg want Bill to fly out tomorrow to discuss the job that they are offering. Wild rush of collecting suit (new one – bought last Tuesday £20), collecting money and packing his case.

Tuesday 10th February 1970

Up at 7.00am. Bill is so excited. This will be the first time he has flown. Suitcase packed – off he goes. Tension all day wondering what he is doing. 10pm phone call Bill is on his way home. They will let us know in 10 days whether or not he has the job.

To be honest I think they thought I would be someone with some commercial experience. I visited their factory near Clichy and met the MD, a one-handed gent, and Prof (Delhaye) who was the technical brains behind the operation. They had stolen a march on American instrument manufacturers (UK ones such as Hilger had abandoned the field a while before in terms of their own products). I had a very brief interview, hung around for a long time, and then took a flight back. Never even opened my case!

The abiding memory I have of this period is of waiting day after day for a response from Coderg. They never wrote or phoned and in the end I phoned them and they were surprised to find I was still waiting to hear from them. Subsequently I resolved if I were in that position – i.e. of employing people I would always take the trouble to advise people of the outcome of an application.

Wednesday 11th February 1970

I went to town to the Family Planning clinic. Horrible nerves – waiting to go in – had a scrape. Cap size 85 mm (I have jumped from 72 to 85 in 2 years). Back to 12 Amity. I felt very excited at the prospect of staying. Evening – so lovely, wonder what Bill is doing – dread going to bed without him. Horrid smell of polish in the bedroom

Thursday 12th February 1970

Get up late. Get dress material (or rather M. did) laze around all day.

Friday 13th February 1970

Theatre in the p.m. "Who killed Santa Claus" – it was very spooky! (*A play by Terence Feely.*) Horrid scene in car going to the theatre. Hate a certain person. M and I certainly enjoyed it even if he didn't.

Saturday 14th February 1970

Stayed in all morning, Dunmore Rd in in pm. Jean there – drank disgusting Martinis.

Sunday 15th February 1970

Church – enough said.

Monday 16th February 1970

UCH. Gyny woman thinks I am still pregnant, could weep.

Wednesday 17th February 1970

Pregnancy test – negative thank god.

Friday 20th February 1970

M & Daph are in Aberystwyth. D has to go and get A and B. Bill very ill – flu and after affects of wisdom teeth – stayed in bed all day and lost a little blood.

Saturday 21st February 1970

Bill better but still very white. Family went up to Coventry to see Ken Dodd in panto.

Sunday 22nd February 1970

Quiet day. Went for short walk. I felt v. shaky. Made a golden cake. Delic. Others came back.

Monday 23rd February 1970

Up to hosp. Back on le.o.d pills as blood count has gone up. I thought it had as I have feeling so sick and feverish. Horrid sore throat for days.

Tuesday 24th February 1970

Bill interview in Worksop. He had the piece of bone that had been troubling him removed. He is so brave.

Sunday 1st March 1970

Have felt quite well during the past days – except of course for this perpetual sore throat. I wonder sometimes if these pills have anything to do with it. I went to the Chem Soc dinner on Friday and so spend all week looking for a dress. Fred has gone to Schaffhausen which meant that we had the car.

Sail On, Silvergirl, Sail On By

Monday 2nd March 1970

Window shopped. Bill rehearsed his colloquium. Bought my dress – blue straight.

Tuesday 3rd March 1970

Dreadful blizzard. It snowed all day – the sky was grey and the birds sang. The Forsythia bush was bent to the ground and trees up the alley snapped under the weight of snow. I borrowed Martins boots and ventured out towards evening. The cool clean air was a tonic in itself. Everywhere was extraordinarily quiet as I crunched through the 16" of snow. The kids were sent home at lunchtime. I felt very light-headed awful sore throat. Bill gave his colloquium today. Evidently it went off v. well. I felt so proud.

Thursday 5th March 1970

Bill stayed at home as no buses were running. We had a lovely day together. The snow plough had been called in to clear the snow.

Friday 6th March 1970

12 pm had my hair set. 5 pm caught the bus to station. 5.40 train. 6.15 St Pancras 7 pm Bill arrives (I could have boxed his ears!) The dinner was very enjoyable, I felt loathe to leave. I <u>do wish</u> that I didn't have to die.

Saturday 7th March 1970

My mother didn't phone last Sunday because she had flue. Bill and I waited in till 3pm and then decided to go for a walk down to the park. People were skiing and tobogganing down Cemetery Hill, it looked great fun. We strolled through the snow until we reached the pavilion where we had a cup of tea (out of plastic cups and stirred with plastic spoons). Wearily we plodded our way homeward.

Monday 9th March 1970

Slept in late, nothing spectacular – Tue, Wed, Thur ditto

Friday 13th March 1970

Prepared Bills favourite – coleslaw and pork. Had it ready at 5.30 no sign of Bill. 7 pm rolls in looking very sly as he has for the past few days. I felt quite well and happy and we

March 1970

set off for James Bond (On Her Majesty's Secret Service). Evidently Bill has been rendezvousing with this blonde in the train for the past week. A pity as I was just beginning to have compete trust and piece of mind. Every night I have been planning how to end it, I don't think that any way is completely painless. Probably the quickest is a hole in the carotid – if I take sleeping pills first. Events like this suddenly bring home with shattering reality the fact that one is completely alone in life. Bill will never be the same to me again after last night. I am very sorry.

I was travelling every day from Bedford to St Pancras usually catching the same train. People tended to stand in the same place on the platform and inevitably you got to chat to people. This is how I met Margaret Thorogood and eventually we would meet up and sit next to each other on the morning train. She was a teacher and I think her husband taught at Harper College in Bedford which was a teacher training college. I don't recall where she worked. As we got to know each other I told her about Jenny and her illness. I suppose for me it was someone to talk to not directly connected with the situation.

I think it was she who suggested that the four of us go out for a meal one evening and it was my suggesting this that so upset Jenny. I think she didn't really hear what I said actually. I remember my mother being quite pleased that we might become friends with another couple. The depth of what this did to Jenny is plain from the diary but I did not realise this until 35 years later on my first reading of the diary. Margaret moved jobs probably that summer and I lost touch with her. She had been just a sympathetic ear and no relationship had developed. I had only ever seen her on the morning train or the couple of times we all went out. Jenny mentions her in a more favourable light later but the upset at the time is plain from her diary.

Started knitting yesterday – I am attempting a pair of gloves. Bad sore throat . Giddy

Saturday 14th March 1970

Bill and I were rather cold to each other today. I feel very angry now with him and want to hurt him in return. He decided that he didn't like the arrangement of our room so we had a great moving around session. We now have the two beds facing the window and the wardrobe and dressing table where the beds were. Andrew came and helped us after a fashion.

Sunday 15th March 1970

Went for a walk – my mother didn't phone as she is still ill.

Monday 16th March 1970

I still feel very angry and am afraid that I took it out on Bill's mother. B. went into college and I was pleased to see him go. In the pm M. asked what was wrong and I couldn't tell her of course.

Tuesday 17th March 1970

B. went in late and was supposed to be home at 8 pm. I bussed into town with him in the morning and went to the bank and did some shopping. Braggins have opened a few new departments and I had a peer around. The have the same carpet as the library – the smell of naphthalene is revolting. 8pm I listened to "War and Peace" – phone, Bill won't be home till 11pm oh hell. I don't care. If I worry about things I only make myself ill, but I can't help worrying.

Wednesday 18th March 1970

B. stayed at home. Things went well until the evening when I felt very peculiar. We were all watching TV, I sitting finishing off my 1st glove when I mentioned something and the inevitable "you're kidding" accompanied by a direct glare rang round the room. It was too bloody much and I ran upstairs and tried to cut my wrists. The only thing stopping me was that I couldn't get the razor to cut. Oh God these moods of utter depression.

Thursday 19th March 1970

Terrible atmosphere. Went into town and bought Bill a pair of swimming trunks. We set off for the pool in the afternoon. He walked and I cycled. Oh it was glorious to feel the cool H_2O round me. I felt very strong and full of life.

Friday 20th March 1970

Still! Did the shopping

Saturday 21st March 1970

Dug the garden and planted the onions

Sunday 22nd March 1970

Did a vast washing. Sat and read. Sore throat getting better. Feel very full and tight around the stomach.

March 1970

Monday 23rd March 1970

Brendan's birthday tomorrow – funny I hardly ever think of him now. I don't think that I ever really liked him that much – it was the fact that out of the whole conflab of everybody I knew, he was the only one who I could have a laugh and feel at ease with.

Inserted in the diary – Bills first published paper!

Today I went up to UCH. Bill and I travelled up to town together. He then set off for college and I made my way to the hospital. As usual I felt an awful sinking sensation in the pit of my stomach as I walked in. Evidently my blood count has gone up tremendously. I couldn't make out whether he said 18 or 80 to the bloke with him but it looked suspiciously like 89,000 on the piece of paper. I felt sick. He says that he thinks my spleen has come up – even though he couldn't feel it. These splits on my hips are stretch marks. On two pills per day.

Tuesday 24th March 1970

Bill stayed at home. We were turned down by Steetley Co – but don't care. Bill worked and I had a restful day – I listened to War and Peace. No sore throat. Margaret came home.

Wednesday 25th March 1970

Bill and Mum went to town in the pm. I sat in the sitting room alone and for some strange reason felt wonderfully at peace. The sun was streaming through the window and everywhere was quiet as a grave. Later I went and bought Bill's Easter present – a big egg.

Thursday 26th March 1970

B. had a headache and looked very white. Family went to town. B. M. and I left alone all day. Typed out a number of letters for B. Sent off M's letter

Friday 27th March 1970 – Good Friday

Received notification of B's interview at Leatherhead. He is go on 6th April at 10.35. Started to write my book. I don't know if it is such a good idea as it make me rather depressed to recount all my past agonies.

See the Autobiography later in this book. I have tried to supplement what she wrote from my own memories and papers she left.

Saturday 28th March 1970

Spent most of the day in the garden. Lovely day.

Sunday 29th March 1970

Bill and I went out to Grafham Water in the afternoon. It was a long drive and I felt terribly sick by the time we got there. The scenery was well worth coming to look at though. The "water" is in fact a vast reservoir and today being a windy one – the sailing enthusiasts were out in full force – some even had their spinnakers out.

Bill and I walked around the edge of the lake had bit a of tea and then set off home. All the way there were huge signs "Thurleigh No!"

This refers to plans to build another London airport at the former Royal Aircraft Establishment at Thurleigh. Some things never change!

Monday 30th March 1970

Rather a tiring day. I went out for a walk in the morning and did the gardening in the pm. I raked the lawn and planted the peas. Felt horribly sick in the pm – could hardly eat. Played Monopoly (Monotony would be a better description!) Watched "Colditz" – awful. No sore throat but pains in bones and frightful pain in back.

Tuesday 31st March 1970

Bill didn't go into college but tried to work. We went out for a lovely walk in the evening. The air was warm and the birds whistled happily as the sun went down. We felt v happy. I listened to "War and Peace". It wasn't all that good this week. Schmidt – Hitler's interpreter was being interviewed.

Wednesday 1st April 1970

Had a luxurious bath. Bill went into College. Steak for lunch and supper. Poor Bill rode his bike down to the station so that he wouldn't have to wait for buses. In fact it turned out he couldn't ride on the bike with the heavy briefcase so had to walk. The paper that Mike and he submitted has been accepted and will probably be published in the next addition of Chem. Acta. Also Mike thought that the first chapter of his thesis was very good!

April 1970

Thursday 2nd April 1970

Felt lousy – light headed, ulcers and back ache! Shopped, lunch then Bill and I did some gardening. I went for a long walk by myself in the evening. Felt depressed. Bought Bill a bottle of beer.

Friday 3rd April 1970

Did shopping for weekend in morning – thought of a good ironical beginning for my biography. Had a rest in pm. In the evening we played a game of "Go" – suddenly the lights went out – a blackout! Bill and I decided to go out to the Plough. It was very exciting rushing along together through the dusk. We had a beer and then drove home. I felt hopelessly sick. No sore throat though.

Saturday 4th April 1970

We did some baking today. I made 9oz of pastry and with this Bill made an apple pie, a steak pie, and some tarts – unfortunately the latter burnt! I made some queen cakes which were very scrumptious.

Sunday 5th April 1970

Went for a long walk in the morning. The others went out for the morning so we were left alone. We had pasta for lunch. I did washing.

Monday 6th April 1970

I wrote up my biography in the am; lunch; shopping. Bill has gone to Leatherhead for an interview. I do hope that he gets on OK poor chap – what an ordeal. This morning the High School rang up and I have an interview next Thursday at 11 am. I am glad as it will take my mind off things. We received an invitation from Margaret Thorogood for next Saturday. Margaret says that she know him as he used to teach French at Pilgrim School. Actually after all my unhappiness over this affair she seems to be a nice girl.

Tuesday 7th April 1970

I decided to have a new dress for the interview and in the afternoon Margaret, a girl called Lucie and myself went into town to by the material. I settled on a dark blue blotchy design. No sore throat but felt tired. Washed my hair.

Wednesday 8th April 1970

Rested in the morning – had a lovely lunch then caught the 1.13 train to London. Hung around for hours before I was seen at the hospital. She says that the cervix is slightly soft. Advises me to have a pregnancy test. I had 10 minutes to catch the train and practically killed myself running for it. I felt very ill when I got home. Bill had supper ready.

Thursday 9th April 1970

Felt ill all day – stayed in bed.

Friday 10th April 1970

Felt ill stayed in bed. Went to see Margaret and John Thorogood in the pm. They were quite a "nice" couple and we had an enjoyable evening. The grapefruit made me feel sick though. Got back at 1am.

We went for a meal at their flat in the centre of Bedford.

Saturday 11th April 1970

Slept in – I cleaned the room. Planted potatoes. Bill went to town to buy some railway track but came back empty handed. Felt sick, sore throat (acid).

Sunday 12th April 1970

Slept in till 10 am. Had a lovely breakfast of porridge, bacon and eggs. Bill and the kids played "Risk" all morning. Had boiled egg and some soup for lunch relaxed in pm. Watched Hitchcock film "Stranger on a train" – very spooky! Couldn't sleep when we went to bed. Bill didn't look very well – he had a headache. Felt v. sick all day.

Monday 13th April 1970

Washing machine broke down. Bill phoned Adams about Coderg. Evidently they have been kept waiting by the other firm. I slept in. Bill phoned while I was still asleep – I jumped up to answer it. Had bath washed hair. Kids first day back at school – perfect peace. We planted the rest of the seedlings and the sweet corn.

Tuesday 14th April 1970

Feel very depressed. The interview that I was meant to have today has been postponed until Thursday. Sore throat and rather a dry throat. – feel sick. Bill has gone to college to give a lecture. I went into town in the afternoon. Bought dress material.

April 1970

Wednesday 15th April 1970

Spent all day making a dress. It is nearly finished.

Thursday 16th April 1970

Got up at 8.30 am. Breakfast. New dress. Just missed the 10 to 10 bus caught 10 past 10 ran all the way when I got to town. Headmistress is v. nice. Mr Brown is horrid, white with reddish hair — very weak face. When I told them that I had to go to UCH he looked straight at my tummy and said in a horrid crude way "Nothing else wrong with you I suppose". Ugh. I got the job mainly because no one else applied I think! On the way home I bought a lab coat and a pair of shoes. I felt very tired when I got back and went straight to bed after lunch.

Jenny had felt well enough to try and get a part-time job and hence this entry regarding an interview at Bedford School for Girls to teach biology. As later entries show it was too much for her.

Friday 17th April 1970

Colours suddenly mean something today probably because the sun is shining for a change. I noticed the red of the carpet as I walked upstairs and the yellow of the bedspread. I couldn't <u>bear</u> to go blind. I typed out a few things for Bill and did the shopping. I really feel that Bill would be far happier married to a wifely person and with a lot of kids around him. I really hope that when he marries again that he will be sensible and marry someone healthy and full of fun and forget these silly years he has spent with me. Last night watching the "Forsyte Saga" I couldn't help reflecting that on the whole I have been extremely lucky. If I had been born in any other time I wouldn't be alive, if I had caught acute L. I wouldn't be alive today; if I hadn't married I would be living at home. Oh there are so many things to be grateful for in life — I mustn't spend my time brooding. No sore throat but feel giddy.

Saturday 18th April 1970

Went for a walk in the evening. It was a lovely and peaceful world as I strolled along admiring the daffodils and the forsythia. I picked some flowers and identified them as round leaved speedwell (Veronica something).

Sunday 19th April 1970

Dashed around getting my notes written up — taking up my lab coat letting down my dress and making an apple pie. Phew — I felt exhausted.

Monday 20th April 1970

Felt giddy and silly. Went up to UCH. The horrid vampire couldn't get any blood and had to try from both arms. The other Dr was there – all smiles "your count is much better this week – only 30,000" Thank god. I was convinced that it was 18,000 last time and not 89,000. Mummy met me and we went to an Italian restaurant. I felt horribly sick. Mummy is so kind. She gave me £5. I was sorry to see her go.

Tuesday 21st April 1970

1st day at school. Felt dreadfully nervous but the girls were rather sweet. One awful child called Stephanie. My bones were aching horribly by the time I got home (pelvic bones). Bill fetched me, fed me and then tucked me up in bed!

Wednesday 22nd April 1970

Didn't go in until 11.40. Bill drove me down I didn't feel as nervous – but had a very boisterous class. Bill fetched me back. I felt better today.

Thursday 23rd April 1970

Work 11.40 – 1.00 Victoria phoned. She hopes to come up and see us. Poor thing, they think she is expecting twins.

Friday 24th April 1970

Vile day. I felt so sick and giddy. The classes were naughty – the staff horrid (I was told off about wearing boots "sets a bad example to the girls"). Fred was ½ hour late in picking me up. We went to see about a moped for me in the evening – but it was too heavy.

Saturday 25th April 1970

Feel terribly giddy and sore throat. Stayed in bed all morning.

Sunday 26th April 1970

A busy day. I made the lunch, ironed my dress and prepared notes for Monday. I felt absolutely ghastly in the morning – sick and sore throat and so on but felt a little better towards evening. Mummy phoned in the afternoon.

April 1970

Monday 27th April 1970

I did the bird with in the morning with the lower IVth. They have rather a nice collection of stuffed birds at the school. We did flight and the wing. Next lesson was seed. I went to see the head (Miss Walham) in the break to ask if I could be let off a few lessons. She was absolutely vile and wasn't a bit sympathetic. I burst into tears and ran out. Mr Brown was nicer and said they would try and arrange a shorter timetable for me. Felt <u>dreadful</u>!

Tuesday 28th April 1970

Staff meeting. Great secrecy. Girl has been taking LSD. Head seemed more worried about the reputation of the school than the girl. I waited hours for the bus after the morning's lessons and didn't get home until 1.45. Nearly 6 hours since breakfast and we didn't have a break because of the staff meeting. Have almost decided to chuck in the job as I really feel awful. What a decision, to stay at home and be bored or to go out and have a bit of excitement and feel lousy. I think that I'd rather be bored and alive, rather than feel ill all the time, thus digging my own grave.

The following table in the diary records the cell count (indicating the state of the disease).

Date	?	Cell count '000	pills per day	
23. 7. 69	S	60	3	
6. 8. 69	S	30	2	
20. 8. 69	S (holiday)	20	1	Spleen gone down
10. 9. 69	S	14		
27 10. 69	P	4		(sickness) preg and tooth out
24. 11. 69	O	12		
26. 1. 70	P	7		Off p for month
23. 2. 70	P	12 (?)		"
23. 3. 70	90	2 per day		
20. 4. 70	O & P	30		"
18. 5. 70	P	7		Off pills for a week!
27. 5. 70	P	13		"
8. 6. 70	P	13.5		Off pills for a month
13. 7. 70	P	48 or 84	2	(flu)
10. 8. 70	P	44	2	(holiday and tonsillitis)
14. 9. 70	7		1 pill every other day	(moved got Sheba)

Sail On, Silvergirl, Sail On By

Wednesday 29th April 1970

Didn't go in. Felt ill all day. Bill wrote to Adams. We were turned down by Coderg – but B. is hoping for a job with Adams.

I think that at this stage Adams was planning to be the agent himself for Coderg and I was still being considered as the sales and marketing person.

Thursday and Friday 30th and 1st of May 1970

I stayed in bed all day on both days. This ruddy sore throat and giddiness is driving me mad!

Saturday 2nd May 1970

Stayed in bed all day with sore throat then in the evening we went out with Margaret and John. I really quite liked Margaret this time. She had a pretty navy blue and white dress on and her hair was done up in a bun. We drove out to the Plough, which unfortunately was packed, and then back into town for a Chinese meal. I felt awful – sick and hot to be exact! Bill looked smashing this evening. He had his hair cut yesterday. We both felt ill all night and I think it must have been the food.

Sunday 3rd May 1970

Sore throat. Sick. Bill felt the same. It really was a glorious day. We had a breakfast of scrambled eggs in bed and then sat out in the garden in the afternoon. We watched a queen wasp feeding on pollen. She was very large and at first we suspected she was a hornet. Mummy phoned – poor Daph has to go into hospital and have her tonsils out. I wrote a letter of resignation to the High School. Bill is going up to Billingham tomorrow – packed case.

Monday 4th May 1970

Bill turned down by electricity board (Leatherhead). I think that he was expecting it. Had a night sweat. Slept till 10 am. Cleaned room. Sore throat (terrible). Bill phoned from Billingham this evening. Poor thing he sounded rather lonely. He says that it is very industrial with a heavy smell of NH_3 in the air. Went to bed early after watching "Up Pompeii" (*TV series with Frankie Howerd.*)

May 1970

Tuesday 5th May 1970

Finished cleaning room. Put flowers in. Sat out in the garden on the Lazy lou. Wrote to Mervyn, Helen and John and Mummy. Bill arrived at 6pm. He looked terribly tired but says that the interview was a success. ST (sore throat).

This is one of my memories of the summer — Jenny sitting on the blue canvas fold up seat. It had a foot and back rest. I kept it and then much later my second wife lent it (without my knowledge) to a friend for a daughter to use on a trip of some kind. It came back broken and probably the children had jumped on it or too many had tried to sit on the foot rest part. This quite upset me at the time because it was a tangible memory of what had been a nice summer for Jenny and her last.

Wednesday 6th May 1970

Lazed around in the sun. It really is hot. Bill is finishing the second chapter of his thesis. We planted some Hawkspur and cottage mixture seeds. Also some peas. ST, fever.

Thursday 7th May 1970

Did the shopping today. We rode up on our bikes. It was early in the morning and the blossom felt heavenly as we cycled up the hill. The magnolias are in blossom now and they really make a splendid sight! The tomatoes that we planted are doing well. I bought a special tomato feed for them today.

Friday 8th May 1970

Long day. It isn't quite as hot today though. The U's went out for a meeting this evening and we were left baby sitting. I typed a letter to Mummy. Victoria phoned and asked if she could come to stay for the weekend. I felt terrible about saying "yes" but she put me in such an awkward position.

Saturday 9th May 1970

Spent all morning shopping, making beds, borrowing sheets and blankets, preparing lunch. They rolled up at 2.10 + dog + baby. After lunch we sat in the garden. The kids and Bill played with the dog. Supper — sat around. The U's went to Valerie's party. (I gave her an epiphyllum and some maize seedlings). Went to bed. I really quite liked John this time and couldn't stand V. She really looked ill though and I suppose that I wouldn't be at my most charming in her condition. Her gory details of a friend were quite uncalled for though and I think done deliberately.

Sunday 10th May 1970

Breakfast of bacon and tomatoes and then down to the river. The weather was vile. They left after lunch and we both collapsed. Bill has been absolutely wonderful this weekend. I don't think that I could have managed without him! (ST sick)

Monday 11th May 1970

Bill went into college. He met Margaret and Sylvia on the train going in. I had a lazy morning and then rushed into town to get some money from the bank and to collect a new Nat Insurance card. Bill got home very late. We had chicken for supper (ST much better).

I have no recollection who Sylvia was. This creates the impression that I met lots of girls whilst commuting on the train!

Tues 12th May 1970

Felt quite well. We went to see "Every Home Should Have One" starring Marty Feldman. It was very funny. We took apples to eat in the interlude and found them more refreshing than the sickly orange juice and ice cream they usually serve.

Wednesday 13th May 1970

Cleaned the room again. Bill went off to London on the 10.20 train. He will spend the day in London and then catch the 5.40 train to Abingdon. It seemed lonely without him. We found a big spider in our room (no ST).

This time the interview was at the Esso Research centre near to Abingdon.

Thursday 14th May 1970

Spent day cleaning room and waiting for Bill to come home. I went up to the library in the afternoon and took out a book on how to keep fit by Sir Francis Chichester. If he can beat cancer so can I! I also took out Cecil Beaton's autobiography. Bill came home at 7.30. I was watering the flowers in the front garden and wondering when he would arrive when lo and behold there he was. He seemed very tired but filled with excitement somehow and quietly told me that he thought the day had been a success. He had no less than four interviews. Each with a different person. The countryside round there is beautiful.

May 1970

Friday 15th May 1970

Restless night. Lot of sweat. Sore throat very bad. Rested all day. Felt quite ill.

Saturday 16th May 1970

Bill and I did the shopping this afternoon while the others were at the Circus. It is a boiling day hot day. As we walked down Greenacres we both gasped at the beauty of the cherry tree in the Rose's garden. Sore throat going – what a relief. Was nearly sick this evening. Poor Bill, he crept over to my side of the bed in the middle of the night – I put my arms around him and comforted him. He is really very sad – such a kind person. His father was very nasty to him this afternoon and he was terribly upset. To be honest I think if I had the choice between being myself and being him – I would choose "me" – mine is really the easy way out – I shall be travelling in another world being rejoined with Granny and Sr Louis, whereas he will be left to battle on in this life. I hope that he finds a really super wife and has lots of kids because he really deserves to. We received a rejection from Titanium Products today (Billingham). Another blow for his self confidence. Received letter from Vic thanking us.

The reference to Sr Louis puzzled me. However amongst her papers is a letter as follows:

> Dear Jennifer
>
> I hope you had a nice journey. We are all missing you very much here. I am hoping to see you again. May Jesus bless and keep you a very good little girl.
>
> With lots of love
>
> From Sr Louis

On the other side is a further letter in a childish hand:

> Dear Jenny
>
> I hope you are having a good travelling. I am very sorry you have left this school. You are a very bad girl for leaving the book.
>
> With love from Alison Sherriff

These letters presumably followed her leaving Ingsdon School (see the autobiography later).

Sunday 17th May 1970

Bill made breakfast. I made lunch and rested for the major part of the day. Mummy rang at 2.30. I listened to the last episode of "War and Peace". I am afraid that it ended on "and they all lived happily ever after" note. Poor Bill has a sore throat and headache. I wrote a letter to the "Times" on their article concerning the sale of foetuses for research. It is my opinion Norman St John Stevens is only having another knock at the Abortion Act. (no ST feel sick) Bill prepared his notes for tomorrows lecture. He hopes that no one will turn up again and then he won't have to give any more lectures this term

Monday 18th May 1970

The day I have been dreading for so long. I felt sick at breakfast, cried all the way up on the train and made myself feel really ill. I couldn't look while I was having the blood count and went to the loo when the nurse was phoning for the results. And then, after all that – my wbc has gone down very well. In fact so much he is taking me off the pills for a week. I have to see him next week though. Mummy and I celebrated by going to the Italian restaurant and then sitting in the park. I had an awful sore throat and felt sick. Nerves I expect. Hilger and Watts phoned up Bill at college and asked him to go for an interview this Wednesday. Luckily no students turned up for his lectures so he won't have to go in anymore.

Tuesday 19th May 1970

Letter of rejection from Esso for Bill, poor thing it was really the last straw. I try not to make too much of it now though as I know that someone continually saying "Never mind" only makes things worse. I cleaned the room and then spend the rest of the day in bed. Bill went to do some spectra.

Wednesday 20th May 1970

I went to a coffee morning at Mrs Gany's. She has a beautiful house – very plush – with oak panelled walls and fitted carpets. I felt terribly depressed and ill though and am afraid that I was what one would term a "social failure". Mrs U was very overexcited when we got back and not having much of a chance to natter at the party went on and on! I could have screamed! I went to bed in the pm then had a miserable walk down to the shops. Bill is rather pleased with the Hilger and Watts interview and will let them know whether he wants the job next week. Unfortunately it would be a nine to five job and he would have to commute to Camden Town. Crash goes our dream of a cottage in the country! Went to see "Romeo and Juliet" (*Franco Zeffirelli version with Olivia Hussey*) in pm. It was very good. I had a sore throat again.

May 1970

Thursday 21st May 1970

Pottered around with letters. Watched Somerset Maugham story on TV. U's went out to The Plough.

Friday 22nd May 1970

Received a letter from the "Times" thanking me for mine. I felt very pleased. Bill received quite a few rejections. I keep quiet now. We went for a lovely long walk in the evening even though I felt sick and sore throaty in the afternoon. As we walked through the park Bill suddenly noticed swarms of tiny ducklings. The were adorable. All the blossom was out on the trees and the air was heavy with the scent. We watched part 20 of the "Forsyth Saga". I took a pill. Margaret returned.

Saturday 23rd May 1970

We watered the garden this morning. Unfortunately the hose didn't quite reach the end of the garden so I had to hold it while Bill filled the watering can and watered the beans that way. We planted out a few more sweet corn but I have now decided that it is better to just leave them outside in their box for a week before planting them. Margaret's boyfriend may be coming and she has spent all day washing her hair, cleaning her shoes and generally making herself look glamorous. She bought at beautiful hat and Indian scarf in Manchester. It is a lovely day – the sun is shining and the birds singing. I feel so well and happy (No ST).

Sunday 24th May 1970

We decided to go to Wrest Park. Bill made up a picnic basket and we set off at 11.30. The day was boiling. We stopped on the top of a hill near Cardington, unpacked the car and set off to find a pleasant spot to eat our lunch. We heard the cuckoo. Investigated tunnel after lunch. It gave me the creeps. As soon as one stepped into the shadow of the tunnel it was cold as a grave. Ugh. We found a dead shrew. On to Wrest Park. It was very hot and crowded. (ST)

Monday 25th May 1970

The others went out for a picnic with Auntie Edie and we were left behind with Margaret and Sam. We ate lunch in the garden and went for a cycle ride in the evening. I felt very tired with ST.

Tuesday 26th May 1970

Bill went into college and M and Sam went back to Crewe. Quiet day except that I spend most of the day washing up!

Wednesday 27th May 1970

Up to UCH. Terrible feeling of dread and fear. WBC only gone up to 13,000. Keeping off the pills for two week. Had lunch in Station Buffet. B. received at letter from Agric research.

Thursday 28th May 1970

Rested (as Prankerd instructed!) Mummy phoned up in pm. Daphne seriously thought to have glandular fever. I feel sorry for her but she does make a lot of fuss, it fills me with contempt really, but I suppose if I hadn't been so "brave" and silent I might not be where I am today. Watched "Olive" very good. (No ST)

Friday 29th May 1970

Oak Apple day. Stayed in bed all morning. Wrote to Mummy. Bill went to the bank. Planted out rest of the tomatoes. Had a very restful day (no ST). Andrew bought his cub uniform.

Saturday 30th May 1970

Bill went to the shops. The family went to the Fete. They started decorating the outside of the house. Poo! What a smell – I can't stand the smell of paint and burnt wood. Bill stood on the scales and broke them! Poor thing he was very upset (no ST)

Sunday 31st May 1970

How time is flying past. What a treat it is to be alive. I have never really noticed the passing of the seasons before, having always been too busy. This year, ironically perhaps my last, I am suddenly seeing everything as if for the 1st time. Bill and I spent ages watching a baby blackbird hopping after its mother on the lawn. It was a great fat thing wobbling along with its mouth open and every so often letting forth the most blood curdling yells! There are also baby sparrows on the lawn – so sweet! Valerie's snowball tree has burst into bloom and under our cherry tree a small clump of white star of Bethlehem flowers has opened.

June 1970

Monday 1st June 1970

What a glorious month. The sun is scorching and I lay out on the lazy lou in the afternoon and did my painting by numbers. Bill went into college and I prepared a stew with green peppers and made a rhubarb fool for pudding. He looked very tired and hot when he came in. (no ST)

Tuesday 2nd June 1970

Fine weather still scorching. I sat outside again and read in the garden. We played badminton in the evening – I almost beat Bill. It ended up 14/13. We could not stop laughing and became very hysterical!

Wednesday 3rd June 1970

Great excitement. Bill has been offered 2 interviews – one with the Chem. Soc. on their editorial staff and the other with Perkin – Elmer. He looked very pleased. Later in the morning a phone call came through asking him to go for an interview with Hilger and Watts. Mum bought some more lettuces for the garden and we put them in.

Perkin-Elmer was an American scientific instrument manufacturer and so a competitor of Hilger and Watts. The reference to the Chemical Society is interesting as my interest in having a writing career certainly goes back quite a long way. Some of the Ph. D. students had great difficulty in writing their theses and quite often after completing the experimental work (and then also having got a job) failed to obtain their degree because they found the writing up so difficult. Most of my career was in marketing jobs and production of technical literature was something I always enjoyed.

Thursday 4th June 1970

Grannies birthday. Bill set off for the interview with the Chem. Soc. people. He looked very smart. I felt lousy today with terrible diarrhoea and headache and very sore throat. I had to do the shopping though and I forced myself to cycle up to the shops. Received a lovely letter from Mummy and replied to it.

Friday 5th June 1970

Still felt awful, stayed in bed. Bill almost landed the job at Hilger and Watts. Yippee!

Saturday 6th June 1970

Dizzy – stayed in bed.

Sunday 7th June 1970

ST stayed in bed. Bill and I watched a baby sparrow in the pear tree. It must have flown from the roof and was too exhausted to fly any further. I had a strong temptation to stroke it but knew it would be cruel so didn't. The irises are standing in stiff rows above the flower beds and yesterday the first rose of the year opened. It smells glorious! The sunflower seeds that I planted last week have germinated and I am hoping that they will survive. We had the hose on last night as it hasn't rained for a month. They are taking the crayfish to the river today.

Monday 8th June 1970

Went up to UCH. It was a scorching day and I wore my red, purple and white trycel dress. I felt terribly light headed and dizzy all morning and was nearly in tears by the time I was ready to see Prankerd. Just as I lurched into the room Mummy arrived. She waited outside. P. looked a bit glum and I remember thinking "Oh God let me die tonight and get this nightmare over with". However he says that the wbc is still "Hunky Dory" (13,500) and I am to stay off the pills for another month.

There was a terrible storm this afternoon. Suddenly the sun went in and a fierce wind began to blow. Then thunder boomed and lightening flashed and the sky hurled a sheet of rain to the ground. The hailstones mixed with the rain were as big as peas and Martin collected some and put them in the fridge! I had a taxi from the station. (6/6d)

Tuesday 9th June 1970

Dad's birthday. Bill went into college. I wished D. a happy birthday and he seemed pleased. The U's went out in the evening. (ST giddy).

Wednesday 10th June 1970

Stayed in bed nearly all day. It was cold and I had the electric fire on. I still feel a bit giddy and have developed tonsillitis again.

Thursday 11th June 1970

Bill received information of the job with Rank (i.e. Hilger and Watts) today. Unfortunately it only gives 2 weeks holiday a year. He thinks he will take it though! He has got on further with Chapter 2 than he thought today so has gone into college. I have been trying to do the crossword little Aunt Dorothy gave me for my birthday but am rather slow. I spent a lot of time in bed today and listened to Anne Bronte's "A Tenant of Wildfell Hall" – very gripping.

Friday 12th June 1970

Went to town and bought a dress. Felt rotten.

Saturday 13th June 1970

Watered garden (sick and S T)

Sunday 14th June 1970

Felt awfully sick and bad S T.

Monday 15th June 1970

Cleaned room (ST). We now have two little tomatoes on our first tomato plant. The peas are in flower and so are the sweet peas. My Helianthous seedlings are 18" high – they certainly grow fast. Hot sunny day. Received letter and newspaper from M and birthday card from Rosy.

Tuesday 16th June 1970

Bill went into college. I had steak and greens for lunch and cleaned the rest of the room. I didn't feel too well (si and ST) and so stayed in bed in the afternoon.

Wednesday 17th June 1970

Rushed up to shops. Sweep came. Rested until 4. Made supper. Knock on window M arrives. Rained hard. Went to bed early.

Thursday 18th June 1970

My 24th birthday. What an overwhelming sense of relief! All through the past year I have been striving to live until this day and now it is here! And yet my year is over – Oh God what a time.

The sun streamed through the windows and I made breakfast for M and I after Bill had gone to college. I received a dress from M., a nighty from Daph and card from Auntie Jean and Victoria. M. and I were left to ourselves all morning and we sat in the garden with Andrew. It was a scorching day and after lunch we went down to the river. We sat under a shade and ate ice cream. Bill came home at 6 pm with the awful news that his bike had been pinched. M. left after supper. The best birthday I have had for a long while.

Friday 19th June 1970

Quiet day. Margaret came home in the evening. I had a bit of a row with Martin as I wanted to watch the "Forsyte Saga" and he didn't. Feel very well.

Saturday 20th June 1970

Bill went off to look at houses in Luton. He has seen two very nice ones on the outskirts. We all sat out in the garden in the evening and Margaret showed us the new fur coat she had bought for 10/- We all think it is cat. I do feel well these days, no sore throat at all

Sunday 21st June 1970

Set off for Luton at 9.00 to see the houses. It was a long drive and I felt a bit sick when we arrived. The house is on a 9 year old estate and my heart went in my boots when I saw it — not a green thing in sight. The people were very charming and said that we could buy the table and chairs in the kitchen. I do hope we get it. On the way home we stopped to eat our ice lollies near a church but had to move on as suddenly the bells started to chime and it was deafening!

Monday 22nd June 1970

Bill phoned about the house but damn oh damn it has gone. Evidently four other couples were after it as well as us. We have put in an offer for the other house in the street though — No 21. Funnily enough 21 is my lucky number. Bill doesn't feel too well and has a sore throat. I feel quite well although a bit sick.

Tuesday 23rd June 1970

Bill very ill but insists on going into work. I had a hectic day; shopped all morning, cleaned room and changed bed. I made us a Chinese meal which took hours to prepare as everything had to be chopped. Feel ghastly with a horrid throat and falling feeling. We both went to bed early and I got up and made us a break – twice! (as Bill was so thirsty). The others went on a car rally but didn't win.

Wednesday 24th June 1970

Bill's birthday! He is 24 today. Poor thing he does look ill. His parents gave him some strawberries and Florentines. (The best way to Bill's heart is through his stomach.) We had a quiet day and unfortunately I spent most of it in bed as I kept feeling I was going to be sick. My parents gave Bill a very nice Nylon shirt and pretty card. Received a letter from the solicitor about the mortgage and also one from my father + a rather pathetic little cutting from Bishop Ward. Oh the arrogance of the man – how can anyone suggest that the whole purpose of the Universe is to be salvation for man's soul. (What ever that may be). The weather is foul now – very cold and dull with a continuous drizzle.

Thursday 25th June 1970

Poor Bill very ill with flu. Drizzly day. Went to pub in country.

Friday 26th June 1970

Bill went in to college. He has taken in Chapter II to be typed today and hopes to get it back on Monday. I feel very hot and feverish today but forced myself to go up to the shops. I drew out £3 from my Post Office. Received letter from Daph. Bill went to see the solicitors about the house. I listened to a program on the "Duchess". She lived circa 1800 and told some very amusing stories in her letters. One concerned a lady in Waiting of hers who always fiddled with a gentleman's buttons as she spoke to him. One day she was talking to a very tall man and being short accidentally began to absentmindedly open his fly buttons!

Saturday 27th June 1970

Terrible night with hot dry aching throat, feverish all day. Stayed firmly in bed. Bill has started house hunting again as the Building Society will only give us a mortgage of £4,900 and the house we had chosen was £5250.

My grant to study Chemistry had been £300 per year with my parents expected to contribute about £30 of that. However because I seemed to cope quite well I didn't get the extra £30 after the first year. I also worked each Christmas for the Post Office and summer holidays in various jobs.

Whilst doing my Ph.D. I had a demonstratorship which meant that I had to supervise a number of laboratory sessions and was otherwise free to do my research work. The salary was £600 pa. The job at Hilger and Watts had a starting salary of £1200 pa. and clearly even though it was my first proper job we could afford to buy a small house within commuter distance of London. Jenny been working most of the time I was working on my Ph.D. and we had some savings to go towards the cost of the house and move.

Sunday 28th June 1970

Flu. Stayed in bed all day. Monday ditto. Awful earache. Bill a bit better but now he has a horrid cough.

Tuesday 30th June 1970

Wretched all day. Unfortunately kept being sick. Wednesday ditto.

Thursday 31st June 1970

Bit better terrible cough.

Friday 3rd July 1970

Cough, feel very sick and light headed. Received Which from Margaret and John. Bill went in collected his typed Chapter II.

Saturday 4th July 1970

Received receipt from Woolwich for the mortgage application. A tiny fledgling hid under the front doorstep all day. We put it into box in the study all night then let it go. I had a terrific night sweat.

Sunday 5th July 1970

Twins and Valerie's birthday. Horrid day spent worrying about the beastly bird. I made myself quite ill over it and can hear it chirping under the hedge. I am sure a cat will get it.

Monday 6th July 1970

Felt quite ill. A Mr Bowmer spent the evening with us. He couldn't speak English so this

July 1970

gave us the opportunity to try out our German on him. A pleasant evening and beautiful sunset.

Tuesday 7th July 1970

Bill and I borrowed the car and drove over to Luton to have a look at the house. I liked it very much, but do wish it had a bigger garden. We had a very happy drive back and stopped off at a pub for sandwiches. Unfortunately Bill was caught speeding by the police. (Sick ST)

Bill took the last part in to be typed and collected the two previous chapters. Quiet day. No reply about my wedding dress.

Wednesday 8th July 1970

Bill did shopping at Sainsbury's. I stayed in b. all day. I am putting on a lot of weight.

Friday 10th July 1970

(Si ST) Margaret at home since Tuesday. Stayed in bed all day. Phoned up about Basset but too dear. They wanted £25 per animal.

Saturday 11th July 1970

Forced myself to go up to the shops. Sent off the wedding present. Didn't feel too well but went for a lovely drive in the evening. We stopped to look round an old church. I love Bill very much. He is such fun to be with.

Sunday 12th July 1970

Washed my hair and spent hours making lunch. We had chicken paprika and lemon snow. I helped Bill make out his tables for his thesis. (si and bad ST)

Monday 13th July 1970

Up to UCH. Bill and I travelled up together. It was very hot in the carriage and we both fell asleep. On reaching Kings X we had a cup of tea in the buffet then parted. I made myself wretched with nerves before going to the clinic. The beastly girl took hours taking blood and Prankerd says that the count has gone up again. I'm on 2 pills per day. Oh hell; when the end draws near though I know that I shall cut my throat and not suffer too much; so I am not going to worry. The weather is wonderful, perhaps a bit too hot though. Bill and I had lunch in an Italian restaurant and got drunk!

Sail On, Silvergirl, Sail On By

Tuesday 14th July 1970

Had to do the shopping although I felt really ill.

Wednesday 15th July 1970

We received a letter from Pembroke but have decided to go to Dorset instead. Feel very shaky and had a blackout at lunchtime. We have booked up at a farm in Dorset for a week.

Thursday 16th July 1970

Bill has gone to college. I wore myself out with the packing and washing this morning. Had a rather truncated conversation with M.U. this morning as I began to say something and was immediately told in a weary voice that she had already heard the story once. What bad manners – when I think of the endless times I have heard descriptions of her sisters house, the farmhouse and her childhood and just listened, trying not to let her see that I am so bored I could scream. Well I know what to do next time! We booked a car today. Oh dear I really don't feel well enough to go away but suppose that I had better make the effort. I seem to be utterly obsessed with thoughts of suicide these days. I sit for hours working out the quickest and most painless way to kill myself and always end up in tears after these sessions, desperately wanting to live. Quite honestly though, what have I got to live for. I dread moving away from here as I know that life will fall into exactly the same pattern as it did at Crane's. I shall be alone all day, I shall be unhappy, I shall be in constant pain. That's the future. And then after that I shall go back into hospital and die. I am not frightened of Death itself, only the transitional state – dying.

Yesterday I sat and watched Bill as he read the newspaper and came to the conclusion that I don't <u>really</u> love him at all. In fact I rather despise him. I think that my wedding day was one of the most unhappy of my life. It seemed to slam the door for ever on Brendan and yet when I think honestly I didn't really love Brendan. I hated him and desired him. I wanted to utterly possess him. I don't feel any of these things with Bill. Poor Bill, he is such as kind person, but so unattractive. Oh why do I write such things, everyone is so kind to me. Yes that's why. If everyone didn't treat me with such exaggerated solicitude, feel so sorry for me perhaps I wouldn't feel such a freak.

Friday 17th July 1970

Have terrible tonsillitis. Probably why I felt so depressed yesterday. Bill went off at 7 and I slept in till 11.30. I had breakfast and then with set teeth forced myself to go up to the shops. I bought all of the things for the journey and then flopped back into bed. M.U. pointed out an article from someone in the Navy for me to read. What pleasant reading. He has leukaemia as well. The only difference is that he is nearly 60 and I am 24.

Saturday 18th July 1970 (added in: Sheba was born)

We got up at the crack of dawn and had a meagre breakfast and then hurried as fast as the car would carry us to Kennings. When we arrived a very dim witted mechanic told us that they didn't have a car for us. Bill was furious. Eventually a very efficient red head (complete in shocking pink uniform!) managed to iron out the situation and one hour later we drove off in a smart green Austin 1100. The journey was murder as we both felt exhausted before we started owing to the big wait at the garage. We stopped for innumerable cups of coffee and ate our picnic lunch on a windy hillside sitting in a field of mustard plants. The sun peeped out every so often and whenever it did a great hail of tiny flies rose from the Matracena matracariodes in which we were sitting! 7.5 hours later we arrived at Monks Wood farm. It was very "farmy" with chickens running under our feet (as we carefully threaded our way through the cowpats) and scraggy farm cats sunning themselves. Mrs Brooks is very young (20's) and has a baby son called Richard. The farmhouse itself has been extensively modernised. From the outside it looks "old worldy" with very old lichen covered stone and thatched roof; but inside it is like a luxury hotel with plush red stair carpet and gleaming white paint and walls. Our bedroom has a fitted carpet which, by the smell of it had only recently been laid. I thought at first that Bill had inadvertently stepped in something. We had a delicious super and then went for a walk in a field. So quiet!

Sunday 19th July 1970

She wants us back at lunch time so we can't do much today. We drove to West Bay this morning and had a look at the sea. My heart sank when I noticed a vast cliff adjoining the beach (of pebbles). As I had feared a certain person was very anxious to climb it, so we laboured half way up and I was forced to call a premature halt though, as my heart was beating so horribly I thought it would burst. We ate a rather vile lunch and then motored off to view a swannery (Abottsbury) in the pm. One paid 2/- and was then permitted to enter a tiny gate. Inside was a stream, alongside which the crocodile of sight seers eagerly tramped. The stream wound its way through the thicket of bamboo and spargavenin to suddenly emerge in a veritable maze of pens; each crammed with tiny cygnets. It was a site to remember! Having passed the cages we then came to the Swannery proper in large numbers of fully grown birds stalked casting a disdainful eye in the direction of the public at irregular intervals. Towards the rivers edge a small crowd had gathered and pushing our way through we discovered that a rather sleepy looking flamingo was the centre of attraction. Every so often it lowered its head under the water and began to jump from one leg to the other. This was stirring up the mud which it strained through its large beak.

Monday 20th July 1970

We set off to have a day by the sea today but it turned out to be rather a dismal affair. We drove to Charmouth and found the beach absolutely packed. Cliffs again so up we staggered + blankets and lunch and spent a really uncomfortable day perched high above the sea on a grassy wind swept eerie. We both felt really rotten this evening and went to bed early.

Tuesday 21st July 1970

After yesterdays nightmare we decided to hire deck chairs and lay on the crowded beach. It really goes against my principles to do this kind of thing – but when one isn't feeling too good – a few luxuries don't come amiss! A fierce wind was blowing as we struggled to get the deck chairs up and after a few minutes reclining a black cloud crept across the sun and large wet drops began to plummet earthwards. Luckily the cloud contented itself with that and blew happily onto another beach before it did much damage. It did clear the place of that horrible animal the holiday maker though we had the beach to ourselves for a little while. At 1.30 we broke for lunch which consisted of a Cornish pasty in a pub. We bought a shell and hat and then drove down to the sea where we went for a long walk on Nat Trust property. I felt very brave walking through a field of cows!

Wednesday 22nd July 1970

Seatown. We lay on the pebbles all morning, which were surprisingly very comfortable once one had worked a hollow out with ones bottom! Lunch in a pub overlooking the sea after climbing another cliff. Lay on sand again. Tea in a café at the top overlooking the sea. Bill has gone a terrible shade of ruddy brown (in the nicest possible sense). When we got home we discovered that a number of people had arrived. I barely survived the ordeal of supper with my plate in.

Thursday 23rd July 1970

Painful breakfast. We drove to West Bay and wandered among the crowds eating prawns and popcorn. I was very cold and we were going to go for a boat trip. Unfortunately the weather was too rough. Had lunch then went up to the ruins of an old fort. We were caught in a cloud – it was a weird feeling.

Friday 24th July 1970

Last day. Spent it on beach at Seatown. It rained all day. Took some photos on returning to the farm. Early night.

Saturday 25th July 1970

Journeyed home. Had a no. of coffee breaks and had a cooked meal at 12 am. Seemed very strange to be home. The others have gone on holiday.

Sunday 26th July 1970

Very quiet day. Bill made a spam casserole, unfortunately it was terrible salty as all the seasoning came out of the spam on cooking. (si ST)

Monday 27th July 1970

Listened to Ken Sykora (*A radio personality*). Did some shopping; the butcher gave a keen look at my ruddy brown face and with raised eyebrows queried "been on holiday"! Bill and Margaret at work.

Tuesday 28th July 1970

Bill at home, lovely day. The sun flower plant (Helianthus) over 5' tall now and I think the flower will be out soon. I have had this awful tonsillitis for 2 weeks now and doesn't look as if it is going to clear up. It makes me feel rather shaky.

Wednesday 29th July 1970

Bill at home. Very cold today.

Thursday 30th July 1970

Bill went in to give the last few bits of his thesis to be typed. Unfortunately the typist has run out of paper. This a terrible blow as we thought that the whole thing would be finished this week. Margaret had a day off today and stayed at home. We did washing in the morning. It is boiling today (80F) and neither of us felt particularly hungry. I made us boiled eggs for lunch. I have put an advert in the local shops concerning my wedding dress.

Friday 31st July 1970

Bill looked tired, I think that he is worried about his work. The insurance man came today and we have taken out a policy that I get the house if anything happens to Bill. What a relief. I often wondered in horror what I would do if I was suddenly left alone. I can't bear to think of anything happening to Bill. The solicitor also rang today and says that we will probably be able to move inside a fortnight. I don't feel a bit excited and if it wasn't for the thought of having a dog and being able to run a house the way I want to (for a change) I would positively dread the move.

When we lived in Tetherdown in Muswell Hill we were visited one day by a representative of the Order of Foresters. He said that someone had recommended us. He played a record which explained the function of his organisation – basically he tried to sell us life insurance. At around this time I did take out a with profits life insurance policy with Commercial Union on my life for £1000 with the intention of providing some funds to Jenny should I die. Of course we did not take out a joint life policy. The CU policy matured in 2007 worth £7000 plus bonuses but was handed over to my second wife as part of our divorce.

Saturday 1st August 1970

An exciting day as we spent most of it in the sales yard. I felt most peculiar going down in the bus, and when we started walking I felt as if the pavement was made of foam rubber and I couldn't control my legs properly. However as usual I survived. Bill bought me a super bike for £6 and he rode it home for me. We have ordered a bed! Bill made up our rocking chair. It's a read beauty with teak seat and black back, arms and rockers. The only trouble is that I feel a bit sick when I rock in it.

Sunday 2nd July 1970

Quiet day. I received an awful fright this morning as when I went to wake Margaret up I found that she wasn't there. She had stayed out all night. I was going to phone the police as I had visions of her having been kidnapped, however at 11am she breezed in. We didn't say anything. Watched a Terry Thomas film. Awful sore throat. Others phoned.

August 1970

Monday 3rd August 1970

They've all gone out today and left me on my own. I spent 2 hours trying to get through to the hospital this morning. Each time I rang it was engaged. Did a vast washing. Felt very sick with tummy ache and bloody sore throat.

Tuesday 4th August 1970

I feel very excited as it is our 3rd Wedding Anniversary tomorrow. We have decided to have a meal at home. I have decided that the only way to get over this tonsillitis is to stay firmly in bed and this is what I did all day. Unfortunately Margaret came home in great excitement this evening and decided to paint the upstairs loo which is unfortunately right next to our bedroom and I can't stand the smell of paint as it always make me retch so had to sit in the garden while she painted. It is a lovely evening and far above me I can see the swallows flitting about catching their supper.

Wednesday 5th August 1970

Our wedding Anniversary. We were very excited to find a little pile of letters on the door mat. Mummy and daddy sent us a very pretty card and also a cheque for £200. We were absolutely <u>staggered</u> and are still not sure whether to accept it or not. Daphy wrote a nice letter and we also received one from Rosy. We had a quiet day with a delicious supper of scampi, raspberries and champagne. All this was too much for my tum and I paid for it dearly. (Si D)

Thursday 6th August 1970

Woke up with tonsils like golf balls and frightful nausea. Stayed in bed all day. We received the contract and covenant from the Solicitor today together with a covering letter. Evidently some of the household articles which the Molloy's have "so generously" given us are on Hire Purchase. They seemed such nice people as well. I forgot to mention that Nasturtium, Golden Rod and Phlox are all out now. The ghodetia has been in bloom for nearly 3 months. It is quite incredible.

Friday 7th August 1970

Yesterday was the 25th Anniversary of his shame. The year I was conceived – I wonder – I wonder. A lonely day on the whole. I spend most of the morning reading up about dogs and in the afternoon I started on the hard crosswords. Well I've learnt two new words today (gelid = icy and tenet = dogma.) My throat is agony still and I have a roaring temperature. I have started to think about the nightmare trip to UCH on Monday. What will be the verdict this time, 2 years or 2 months. O balls, they don't really know as they had given me up as a gonna last year anyway. Don't know how much longer I can hold out though.

Saturday 8th August 1970

The others will be back this evening. We received a letter telling us that we will probably move in on the 21st August from the solicitor. Also received the photos – what a <u>sight</u> I look and I used to be so pretty. Now that Bill has finished his thesis I can see that the storm will break and he will be hell to live with for the next few weeks. It is always the same. I suppose that he has to vent his spleen on someone though. It is raining today. "The very heavens do weep". (*When heaven doth weep, doth not the earth o'erflow? – Titus Andronicus, this seems the most likely reference*) It was nice to see the family again and hear cheerful voices. I noticed yesterday that the stretch marks have gone from my hips. They have taken a year to fade.

Sunday 9th August 1970

Quiet day

Monday 10th August 1970

Train strike so had to get up at 6.45 (7.15 actually). After a hurried breakfast I went round to Valerie's at 7.45 and caught the train at 8.48. How ridiculous it is to have to leave the house an hour earlier than I need just so that I can get a train. These buses. Horrid nerves. It was pouring with rain in town. I heard the nurse say 2.20 then 40 (14), 400. The latter must have been the wbc which means that the count has hardly moved in the last month. I went into a state of shock on hearing this – the cold hand turning my innards to water feeling. He says that the pills are turning my skin black.

Tuesday 11th August 1970

Phoned up M. to tell her not to dispute Gt. Grandpas will.

Wednesday 12th August 1970

M. phoned this evening to say that Daph had passed her English with the same grade (D) but had only got an 'O' level pass in History. Poor thing, I feel terribly sorry for her. I am very doubtful about her getting into Wolverhampton as the legal minimum standard for degree entrance in this country is 2 A's.

August 1970

Thursday 13th August 1970

Spent all morning in town and have bought a Hoover, bed for the spare room and Bills shirts. Also spade, fork and shears. Am exhausted! (ST)

Friday 14th August 1970

Did the shopping on my new bike. It is rather heavy going up hill on it but lovely coming down. Bill went into college and had a booze up and sandwich with the "boys" in the afternoon. He said that they had got through 84 pints of beer and 1 bottle of whiskey and 12 cans of lager. The Hoover arrived at 5pm. It's a real beauty and we couldn't wait to try it out. I had a horrid headache all day.

Saturday 15th August 1970

Sent off the Hoover insurance. Bill bought the washing machine and liquidiser and a hair dryer. We felt for some inexplicable reason, rather quite guilty at spending so much money on ourselves at once. We have pinched and scraped for so long though that we deserve to treat ourselves to something. It really was very kind of Mummy and Daddy to give us £200, without it we just couldn't have managed.

Bill also spent many hours at the sales yard today and has bought a really super desk for his study. It was an army desk and has a green leather top and filing draw (£5). Bill also bought a chest of drawers for £1 – it has woodworm.

Sunday 16th August 1970

Felt aggressively well last night. I could have pushed a house down. Got up late today though and felt very light headed. Bill has bought nearly everything down from the loft and has stacked it in the study. There was a tremendous storm last night and we came down to find the sunflower flat on the ground. It only needed another day to fully open. I could scream as we have watched it growing for months and just as we are about to see the flower the damn plant falls over.

Monday 17th August 1970

Bill's first day at work. I had everything for him and put the bacon in the grill etc so that all he had to do was to jump into his clothes and switch on a plug. He caught the 7.10 train by the skin of his teeth. Today he went to the training place and worked with a bloke from Vienna who is on a course here. When he has finished he will return to the continent to represent the firm. Bill enquired about removal expenses and was told that he can make a claim for half the cost. Let's hope that it is accepted. The liquidiser and hair dryer arrived and we put them together and we had a few trial runs. I painted the £1 chest of drawers white. (G no ST).

Tuesday 18th August 1970

Second day at work for Bill. He didn't spring out of bed with as much alacrity as yesterday I must say, but he didn't get to sleep until 11! It has been a strange day weather wise – with great gusts of wind and heavy showers and then suddenly peace, tranquillity and sunshine. It is amazing how the birds sing after rain! I went for a walk in the garden at dusk and looked at the bees tucked up for night in the golden rod.

Wednesday 19th August 1970

Pouring with rain this morning so Mum drove Bill down to the station. She looked ghastly later on in the morning and stayed in bed for the rest of the day. Dr Moody called in the evening. He thinks it is the change of life. Martin and Andrew were very good today and did the washing up twice.

Thursday 20th August 1970

Mum much better today. I phoned the solicitor and he says that the completion date is definitely the 21st tomorrow. On hearing this I hurriedly phoned for a van, had the telephone maintained etc. In the pm Mum and I went down to Lime St to look for a table – after trailing around for hours we eventually found just what we wanted in the old junk shop. We also bought 3 chairs. Two to go with the table and one for Bill's desk. Bill and I went down to collect them in the evening. (no st)

Friday 21st August 1970

Have hired a van for Sunday. This morning I phoned up about a puppy; the woman works for the RSPCA and evidently has hundreds of unwanted pups. I think that it would be better to move in first – settle down and then get one. Everything happening at once would be a bit too much. Bill did the shopping at Sainsbury's. Mum and I packed all our clothes and changed the sheets. Wow I felt awful. (St and cough)

Saturday 22nd August 1970

Mum and Bill have gone over to the new house today to give it a good clean. Mr Molloy will hand over the keys to Bill. We are all packed up now and raring to go. I wish I didn't seem so tired. The van came this evening and we spent hours piling all our junk into it.

August 1970

We have decided to do two trips. Lovely peaceful evening. I have given the U's our set of Dickens.

Sunday 23rd August 1970

Bill went off at 8.30 with Dad in the van. They unpacked the 1st load in Luton and then Dad came back for me. After much discussion it was then decided that I should go in the car with Mum and Andrew and Martin should go in the van. I was a slow journey and Mum has to drive carefully and not get excited. I felt very strange to be stepping over the portals of <u>our own house</u>. We had a picnic lunch in the kitchen and then unpacked most of the stuff. We had to sleep on the floor as the beds have not come yet.

Monday 24th August 1970

1st day in our new house. Had a terrible night – hardly slept a wink. Very lovely cold day. Felt terribly sick and S. T. Bill cycled down to the station. Wrote to M.

Tuesday 25th August 1970

Washing machine in. Rather a lonely day haven't spoken to a soul yet.

Wednesday 26th August 1970

Mummy came up for the day – it was lovely to see her. I felt rather proud of the place as it does look tremendously plush when compared to 12 Amity.

Thursday 27th August 1970

Yesterday phoned up about dog.

M. came. She left early as she had to do the shopping. Policeman + wife + 5 puppies arrived at 4 pm. Evidently they had been driving around for an hour or so and eventually had to swallow pride and phone me for directions. I raced out to Halleford road and directed them here. The puppies were a motley crew of mongrels and I didn't like any of them over much. However, after much debate decided on the baby of the brood. The others had feet like dinner plates and would have grown into <u>monsters</u>. We have called her <u>Sheba</u>. The beds came!

Saturday 29th August 1970

Terrible night as Sheba spent most of it crying. She is minute – white and black saddle, black head with white and brown stripes and navy blue eyes.

Sail On, Silvergirl, Sail On By

Sunday 30th August 1970

Bill went off to get the paper as they don't deliver around here. Lazy day. ST all week.

Monday 31st August 1970 – Bank Holiday

Bill has had a lovely weekend. The weather wasn't very marvellous today so we sat over the fire for most of the time. Sheba is a little scamp but very sweet. We gave her a bath today with her sponge. Wt 4 lb. Height the length of my hand.

Tuesday 1st September 1970

M. Phoned to say that Daddy had flu and she had to stay at home and look after him. I was annoyed as I had rushed around getting everything ready for her arrival. Also it felt rather lonely without her. The man came about the washing machine in the afternoon and was beastly. He said that by phoning up the manager and saying that I wasn't pleased with his work I had nearly lost him his job. I apologised, but pointed out that it was hardly worth paying out £100 for a washing machine if it didn't work. Strangely I don't think that he took the point.

Wednesday 2nd September 1970

M. rolled up at 11.45. We had a quiet day. I think that she liked Sheba. M. went up to bed when Bill came home and he remarked that you could hardly know that she was here. No ST – feel very well. Went to Family planning.

Thursday 3rd September 1970

M. got up early and made our breakfast which was very kind of her. We went for a walk in the country this afternoon. Ten minutes walk from the front door are open fields. I really is wonderful. I am glad now that we didn't get our dream " cottage in the country" as here we have the best of both worlds – i.e. shops and country side on our doorstep.

Friday 4th September 1970

Went shopping. Found a new kind of food for Sheba " gravy". Brenda came over for coffee. M. told her I have leukaemia. I was relieved. Went to see Dr McGill today.

September 1970

Saturday 5th September 1970

We spent most of today preparing for Sue and Ben's visit tomorrow. This means that I can devote all my energy to entertaining when they come and not have to keep rushing out to peel potatoes. Watched our "new" TV.

Ben was also working at the Northern Poly finishing off his Ph. D. and I travelled with him on the train from Bedford. Sue was his wife. They lived in Luton.

Sunday 6th September 1970

Sue and Ben were supposed to arrive at 4 however at 5.10 they still hadn't turned up and we were beginning to wonder if had made a mistake. 5.15 they arrive. Tea – chat; then tour of the house followed by supper. Very pleasant evening although I thought that they overstayed. No ST – feel well.

Monday 7th September 1970

M. arrived at 11.45. Poor thing she had just missed the early train by 2 minutes. Sheba was pleased to see her and thought aha someone to bully. She's growing at a tremendous rate. Went to Dr McGill in pm (cervical infection).

Tuesday 8th September 1970

Daph. phoned up this evening to say that she had heard from the hostel at Wolverhampton who wanted to know if she had a place. She sounded very unhappy.

Wednesday 9th September 1970

Quiet day. M. insisted on doing a lot of cleaning though and thoroughly wore herself out. Bill seems quite happy at work. Fielder is away again and Bill is in charge. The viva should be coming up soon.

Thursday 10th September 1970

M. went at 12.50 and had the rest of the day to myself. I did some shopping and then read the book I borrowed from the travelling library on Tuesday. U's came in the evening. Mum looked <u>ghastly</u>. We gave them a snack and then drove them to the airport. I was very disappointed at the shabbiness of the terminus. We didn't get to bed until 1 am.

This refers to Luton Airport which was about 20 minutes away.

Sail On, Silvergirl, Sail On By

Friday 11th September 1970

Miserable day on my own. Sheba was very sweet though. M. phoned to say that Daph has been turned down by Wolverhampton. Bill has gone to Oxford. He said that he would be home by 5pm and I had supper ready then. It is now 10.45 pm and he still isn't back. I feel very worried.

I think this occurred when I had been to a sales conference for Hilger and Watts which was actually in a hotel in Banbury. After my talk I had stayed on for the dinner and then given the time and having drunk wine I arranged to have a room there for the night even though I had no night clothes.

Saturday 12th September 1970

Went to Luton to do the shopping. Pouring cats and dogs but felt very well and strong. We parked in the multi-storey car park. Went to see Sue in the record library.

Sunday 13th September 1970

Packed for Bill, we went for a drive in the country this morning. It was lovely. I adore the Autumn. Bill went off at 1pm and once more I was left totally alone. M. turned up at 5 o'clock. She brought at mop and some raspberry canes with her.

Monday 14th September 1970

Up to UCH. My God what a hellish journey it was. The bus ride seemed to take hours. The train was late and then poor M. had to stand all the way as nobody would give up their seat. Well, the wbc has thank God, gone right down again this week and I am on levod now. Had a lunch of sausages and bacon – delicious. Bill phoned – he has a lovely voice on the phone. The cervical smear showed inflammation and I have to stay on the Triple Sulpha cream.

Tuesday 15th September 1970

We decided to wash all the curtains today. It took hours but they look much better. I had thought that the sitting room curtains were grey and red but having washed them I now realize that they are white and red! Watched TV in the evening.

Wednesday 16th September 1970

Tea in bed again this morning – it is just like being in a luxury hotel. We had a quiet day and I rested all afternoon as I am going out in the evening.

September 1970

Thursday 17th September 1970

Ghastly time last night. The assembled "young wives" were all pretty ancient. I sidled into the hall and sat next to the only person under 50 in the place. She was a rather drippy bespectacled individual and I felt bored stiff listening to tales of nappy rash and teething problems. The Crimplene "party" turned out to be a grand selling riot. I didn't buy anything and left early. Bill came home at 6.30, I felt rather depressed as he told me of the lovely things he had been doing – theatre visits, parties till all hours, climbing over college walls to get back into hall. If I let myself I could feel a bit bitter but poor thing it is not his fault I have to stay cooped up in bed all day. It seems such a little time ago I was young and gay though.

The event was an international conference on Raman Spectroscopy in Oxford. I attended for Hilger and Watts and stayed in Oxford for the duration of the conference. I remember that it included a theatre trip to London where we saw "Fiddler on the roof" with Topol. I did feel guilty at leaving Jenny behind but have no recollection of the incident regarding climbing over a wall to get back into college.

Friday 18th September 1970

M. came up this morning. She arrived at 10.30 but it seemed like late afternoon as we had been up since 6 welcoming the U's back to Merry England. They had a lovely time and brought us back some cheese and a little picture made of pressed flowers. M. and I went a walk to the airport in the pm. It was exciting watching the enormous jets shake off their fetters and with a roar leap into the sky. We smelt aromatic poplars but couldn't trace them. Sheba is becoming very obstreperous she bit M. yesterday and tried to savage my foot this afternoon. I was collecting the washing and became rooted to the spot. Each time I tried to take a step towards the house she pounced on my foot and bit it as hard as she could. Eventually thinking to myself that the best form of defence is attack I lashed out at her and ran, with all my might, inside.

Saturday 19th September 1970

The U's come over this afternoon. Martin brought Sheba a squeaky toy which she is scared stiff of. We gave them tea after which they left. Margaret liked the house but declared that she would redecorate it if it were hers. I think that she will come down to earth with a bang one of these days.

Sunday 20th September 1970

Went to see Ben and Sue. Their daughter Nicky had a terrible cough and cold. The meal was ghastly although we didn't dare to leave any. Went for a lovely drive in the country this morning and picked blackbugs.

Monday 21st September 1970

Quiet day. M. phoned in the morning which was kind of her. Bill went to Leicester today and got back at 3. Sheba to the vet where she had the 1st of her triple injections. She was very good and hardly cried at all. The vet, Herr Schwartz, was small enormously powerful man. There was a statue of a little boy spending a penny in the waiting room and as we left I noticed that someone has " switched him on".

Tuesday 22nd September 1970

Sheba very quiet but seems well. I went to the library in the pm and also bought Christmas presents for the twins. Bill had a hard day as Fielder was away again.

Mike Fielder was in charge of the section in which I worked at Hilger and Watts – basically I did marketing support for the UK sales force and overseas agents. All quotations had to go through the section and we produced leaflets and sales support materials.

Wednesday 23rd September 1970

Been feeling very well these last few weeks – no sore throat or sickness. Went to the Dr this evening. He was very kind and said that he had been reading up my hospital notes which were very promising. I was going to ask him for some sleeping tablets but changed my mind as he says that I will live for another year or so yet. I felt deliriously happy as I walked home. The sun was warm and the earth smelt good.

Thursday 24th September 1970

Did the weekend shopping. I finished painting the cabinet. Mrs U. phoned up to say that they are having their celebration (25th wedding anniversary) on the 10th of October.

Friday 25th September 1970

Daph. Phoned up at lunch time to christen their new phone. She said that there had been a disaster in the copper mines and we worried in case Mick had been involved. M. phoned at 5 pm and as usual on the phone was very brusque and sounded unhappy. I sometimes wish that she wouldn't phone.

Daphne's twin Rosemary had married a man she met at a party or some event in Oxford. They had married very quickly because he had a job in Zimbabwe lined up and had to take it up immediately on completing his degree!

September – October 1970

Saturday 26th September 1970

Terribly hard day. Changed the path and dug a new flowerbed, put up cabinet and clock.

Sunday 27th September 1970

Felt very ill with back ache. Went to pot in morning and had a restful day.

Monday 28th September 1970

Spent the entire day doing the housewifely things I am expected to do – i.e. cleaning, cooking shopping and making love. All that women are good for I suppose!

Tuesday 29th September 1970

Received photos of Sheba from M. Considering the camera they were taken with they haven't come out at all badly. I felt ghastly all day and had to stay in bed. I kept vomiting everything I ate and had a soaring temperature and headache. Funnily enough when I feel as ill as that suicide is the last thing on my mind, all I want to do is to get better.

Wednesday 30th September 1970

Nausea still but ST gone. Sheba had me in tears again as she kept attacking my legs. When one is feeling ill anything unpleasant seems the end of the world. I really think that if she still has this trait at 6 months she will have to go. My legs are a mass of scars and bruises. Bill says that I should correct her but as soon as I try to catch her, kick her or scream at her she has gone – to her it is a lovely game.

Slunk out to the Woman's Guild. So boring listening to tales of peoples kids all the time. After listening to one Mum extolling the charms of her multifarious offspring for over twenty minutes I became filled with a mad urge to scream at her "I have 12 of my own at home, you know, and one has 2 heads". Luckily I checked myself in time and when she did get around to asking me in condescending tones if I "had any" - I mumbled "no, my husband and I haven't had time" which I suppose sounded equally as bad!

Thursday 1st October 1970

Busy day shopping and cleaning. I cleaned the windows and washed down the Venetian blinds. Bill was his usual taciturn self and apart from the few uninterpretable grunts he could have been to the moon today if what he tells me is anything to go by.

Oh <u>God</u>, I wish I had someone intelligent, witty and scintillating to talk to. What fun B and I used to have – how we used to laugh and row together. How we used to <u>live</u>.

It has been very windy today and a pane has broken in the garage window.

Friday 2nd October 1970

Usual domesticated day shopping etc. Mrs U. and Mummy both phoned this evening. Mrs U. much better but still not A1. M. Feeling sick all the time – I suppose that is the change of life.

Saturday 3rd October 1970

Up at 8.15. Bill made breakfast and then started on the garden. He has dug up the grass under three of the flag stones and relayed the two in front of the kitchen window. Poor thing looked very white and shaky afterwards. He thinks he is going to be in for a cold.

Sunday 4th October 1970

Bill ill. We went for a walk in the morning and B carried Sheba. He thinks that she is too big to carry to the vet. We will probably order a mini-cab. Felt sick and ST

Monday 5th October 1970

How this year is flying, I had a semi nightmare last night (semi in the sense that I wasn't really asleep) all about the future how I will have my spleen out eventually and be in mortal agony and then probably die of suffocation – how I wish I hadn't read that medical book. I felt really ill today but forced myself clean the floors as they are such as mess. Bill came home soaking wet and swears that will be his last cycle ride. He went to bed straight after supper and was asleep at 9.15.

Tuesday 6th October 1970

Sun is shining – it's a lovely day. I was up at 7.30 but crawled back to bed as it is <u>so</u> cold. Slept till 10.30 and woke with a violent headache. Sheba was very naughty and bit my leg again. She doesn't look very well and keeps coughing.

Wednesday 7th October 1970

A lovely sunny day and when I got up I quickly ate breakfast and then did a washing. It had only been out there an hour when the rain came down. Luckily these nylon/cotton shirts dry very quickly. Received letter from Daph. and replied. Si. ST. Giddy. Bill looks much better.

8th October Thursday 1970

Sheba 12lb. Not feeling too good today – probably going down with flu. Went out to shops and did weekend shopping. Met Eavy in the butchers, she looks quite ill.

9th October Friday 1970

Did some silly exercises today. I always get one of these keep fit moods when I am going in for something. Temperature.

Saturday 10th October 1970

Feel sick and hot and bothered. Bill phoned up the U's to say that I wouldn't be coming. I'm really disappointed as I have been looking forward to seeing the garden and so on for weeks. When Bill had gone I decided I had better clean the sitting room for M. and D. coming tomorrow. I couldn't finish as I thought I would have a heart attack. Bill got home at 10.30 – appeared with turkey and 12lb of tomatoes.

Sunday 11th October 1970

Terrible nausea and headache. M. and D. arrived at 4 and I put on a desperate act to appear normal and gay. Bill made a curry for supper. The very smell of it made me retch.

Monday 12th October 1970

Violently sick. Didn't go to Hospital

Tuesday 13th October 1970

Violently sick all day – want to die.

Wednesday 14th October 1970

Same

Thursday 15th October 1970

Same

Friday 16th October 1970

Kept being sick so decided to call the Dr. He was a very nice man when he eventually arrived but almost had me in tears as he said it would be better if I went to see him in his surgery. He has given me some medicine and thinks it is gastric flu.

Saturday 17th October 1970

Bill got the Kaomycin. It is foul – so bitter and I have to drink a half a tea cup full at a time. Wasn't sick today but terrible nausea. Didn't go out with Ben and Sue.

Sunday 18th October 1970

Ditto. Had an egg for lunch – it took about half an hour to get it down. Mum phoned.

Monday 19th October 1970

Violently sick all morning. Fish for lunch – ugh. Bill is meeting Mike to discuss the Viva on Wednesday.

End

So the diary ends on an inconclusive note with Jenny having been ill for a period. At this time the UK was being converted from town gas to natural gas and there was a cold period when there was no heating in the house whilst the changeover of our street took place.

I don't remember the date but one evening after returning from work and finding Jenny not feeling well I suggested that we go for a little walk to get some fresh air. We only walked a little way and went back. Her legs swelled up horribly and I called the doctor. She was taken to Luton and Dunstable Hospital that night. They felt that they could do nothing for her and she was transferred to University College Hospital. She was placed on a ward in the red brick building which is currently (2007) undergoing conversion/ renovation. I think we expected her to be out quite quickly as she was in her first stay. I think it was in November that this all happened.

Her stay became more protracted as the treatments failed to bring the condition under control. She was in an open ward with a number of other women and of course it was a depressing place. I visited every day and sometimes she seemed quite well again and we would go for a walk down the corridors and take a look outside. She told me of one distressing incident of a woman on her ward keeping everybody awake one night screaming and jumping up and down on her bed. The woman died the following morning.

I continued with my job and would call in the evening on my way to the station. I tended to eat a meal at a restaurant after the visit and then catch the train home and go to bed. We thought that she might get to come home for Christmas but it came and went.

Victoria remembers visiting her during this period and at one point she recalls Jenny saying that she regretted all the time that had gone into studying to get into University.

The diaries make clear that this had been a constant preoccupation for her. On the other hand I only worried when the exams were imminent.

Sometime in January/February it was recommended that Jenny have her spleen removed. The operation took place at the beginning of February and she never really recovered, having a drain in her tummy till the end. Looking back now I wonder if it was worthwhile because she suffered dreadfully from having the operation. People tend to ask more questions of doctors nowadays – what impact were they expecting the operation to have on her life expectancy anyway? Her notes earlier indicated that she expected the worst from this intervention.

We tried to look forward and I brought in a selection of holiday brochures after Christmas for us to look at regarding a holiday in the coming summer. She tried to perk up at that time and I think the nurses made a special effort with her. However she continued to decline. I had taken to going back to Bedford at the weekends and had gone to the cinema that Sunday with Martin to see "Lawrence of Arabia". Whilst the film was on, a slide appeared on the screen asking Mr Unsworth to go the foyer. I phoned home and was told that the hospital had phoned and suggested that I go down immediately because Jenny had taken a turn for the worse. I drove down and parked the car in Grafton Way directly next to the hospital on a double yellow line. Jenny was in a side room unconscious with an oxygen mask on. She never regained consciousness. I stayed with her (except for overnight when they arranged for me to have a bed in the modern part of the hospital). She progressively got worse with a film on her teeth and lips and fungus on her ears and her breathing deteriorated. Her mother spent part of the time with me and I was able to go out to eat. Eventually on the 25th February at 5 o'clock she died. She took a deep breath and then just stopped breathing. I said goodbye and called the nurse and felt quite literally a weight lift from my shoulders. I called home and my mother came down by train to take me home. My car was still outside on the yellow line, untouched and without a parking ticket, and I drove us back to Bedford.

When I came to go through the trunk from the loft where I found the diaries there was a set of about ten notelets that Jenny had written after that Christmas to thank people for presents, but that had never been sent.

A death like this makes one suddenly realise how many assumptions we make at a young age about life without realising – having children, even grandchildren, careers, holidays, just time with one person for the rest of your life. It is a shock to find how many of these things are fragile, and to realise that other things are going to happen in life that you can do absolutely nothing about. My mother surprised me sometime much later (early 1990s) by stating that she had never worried about me because I had always bounced back! All I can say is well maybe – but I am sure life will hold further shocks.

Autobiography of Jennifer Holly Stephens
(fragment)

I was 6; the wind was screeching and plucking around the tall gaunt house; the trees were moaning. It was late in the afternoon. The place a boarding school in the middle of the fast dwindling "English countryside". A tomb for youth.

Not knowing how to pass the time – it being a Sunday afternoon. The idle hour between one dreary church service and the next, we sat gloomily around the fire. A nun all eyes and ears sat quietly knitting in the corner "Please sister", bob, downcast eyes, "may I tell the girls about their names?" A rustle of starched habit , a flipping through the pages of "<u>the</u> book". "Yes, Marie Anne, but no noise. Bob, downcast eyes, flurry of excitement. Slowly we worked down the list of names:

A B C D E F G H I J

    Anne —

    Ellen -

    Fanny

Jenny – suppressed giggles from the reader "a white ghost". What a shattering revelation! It seems the ghost has haunted me through the years that followed.

Some modern scientists hold that cancer may have deep psychological cause. Perhaps it has, I don't know; what I do know is that at the age of 17 my white ghost came home to roost – I contracted leukaemia. This, then, is an autobiography, a story of that child, a short one perhaps but no one but immediate friends and family will read it. It does however give a strange sense of reassurance to recount these years, perhaps, and I am writing for the purely selfish reason of being able to recount my life. I think in many ways that it has been an unusual one but then perhaps all the more reason for writing it.

When I was a child – yes still a child at the age of ten – I was presented with a diary. It was an insignificant little affair with over romantic blue tits for ever flirting on the front and inside thick coarse paper with the smell of the printers ink still fresh on them. But to me that diary opened up a whole new world – the world of self expression – of secrets entrusted to an ever patient uncomplaining friend.

I can still feel the thick brown paper in which it was wrapped. As I turned its delicate pages a whole new world began to reveal itself to me. At last, here was a friend, my secrets once whispered onto these pages would be safe. I was a lonely child.

Now at the age of 23, with little life left to me, I feel the urge to browse through these idyllic days once more, to see things through the eyes of a child. To, as it were, relive my short but eventful early existence. It may amuse you to wander down these avenues with me. And providence permitting to arrive.

Early influences

Before embarking on this exercise, I suppose that it would be easier for the reader if I sketched in a few of the leading characters.

My mother – in her youth a beautiful woman, small, petite with perpetually tanned rosy face and shock of flaming red hair. We are of French – ish extraction and this is revealed in both colouring and temperament. Mother was a nurse – like all that breed bursting with medical facts and figures; consequently the small part of my life spent with her was a constant treadmill of hand washing, tooth brushing and fear of obesity and the "curse" – a mysterious complaint with which I was all too soon to become familiar.

My father – again – I paint the picture in youth – both M and F were to change considerably, both in temperament as well as in looks, in later life. In youth – a dark gypsy like individual – second cousin to my mother – and if we are to believe him forced into marriage against his will. At school he is said to have led a very wretched existence and through the rest of his life was intent on revenging himself on those unfortunate to come under his influence – viz. his wife and children.

Towards the end he showed distinct paranoid tendencies.

The other characters of importance at this juncture are my mother's parents. These contented individuals had spent the greater part of their married life in India; consequently my early childhood was flavoured with grand tales of the east and many of our toys were priceless pieces of jewellery, trays and other ornaments presented during Grandpa's service by grateful maharajas or members of the "club".

Grandpa was a small man, but tremendously strong. If pressed he would, with ear shattering shouts and exaggerated waving of arms, bend a poker in two before your very eyes. Unfortunately he could never bend it back again and these awe inspiring displays always had to done in great secrecy when Granny, the tyrant of the house was safely out of the way.

Grandpa had laughing grey eyes, and he was bald except for a fringe of hairs around the very perimeter of his head and a dangerously thin lock which crept over the top of the top of the shining expanse of bald pate. This pathetic lock was his pride and joy and he would spend long hours in front of the bathroom mirror carefully greasing it and then with infinite tenderness and the air of an artist at work lay it at the most flattering angle possible on his bald head. Unfortunately, Grandpa was fat and Grandpa loved his food – hot spicy food which poor Granny spent hours preparing.

Grandpa also had a tendency towards constipation and in order to relieve this distressing complaint used to crunch his way through platefuls of "All-Bran".

But enough of him, he will come in later.

Granny, a tall well-built woman with the carriage of a Sgt. Major – but with the kindest brown eyes and warmest heart I have ever known. The terror of the kids in the neighbourhood and eternal champion of her grandchildren.

My Great Grandpa was and is a small dapper figure. He wears grey tweeds and smells constantly of stale tobacco smoke. His head is a tiny mop of white hair, slim, tidy features, pointed nose, moustache and piercing lustful eyes. His hands are small with long thin fingers and he has the habit of clutching the index finger of his left hand in the palm of his right hand and slowly rubbing it back and forth as he talks. Despite his 100 years he holds himself well and never uses a stick.

Thus the stage is set.

Early life

As is not unusual I remember virtually nothing of my early life – the nappies, bottles, humiliation of having my bottom powdered, and so on are mercifully buried in my subconscious. It must have been a dog's life – on the whole, though, I think that dogs have a rather splendid life these days. In America at least, where vast amounts are spent on seeing that our canine friend has every luxury possible.

At the nappy bashing stage mother, father and I were happily ensconced in a cellar in Newcastle. Father was studying at the University – or rather, trying to study – because the combined effects of my contented belching and screaming and the hysterical yapping of the landlady's dog drove him to the extremes of tying the dog to the pram, ensconcing me in the vehicle and pushing us out into the snow. I was an enormously fat child so belched and gurgled just as happily. Unfortunately the dog died.

The winter of 1946/47 was notoriously hard and I remember stories of my father borrowing my pram to go and fetch coal for the fire from the gas works in Bury.

The next stage in my life is one of me awakening. I actually began to live, or rather remember – the memories come flooding back.

Africa

The heroine now makes her way to the black continent of Africa. Father, having failed his degree and been sent down in disgrace, was bent on finding his fortune in distant lands. The mini migration was composed of Father, Mother and a round fat, red ugly bundle who had now reached the venerable age of 18 months.

Father's parents were glad to see him go. "Make something of his life at last – about time humphed the old fellow". The "other granny" – a name which became run together so that it sounded like "thothergranny" – an immensely tall, skeletal woman who always talked of "gels" instead of girls, saw us "orf" with a sigh of relief. At least we were out of the way!

The passage by ship to the British Cameroons took three weeks. The other day I unearthed some photos of Mother on the boat – it was a banana boat – and she looked young and beautiful with not a care in the world. A few years ago she told me that the captain of the boat was mad and after the voyage had committed suicide. He looks such a pleasant person in the photos.

The actual arrival in Africa was a terrifying experience for Mother. She had to take a launch down river to the settlement where father was already living and was then taken by primitive railway – a single carriage running on one track through the bush. The horsepower was provided by two men who pushed and puffed us up the slopes and jumped on and shrieked with delight as we sped down the inclines. The natives crowded along the lines as we made our undignified way inland. Pot bellied children covered in flies and hideous sores, insolent women who glared balefully. Rustling though the undergrowth mother swears that she saw men with knives. All very alarming.

The house we occupied was on stilts so that snakes couldn't get in. We had a few servants and I had an ayah who was called Prudence but whom I called Prunes. I remember absolutely nothing about her. In fact most of my memories of this idyllic stage are very sparse.

Autobiography of Jennifer Holly Stephens

At the end of the garden were the servants' quarters and I can remember toddling down to spend endless happy hours amongst this band of giggling individuals with their rolling eyes, flashing teeth and yellow hands. My favourite was a man called Joseph. Old Joseph could really spin a tale. Scarcely daring to breathe I remember hearing tales of elephants and monkeys, snakes and men. It was Joseph who showed me my first snake – an enormous fellow hidden amongst the bananas which the servants used to hang up to ripen in a little shed. It twined and curved amongst the hands of glistening fruit, before it quietly dropped to the ground and flowed into a crack in the wall. It was he who told me that the monkeys used leaves as umbrellas when the rains came down. And so it came about that my innocent games with this gentle man came to an untimely end. For one day, busy as usual watching the monkeys, I happened to remark to the unfortunate man that he looked "like a black monkey" – a childish compliment. After all I was very fond of monkeys! Suddenly out of a corner of the veranda rose a demonic face – Father had been listening. Nursing a frightful hatred for the Africans, which he relieved with constant whippings and torture, he felt it time to put these pleasant tête-à-têtes to an end. So it was that with awful fury he descended on us, carried me back to the house and as a punishment for this outrageous deed forbade any sweet thing to enter my foul mouth for an indefinite period of time. On his majesty's pleasure, so to speak! The dismal result of this unhappy series of events was that I became skeletally thin and was eventually carried half dead to the nearby hospital with acidosis.

Africa, that part anyway, is a dismal place for adult and child alike. Our attempts to keep chickens were foiled by the perpetual night raids by Africans and day raids by hawks. I can remember to this day the terrible screeches as some unfortunate bird was carried off into the sky until it was a fluttering dot on the horizon.

The insects were another hazard to both man and beast. Once out walking mother and I inadvertently wandered into a column of army ants. These voracious feeders have been known to eat a horse down to the bare bones in a matter of hours. The Africans quite rightly have a hysterical terror of the creatures. The columns often reach a village at night whilst all the occupants are sleeping, silently munch their way through the inhabitants and leave behind a village of ghosts and skeletons the next morning. The natives hold that the ants quietly swarm all over you and then as the result of some mysterious signal all bite at once. Luckily our encounter with them had happier results. We leapt – or rather Mother leapt and I was hurtled – into a bath of cold water, so drowning the little devils before they did much harm.

As well as suffering from acidosis in Africa, I also picked up filaria, an insidious blood parasite which leaves the victim rather weak and unhealthy looking but not desperately ill. Consequently I carried my unwelcome guests around with me (the parasite is a microscopic worm) for over eleven years before anyone took the trouble of carrying out a blood test on me.

Home to England – Granny and Grandpa and all that was friendly and kind. I was sick all the way home and was thoroughly despised by all my travelling companions – or so I am told.

Row upon row of grey terraced houses. Grey slate roofs, grey walls, grey curtains, grey people. Even the pavements are made of this apologetic colour. London, London what a fluttering heart quickening of the breath the name brings to those who love the city. The smell of soot, cabbages and people. A collection of villages, a hive of activity.

It was to a small suburb of this vast metropolis that father was transported amongst, we must hasten to add the inevitable screeches of Mother, shoshings and snappings of Father, rattle of porters and so forth. Quite a cavalcade. Dunmore Road is situated in the quieter suburbs of Wimbledon. It is not too far from the common and yet near enough to the local shops. One makes an abrupt turning off the main road, passes some tennis courts, makes another sharp turn to the left and there one is. A drowsy little street on terraced houses with cottage gardens and a row or cherry trees on either pavement.

Progressing down the road one eventually comes to a well-kept house with the number 7 bold and clear in the stained glass of the front door. The brown gate swings open rather creakily sending shudders down the leaning fence to which it is attached. The front door opens, a plump woman runs down the path snatches up the little bundle from Cyny's arms and bursts into tears of happiness. Home. It has been a long time.

A new baby is expected

Auntie Jean, Mother's sister, has yet again managed to get herself into what is coarsely termed "The family way". The father is a Scotsman and rumour has it that the dirty deed was done in one of the graves he is employed to dig! Very ghoulish. Grandpa has put his foot down this time though and as well as a baby there will be a wedding. The blushing bride dressed rather surprisingly, or not so surprisingly, in black, is still simpering in the photo on the drawing room mantle piece. The groom looking incredibly young, with a naked boyish, face gazing in a suitable doting fashion on his beloved. Proud parents stand either side.

Soon after a "premature" baby arrived – all eight pounds of it. The mother, bride of a few weeks ago, has been incarcerated in the back bedroom and there is a constant hurrying to and from the delivery room. Bowls of steaming water, kettles, towels, cotton wool, all find their way through the ominous black door. Tortured shrieks are heard endlessly. Morning passes into afternoon, afternoon into evening and then unexpectedly at last peace. The stillness is unbelievable. A girl, a girl. Everyone is so happy.

After much argument and heart searching the new arrival is to be called Victoria. A good patriotic name and a diplomatic one as well, the father of the new now mother rejoices under the name of Victor.

The days after the birth are ones of pent up excitement. I am allowed in to see the small person who to my childish mind looks rather like a fat little pig dressed up in baby's clothes. Five minutes of gazing and then I'm hurried off. "Now, Jennifer, you must be a good girl, I know you can if you try," Granny coos at me. All I can think of are the terrible screams of the delivery room and the fear that no one will love me anymore. I determine to be as obstinate as possible and toddle upstairs trailing a red pencil along the wallpaper.

Two weeks later, a large lady appears at the house, posts in the dining room behind a cup of tea and declares that as she has come all the way from Scotland expressly to see her delicate (premature) grandchild she will not leave without doing so. This lady was in the nature of what was once referred to as a "character". Her voice was loud, her figure large and her ageing face covered with such a profusion of rouge, mascara, lipstick and powder that one had the impression that she had stuck it on in the morning and took it off at night and fixed it on a hat stand, which she probably did. While Granny was desperately plying her with tea and making hasty stage winks at Grandpa, Mummy and Auntie Jean were flying around upstairs wrapping the child in vast quantities of swaddling clothes. By the time that Mrs Shanks came upstairs only its tiny face could be seen. Having prodded to make sure it was alive, that strange lady then sailed down the stairs and disappeared through the front door never to be seen again. She had done her duty!

Now began a time of bliss, with tea parties on the lawn, endless sunny days. There was an old pushchair at the end of the garden and on arrival of the baby this had been salvaged from the nettles, given a new coat of paint and a squirt of oil thus to be reinstated as a form of transport. It was to my mind the most uncomfortable contraption with springs sticking into one from every direction; however; if one looks back through the family album there are numerous photos of an enormous baby draped over a tiny figure, both crammed into this crazy contraption. In one of these pictures two hands are springing from the baby's neck and a nose has sprouted from the top of its head!

Although we are a large family with numerous Uncles, Aunts, Cousins, Great Aunts and such like scattered around the globe, we have an appalling tendency to confuse the issue still further by bestowing the title of "Aunt" or "Uncle" onto any good friend of the family. It never ceased to amaze me as a child that the local butcher and baker were my Uncles, the woman next door my Aunt and so forth. It was a happy secure world!

Of the numerous relatives, however, we did have one of whom we were told to be especially proud – our Great Grandpa. This venerable old gentleman would stroll over to house occasionally to spend the day with Granny his favourite daughter.

I hated his coming as at the time he seemed rather a cantankerous old person who came over expressly to steal the day from us all. As we invariably spent the day playing in the street with our balls and skipping ropes we kids were the first to see the little figure hurrying around the corner at the end of the road. I would rush in screaming the news and by the time the old gentleman reached the front door, Grandpa would be safely locked in the sitting room "having a snooze". Granny would have rushed upstairs to put on a clean dress and do her hair and would have been sat down on chairs to spend the rest of the day listening to boring "memories". How we dreaded his coming! At last the awful moment would arrive, there would be a knock at the door and through the cracks the whiff of stale cigar smoke sent us into fits of giggling and Granny would then fling open the door as if she expected a tradesman, give an affected gasp, throw up her hands, beam and with mock hysteria scream "Father, Father how wonderful to see you". Then a great hugging and kissing would start as we watched sniggering through the dining room keyhole. Eventually after his coat had been hung in the hall, his shoes carefully wiped and his neat little bag placed in a safe place the great moment would arrive and he would stumble into the dining room where we were waiting. Then some more kissing; we always had to kiss him on the mouth I remember and as one went close he would curl his thin fingers around your arm in a tight little pinch and look in a burning hungry way into your eyes. It made me feel weak.

In retrospect, I wish now that I had listened more attentively to his "memories". He must have had a fascinating life. His family came from East Anglia but most of his early life was spent in India. He then became a doctor in the Indian Army. I remember some of his stories, however the most grisly ones. One of his duties in the Army was to attend at the executions of errant soldiers, and if we are to believe him they were very plentiful. He took a delight in telling the gory details of these executions and of how afterwards he had to go round making sure that the prisoners were well and truly dead.

Great Grandpa was an incurable flirt. His first daughter was illegitimate, which was in those days a terrible stigma and was always shown on your birth certificate. He did, however, marry the mother but after that his life was a long chain of extramarital affairs. Luckily for the poor woman, it doesn't seem to have worried his wife unduly and she in turn went for a short time to live with another man and had a child by him. After having had a large number of children, though, her uterus became misplaced and she became very fat and ugly. She could of course have had an operation but, as Dr Great Grandpa knew, in this condition she could not have any more babies. He therefore didn't let her have the op and as consequence of this she died very young. Granny used to have a portrait of her as a young woman and the mantelpiece and I used to sit and stare at it when Great Grandpa came and wish that she was still alive.

Well, Great Grandpa, it seems, will go on for ever; at the time of writing (1969) he is still alive, although well over a hundred years old. Who was it who said that the wicked prosper?

School

Some time in my young life, I had been deeply impressed by the fact that it was my fate to be sent away to school and I remember begging my mother to promise me that she would never subject me to that fate. Hence it was with a slight feeling of foreboding that I hear that we were going into the country for a holiday one sunny, summer day in my fifth year.

We duly arrived at a large country house but, horror of horrors, the place was filled with schoolgirls, and gliding here and there were ladies dressed in funny clothes. They had long black dresses on and great sails on their heads. I clutched at my mother in terror; hatred at her treachery mingled with a paralysing knowledge that I was to be abandoned amongst these strangers possessed me and desperate feeling that I would go through anything as long as she didn't leave me. We were greeted by a person in "sails" and taken through a long corridor smelling of polish and filled with peeping and giggling girls down into a basement. I tore at mother's dress in a frenzy and first whispered then said very loudly "Let's go home now". Once "in" the basement the door was closed and another figure loomed over me, took my hand and pulled me away. She asked me my name, but I was too terrified to speak. Then she asked me my age smiling kindly at me, I began to reply when I suddenly heard the door opening, whisked round and there was Mother quickly disappearing through the door while the nun stood with arms outstretched to stop me following. My blood raced. I screamed and tried to run past but strong arms held me back. I kicked and bit, shrieking and crying to no avail. Meanwhile a group of girls had come into the playroom, for this was what the basement was. Seeing them I shrank against the row of lockers next to the door through which Mother had disappeared, and crouched there immobile with fear. I wondered if they would start to stick needles in me and make me sick like the other ladies had done in hospital. One girl came forward, picked me up, sat me on her knee and dried my eyes. Then, she stood me on the floor in front of her and said that she knew my name was Jenny, and hers began with a J – and was Janet she was going to look after me! I glared at her and mumbled that I didn't want to be "looked after – only to go home thank you". Whereupon she laughed and said could I count up to five, that being my age. 5? Five! **I** could count up to 1000 (!) which I promptly proceeded to do.

So opened the happiest years of my childhood. How I would have jumped with joy had I known what happiness I was to find in that convent nestled in the bosom of the Devonshire countryside. What friends I was to make and what love I was to bear those frightening ladies in sails!

Ingsdon Convent School

This old school, run by Roman Catholic nuns, is located between Torquay and Newton Abbot. A bus from the school used to collect those girls who lived in London and came down on the train from Paddington at the beginning of the term. We would all pile in and the old vehicle would grind and wheeze its way through the country lanes until, suddenly, it came to the main road. Here it would pause then shoot across into a driveway on the opposite side of the road, where, partly hidden by the bushes which lined the entrance to the drive, stood a large blue sign with "Ingsdon Convent School for Girls" painted proudly in while letters upon it. My stomach always gave a little lurch as I read the sign. A queer feeling – a mixture of fear, excitement and relief.

The old bus then wound its way up the long hill, past the keepers lodge, past the old chestnut tree up a very steep slope, round a corner and then "crunch", the gravel of the school grounds was under the tyres. We ground through the gates and then rumbled to a halt outside the school itself. All through the long drive girls had been chattering gaily, telling of this and that that had happened to them during the holidays, yelling down the bus to someone they'd only just noticed or hastily shoving sweets down the lining of their clothes (including the pockets of their knickers) so that the nuns would not find them, but as soon as the bus stopped it was all silent. A nun glided into the bus, quietly told us that we were to go straight to our dormitories and sit on our beds until our trunks were unpacked and quietly glided out again. The term had begun!

Ingsdon itself was once a monastery, or so a rumour has it. It is a large white building set in superb grounds of rolling lawns, beech trees, sunken gardens, grottoes and on the slope in front of the main entrance a dazzling white statue of St Michel killing the dragon.

To this day I cannot smell clover, or hear the cuckoo without thinking with painful nostalgia of that wonderful, wonderful childhood I spent in the heart of the Devon country side. The life of a convent is one of serenity of the unhurried and dignified passage of time. When she enters the convent the nun is by the very act pledging herself to a life of hard work and devotion. This convent had nuns from all over the world inside its cool white walls. Black cheerful faces from Africa and India, plump rosy faces from County Cork and the sallow beautiful faces of the French with their liquid almond eyes. The common language spoken by all the nuns was French. In every corridor one would come across stately figures gabbling quietly. The child is quick to pick up a phrase, though, and we soon learnt to count and give "secret messages" in this intriguing language.

Autobiography of Jennifer Holly Stephens

All the work of the convent was done by the nuns themselves. Each nun was trained in her task and seemed quite content with her lot. The farm and vegetable gardens of the school were run by jolly fat nuns. They would always be singing and tinkling with laughter when we passed them. The very heavy work was carried out by a husky Devon farmer – who, strangely, was called Mr Gardener. We were all rather frightened of this rough coarse man. He never smiled and seemed to epitomise what we were told was the "big bad world" we were being prepared for and would one day have to venture into.

Our clothes and sheets were washed and ironed in a grim dungeon-like cellar where nuns in grey habits toiled ceaselessly. Their faces always seemed as grey as their garments and I used to feel tremendous pity for them and often wondered what they had done to deserve such a horrible life.

The elite of the society were the cleaning and teaching nuns. The cleaning nuns never seemed to be exerting themselves unduly. One would come across them idly polishing a holy statue or rubbing a duster down the banisters of the main staircase. No doubt they did work hard when we were at our lessons though, as the dormitories and corridors were always sparkling clean and smelt incessantly of the dark orange polish which was used all over the school!

Unfortunately the biography ends here. It is mentioned in the diary with the implication that a lot had happened in her short life – a lot of it unpleasant – and that she doubted whether she should write it.

She was born June 18th 1946 at Redruth Women's Hospital in Cornwall to Donald Robert Stephens, with a rank of Captain in Hodsons Horse and Cynthia Grace Stephens formerly Stephens. The birth was registered by Cynthia on the 17th July and their residence is given as Tor Bracken, West Penwith, Treen near Penzance.

When I met Jenny at college her home was in Wimbledon just near to Raynes Park railway station – Shakespeare Villas in Amity grove. It was a Victorian house and the lounge fireplace still had an original surround with tiles illustrating scenes from the Bard's plays. At that time Jenny's father worked as a postman. I don't think her mother worked then although she had been trained as a nurse. I believe that she and Donald had met in Edinburgh when she was undergoing training during the war at the Royal Infirmary, Edinburgh. Donald had at some time found religion and Jenny clearly believed that he was a complete hypocrite. He insisted that before he would agree to our marriage I become confirmed, which I did at Crouch End C of E church. So I suppose that I was also a hypocrite for agreeing to do this, not being a believer then or since.

The Stephens's life plans had obviously gone seriously awry – he had failed at university and failed as a plantation manager in Africa (and Jenny implied that he had assaulted workers whilst there). However there was worse to come.

They decided to buy a farm near to Mevagissy in Cornwall. We stayed in Mevagissy on one of our holidays before she became ill and she managed to find where the farm was from her childhood memories. Unfortunately it turned out that the farm had been sold to a number of people and the Stephenses lost their savings from working in Africa and had no farm and no money.

The family returned to London and lived with the grandparents in Dunmore Road (also close to Raynes Park Station) in one room (Auntie Jean and Victoria were also living there at the time). They were to play a very major part in Jenny's life as she grew up. Perhaps they looked after her whilst her parents found their feet again. Unfortunately they died just before I met Jenny, quite quickly one after the other, and a major part of her security was lost. Jenny was certainly living at 7 Dunmore Rd in May 1961 when she and Victoria got involved in a scheme to graze a donkey on Wimbledon Common. Eventually the request was rejected!

It is not known at what time Jenny left Ingsdon School but in 1962 she got her O-levels in English Language, English Literature, Geography, Household Cookery, General Science, and Human Biology whilst at Joseph Hood Girls' School, Raynes Park. At Ewell Technical College she obtained an A-level in English Literature (1963), O-levels in Biology and Chemistry (1963), O-levels in Botany and Physics (1964), and A-levels in Chemistry and Zoology. It is believed that she transferred to Ewell Technical College in order to do A-levels for University entrance but also had to obtain more science O-levels. I suppose that her A-level English Literature and her drama studies explains the frequent quotations from poetry and literature. The diaries also contain a couple of references to a possible acting career, but we never discussed this and I don't know at what point she decided not to pursue that further.

Jenny's grandfather's funeral was on the 8th January 1963.

There is an invoice in the file from Messrs Hilder, Thompson and Dunn:

49, St James St
London SW1

Mrs Stephens
7 Dunmore Rd
Wimbledon
SW 20

To Professional Charges with reference to the case brought by yourself and on behalf of your daughter against your husband in the Wimbledon Magistrates Court for assault – taking instructions and your statement of evidence correspondence with you and the Police attending conducting case and later attending court again when your husband was find £2 on each of the three summonses and was bound over in the sum of £20 to be of good behaviour for 12 months and £5. 5. 0. were awarded to you. £12. 12. 0

8th February 1961.

Jenny is referring to this when she decides to have one of her front teeth out and use a plate because of the constant pain she was getting from the tooth that he damaged.

According to a Notice of Sale the house in Dunmore Road was auctioned by Order of the Public Trustee re Mrs E (Emily) Stephens deceased on 27th May 1964 at 6pm.

Jenny appeared in a number of plays with the Pioneers Dramatic Society and playbills are shown in the photos and documents section. The following letter is in her file and refers to the time she was looking for accommodation near to the Northern Polytechnic:

9th October 1965

West Wimbledon

TO WHOM IT MAY CONCERN

Miss Jennifer Stephens has asked me for a reference in connection with her application to join a YWCA hostel.

I am a barrister at law in the Government Legal Service, and in my spare time a lay reader for the Church of England, in the course of which I came to know Miss Stephens some five years ago. Further, both she and I were engaged in an amateur dramatic group, Miss Stephens frequently playing a leading role, and myself as producer.

I believe that I am therefore in a position to appreciate Miss Stephens' character, and I can say without hesitation that I have found her always to be a most loyal, hardworking and helpful member of the cast, getting on well with her colleagues, and fitting in easily with the smooth running of the group.

These qualities I am sure would enable her to associate well with the members of a hostel.

Maurice A. Rao

List of Characters and Family Backgrounds

The main protagonists:

Jennifer Holly Unsworth née Stephens – "Jenny"

William David Unsworth – "Bill"

The Stephenses:

Cynthia, mother died 2007

Donald, father – "Dick"

Rosemary, sister – "Rosy"

Daphne, sister – "Daphy"

Victoria, cousin

Jean, aunt – "Auntie Jean"

The Stephenses had Scottish, English and German roots and a long time connection with British India. Jenny's great grandmother on her mother's side had been a doctor in India in the early 20th century (as had her great grandfather mentioned in the diaries and biography) and her grandfather Victor had been an engineer with a senior position in the Indian Railways. He and his wife (Emily) had retired to the UK and bought the house in Dunmore Road after the partition of India in 1947. They would have preferred to have stayed in India for the rest of their lives but were persuaded it would be unwise to do so. Donald and Cynthia were in fact second cousins. Jenny's great grandfather Francis Watkin died shortly before her. Cynthia and Jean also had a brother called John who was apparently quite swarthy and had spent his adult life in Italy because of the discrimination his dark skin caused him in England.

The Unsworths:

Fred, father died 2007

Marian, Mother died 2003

Margaret, sister

Martin, brother

Andrew, brother

The Unsworths originated in the North of England – Bury to be exact. Fred was an engineer and at the time of the diaries worked in Bedford as a manager at Swiss owned George Fischer, a firm producing castings which had originally been the Bedford Britannia Iron and Steel Works. His father (Albert) had also been an engineer and millwright and had been part of a very large family. Fred's grandfather had been a ship's butcher and had travelled the world before having a butcher's shop in Bury. Fred's mother had been killed after a dreadful accident involving falling into an open fire whilst already incapacitated. Marian came from Dukinfield in Cheshire and her father had been a mill worker.

Consequences

Events as described in this book do have consequences and it is interesting to try and elucidate what they were. Of course we can't always say what caused what and maybe some of the things that happened would have happened anyway. Cynthia, who had been abused by Donald for many years, left him shortly after Jenny's death, although they didn't divorce. Daphne never married and in her later life looked after Cynthia when she became ill. Victoria was strongly affected by the death and says that it had a major impact on her life.

Fred and Marian stayed in Bedford, he in the same job for many more years and then perhaps when it was getting too late in a career sense they moved to Yorkshire where he first worked for an engineering company in Keighley and then in Kirkbymoorside. However the latter job lasted only a few years and they moved back to Bedford where he never worked again – the spirit knocked out of him after the sortie to Yorkshire, or perhaps it was the tragedies in his life? Martin was greatly upset by Jenny's death and had not been aware of the severity of her illness which probably exacerbated things –

List of Characters and Family Backgrounds

he was only 14 at the time. When Fred and Marian moved to Yorkshire he opted to stay in Bedford and got married and started a family.

As to myself – I suppose I put it behind me quite quickly and I certainly did my grieving very intensively for a short period. I remember sobbing my way through the funeral at Merton Crematorium and then afterwards at her parents' house. I could simply not talk about it to my mother or father although, much later, just before they died, I thought perhaps I could have, but of course by then it was too late – and would it have mattered anyway?

I remember reading C.S. Lewis's Narnia books (which I think had been bought for Andrew) when in Bedford shortly after Jenny died, and coming to the last section where they are all reunited in "Sunlit Uplands". As I finished I looked up and my mother was intensively looking at me as if she knew exactly what was going through my mind. So we did communicate without speaking.

Photos and Playbills

A very young Jenny and her mother!

Jenny with twin sisters and grandmother.

Stephens family shot – from right – 4th Donald, 6th Cynthia, 7th Jenny, 9th Daphne, 8th Rosie.

A moody teenager.

Sail On, Silvergirl, Sail On By

Seen at the prizegiving at Ewell Technical College last week are Derek Marles, Jennifer Shepherd, Tony Fifield, Rosalind Fortune and Elizabeth Blacklaws.

Shot from the local paper.

Jenny goes to University.

In the garden at 22 Tetherdown

With Sheba in Luton

Holiday in Norfolk

Wedding Photo.

Bill and Jenny

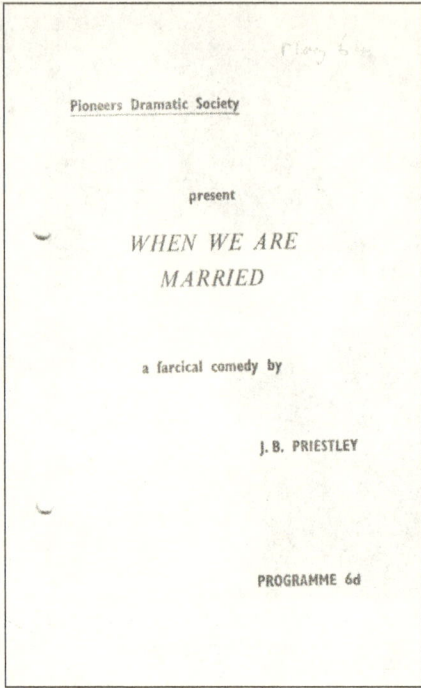

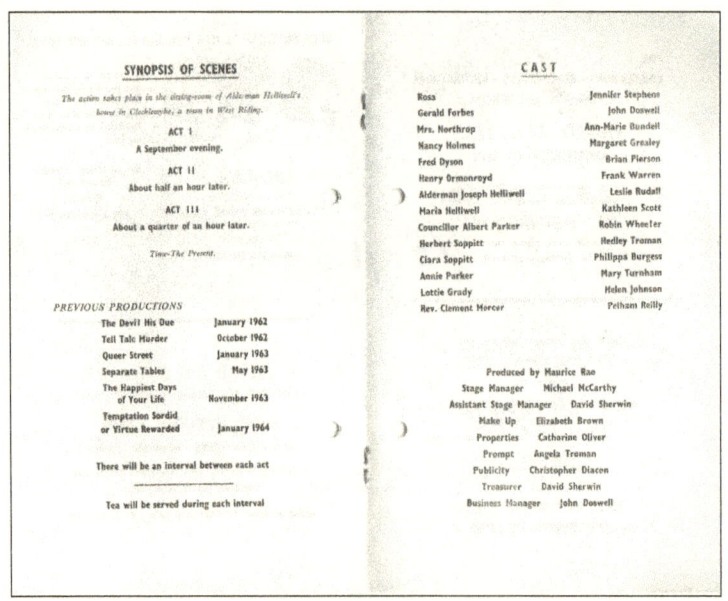

Sail On, Silvergirl, Sail On By

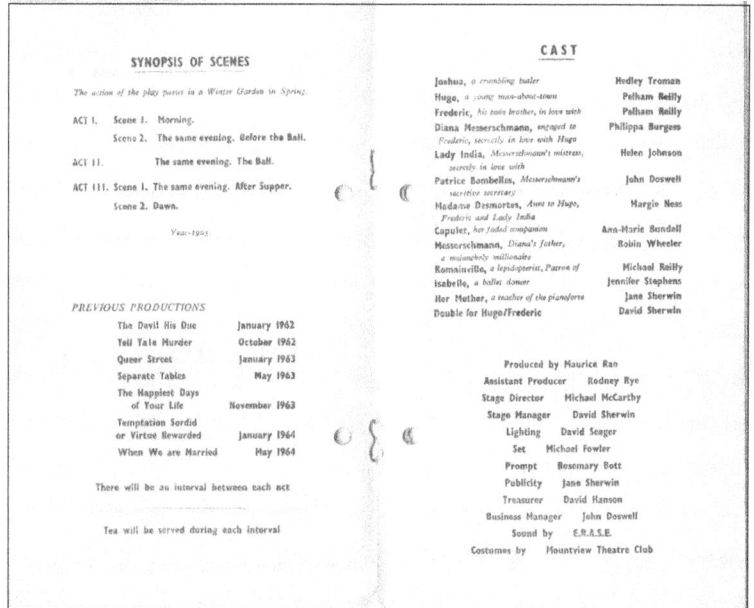

NORTHERN POLYTECHNIC THEATRE

HOLLOWAY ROAD · LONDON N.7

Licensed by the Lord Chamberlain to R. H. CURRELL

The Northern Polytechnic Repertory Company

presents

Brush With a Body

A Play in Three Acts by
MAURICE McLOUGHLIN

30th & 31st MARCH,
1st & 2nd APRIL, 1966

programme · sixpence

Brush With a Body

characters in order of appearance :

Sarah Walling	Jenny Stephens
Cynthia Walling	Herald Braune
Mr. Flaherty	George Hawkins
Mrs. D'Arcy	Marjorie Barltrop
Henry Walling	Roy Walsh
Paul Martell	Peter Sheltrum
Sybil Walling	Constance Hunt
Detective Inspector Hardy	Don Anderson
Sergeant Bray	Terry Horne
Rosita Hernadez	Leonie Waller
The Hon. Pamela Colefax	Carolyn Oakden

The Play produced by John Woodnutt

All performers are amateurs and registered members of the Northern Polytechnic

SYNOPSIS OF SCENES

The action of the Play passes in the morning-room of Sybil Walling's house in Hampstead.

ACT 1
A summer morning.

interval

ACT 2
The next morning.

interval

ACT 3
Immediately following.

A warning bell will be rung before commencement of each act

REFRESHMENTS ARE SERVED DURING THE INTERVALS

Stage Manager : MICHAEL HANNAN
Asst. Stage Manager : DOREEN O'BEIRNE
Script Continuity : JILL PRESTON
Scenery by STAGE SCENERY LTD.
Furniture by OLD TIMES FURNISHING CO. LTD.
Lighting and Sound Effects by PAT SMITH
Additional Lighting Apparatus by
STRAND ELECTRIC & ENGINEERING CO. LTD.
Sound Equipments by THE DEPARTMENT OF TELECOMMUNICATIONS
Presentation of the play is by permission of
SAMUEL FRENCH LTD.

The Committee records its thanks to all Stewards, Programme Sellers and Helpers during this production

www.ingramcontent.com/pod-product-compliance
Lightning Source LLC
Chambersburg PA
CBHW051750040426
42446CB00007B/298